King Arthur and the Myth of History

Florida A&M University, Tallahassee
Florida Atlantic University, Boca Raton
Florida Gulf Coast University, Ft. Myers
Florida International University, Miami
Florida State University, Tallahassee
New College of Florida, Sarasota
University of Central Florida, Orlando
University of Florida, Gainesville
University of North Florida, Jacksonville
University of South Florida, Tampa
University of West Florida, Pensacola

King Arthur and the Myth of History

Laurie A. Finke and Martin B. Shichtman

University Press of Florida
Gainesville · Tallahassee · Tampa · Boca Raton
Pensacola · Orlando · Miami · Jacksonville · Ft. Myers · Sarasota

Copyright 2004 by Laurie A. Finke and Martin B. Shichtman
Printed in the United States of America on acid-free, recycled paper
All rights reserved

14 13 12 11 10 09   6 5 4 3 2 1

First cloth printing, 2004
First paperback printing, 2009

A record of cataloging-in-publication data is available from the Library of Congress.
ISBN 978-0-8130-2733-3 (cloth)
ISBN 978-0-8130-3415-7 (paper)

The University Press of Florida is the scholarly publishing agency for the State University System of Florida, comprising Florida A&M University, Florida Atlantic University, Florida Gulf Coast University, Florida International University, Florida State University, New College of Florida, University of Central Florida, University of Florida, University of North Florida, University of South Florida, and University of West Florida.

University Press of Florida
15 Northwest 15th Street
Gainesville, FL 32611-2079
http://www.upf.com

The fact is that there is no historical evidence about Arthur; we must reject him from our histories and, above all, from the titles of our books.
David Dumville

No figure on the borderline of history and mythology
has wasted more of the historian's time.
J.N.L. Myres

Contents

List of Illustrations ix

Acknowledgments xi

1. "To Mend the Interrupted Sequence of Time": The Narrative Logic of Medieval History 1

2. Profiting from the Past: History as Symbolic Capital 35

3. The Romance of Empire: Vernacular History and the Structuration of Power 71

4. Discontinuous Time: History in the Eyes of Its Losers 103

5. Mapping Ambition: Imperialism, Nationalism, and the Logic of Seriality in the *Chronicle* of John Hardyng 133

6. Patronage, Printing, and Symbolic Economies of Nationalism in Caxton's *Morte Darthur* 159

7. Paranoid History 186

Afterword 215

Notes 221

Bibliography 239

Index 255

Illustrations

5.1. Detail of Map of Scotland   143

7.1. Knight with Swastika. Labadie Collection, University of Michigan Library   187

7.2. Knight with Swastika. From *Die Kunst im Dritten Reich* (*Art in the Third Reich*)   187

7.3. The Flagbearer   188

7.4. Otto Rahn at Montségur   211

Acknowledgments

This book is the result of twenty years of collaboration and friendship that began in 1983 when we met at the University of Oklahoma and decided to collaborate on a collection of essays that in 1987 became *Medieval Texts and Contemporary Readers*. We enjoyed the process so much that we decided to try to write a book together. People sometimes ask us why and how we have managed to sustain this odd professional relationship at such a distance for so long. The why is easy. We had fun and enjoyed the give and take of sharing our ideas and completing each other's sentences. The how is more complex. In the early days we got along by telephone, the U.S. mail, and the occasional face-to-face work session. We wrote at conferences, in bars, separately at home, and together when we could find the time. This book has been nurtured by nearly a decade of trips to Kalamazoo, Ypsilanti, and Gambier and a lot of Thai food (many thanks to Thai Bistro in Canton, Michigan, without which this book would not have been written). But it was also helped along through the years by email, fax, and instant messenger, technologies that simply didn't exist when we first began writing together and that, by providing nearly instantaneous forms of communication (both synchronous and asynchronous), increasingly made the kind of collaborative writing we do practical. Our families were necessarily also part of this collaboration and we offer our thanks to Robert, Stephen, and Hannah Markley and Maryann and Matthew Shichtman for their patience, understanding, and support.

But in the final analysis all books are the result of the collaboration among a host of people and institutions. We would like to thank the following persons for their advice and criticism, encouragement and assistance in the preparation of this manuscript: Dorsey Armstrong, James Carley, Robert Citino, John Coldeway, Marcia Dalbey, Michael Harris, Donald Hoffman, Robert Holkeboer, Valerie Lagorio, Russell Larson, Jami

Peelle, Paul Remley, Felicity Riddy, Anna Roberts, Christine Rose, Ronald Schleifer, Mary Suydam, Michael Uebel, and Bonnie Wheeler have all been wonderful colleagues and friends. Our readers, Kathleen Kelly and Patricia Clare Ingham, offered both encouragement and criticism; we are indebted to them and to other anonymous readers for pushing us to make the best arguments we could and saving us from embarrassing error. Julie Herrada of the University of Michigan's Labadie Collection, Renee Klish of the U.S. Army Museum, and Stephen Roper of the British Library were invaluable in helping us track down the images in our book. Our editors at the University Press of Florida, Amy Gorelick and Susan Albury, deserve high praise for their efficiency and professionalism throughout the editorial process. Many thanks to Deborah A. Oosterhouse for her rigorous but sensitive copyediting.

Many of the arguments in this book were first tested in the classroom and we thank our students, past and present, who have been a constant source of inspiration and stimulation. We have especially appreciated their trenchant questions and their unwillingness to be fobbed off with conventional answers. We are grateful to audiences at the University of Washington, Portland State University, Miami University, Eastern Michigan University, and Kenyon College where we presented earlier versions of the material in this book. Faculty Development Grants and a 1997–98 Sabbatical from Kenyon College, as well as a 1993 Faculty Research Fellowship, a 1998 Sabbatical, and a 1999 Spring/Summer Research Award from Eastern Michigan University, supported the research and writing of this book. A publication grant from Kenyon College assisted in the manuscript preparation.

An earlier version of chapter 2 originally appeared in *Arthurian Literature* 12 (1993); a portion of chapter 4 appeared in Anna Roberts, ed., *Violence Against Women in Medieval Texts* (Gainesville: University Press of Florida, 1998); and a portion of chapter 6 appeared in *Arthuriana* 8 (1998). We thank these publishers for granting us permission to reprint. We also thank the British Library, the U.S. Army Museum, and the Labadie Collection of the University of Michigan Library for permission to reproduce materials from their collections. We are grateful to St. Martin's Press for permission to reproduce extracts from Rosamund Allen's translation of *Lawman's Brut* and the University of Exeter for permission to use extracts from Judith Weiss's translation of Wace's *Roman de Brut*.

Finally, we see this book as part of an ongoing collaboration between scholars of medieval literature and critics interested in literary and cultural theory. Such a collaboration is, we believe, both appropriate and necessary, and unfortunately all too rare. We continue to believe, however, that it offers opportunities both to reread texts and to rethink the boundaries of our disciplines.

1

"To Mend the Interrupted Sequence of Time"

The Narrative Logic of Medieval History

No history of the British Isles would be complete without some mention of the feats of an early British king, prince, chieftain, or "Duke of Battle" (*Dux Bellorum*)[1] named Arthur who achieved immortality in an apparently hopeless campaign to repel the hoards of Saxon invaders threatening sixth-century Britain. Whatever grain of truth this story may have possessed has been hopelessly obscured in the mists of Celtic prehistory and in the romance, nostalgia, and fantasy in which it has been wrapped from its inception. As late as the 1950s, no less a historian than Sir Winston Churchill wrote of King Arthur in the first volume of his *History of the English Speaking Peoples, The Birth of Britain*:

> we prefer to believe that the story with which Geoffrey [of Monmouth] delighted the fiction-loving Europe of the twelfth century is not all fancy. If we could see exactly what happened we should find ourselves in the presence of a theme as well founded, as inspired, and as inalienable from the inheritance of mankind as the *Odyssey* or the Old Testament. It is all true, or it ought to be; and more and better besides. And wherever men are fighting against barbarism, tyranny, and massacre, for freedom, law, and honour, let them remember that the fame of their deeds, even though they themselves be exterminated, may perhaps be celebrated as long as the world rolls round. Let us then declare that King Arthur and his noble knights, guarding the Sacred Flame of Christianity and the theme of a world order, sustained by valour, physical strength, and good horses and armour, slaughtered innumerable hosts of foul barbarians and set decent folk an example for all time. (60)

The subject of this book lies in the gap between Churchill's indicative and subjunctive, between his claim that the glorious stories of King Arthur *are* all true and his belief that they *ought* to be true because they represent what, for him, is best about the English nation. Our analysis of the ways in which historians in the Middle Ages and in the late twentieth century have used narratives about Arthur *as history* examines the slippage in history between "belief" and narrative (Churchill's assertion that the story of Arthur is a "theme" as significant as the *Odyssey* or the Old Testament) on the one hand, and "seeing exactly what happened" on the other. It joins contemporary theoretical debates about the nature and function of history,[2] exploring the gap between the claims of history to record "what really happened" against the assertion that history creates a "useable past," a past from which its authors would like to be descended, to paraphrase Hayden White.[3]

Traditional Arthurian scholarship, when it has taken up the question of Arthur's historicity, has been largely concerned, as Churchill is, with locating the origins of a Celtic chieftain named Arthur. In this book, however, we distance ourselves from the debates over whether or not such a king actually existed. Instead, we consider why, in the twelfth century, a set of narratives about King Arthur suddenly emerges full-blown, virtually from nowhere (from the margins of the Norman empire), as an important subject of historical writing (at the center of the Norman empire) and why Arthur has since continued to be an enduring cultural and semi-historical figure. We contend that King Arthur has been used by historians—medieval and modern—as a potent, but empty, social signifier to which meaning could be attached that served to legitimate particular forms of political authority and cultural imperialism. In the twelfth century, the recent history of Norman conquest and colonization, the displacement of the island's previous occupants, and the uneasy cohabitation of the Saxons, Irish, Welsh, and Scottish inhabitants of the British Isles could be masked by appeals to an archaic, holistic past, so that, at its birth, the Arthurian legend was isolated from the immediate political and historical context of its production. Churchill, writing as an historian in the shadow of fascism and impending world war, continues this glorification of an archaic, "primitive" past by casting Arthur as a symbol of all that is noble in the fight against fascism: he represents the forces of "freedom, law, and honour" ranged against "barbarism, tyranny, and massacre."[4] However, our study of the chronicle tradition further suggests that historians have transformed Arthurian stories to negotiate power relations among influential and often conflicting factions, especially during times of cultural and political destabilization. Churchill's encomium to Arthur's nobility carries with it disturbing whiffs of a European imperialism tinged with militant masculinity. To hold Arthur up as the guardian of the "Sacred Flame of Christianity" and "a world order, sustained by valour, physical strength, and good horses and armour," to applaud his slaughter of "innumerable hosts of foul barbarians," at least unconsciously gestures toward the cult of military masculinism and racial and nationalist politics that fueled the Nazi propaganda we examine in our final chapter. This potential, we argue, has existed in Arthurian narrative from its very inception, the heart of darkness in a myth of political authority.[5]

The cultural and historical forces that created Arthur as a cultural signifier of feudo-dynastic expansionism from the twelfth century down to the Wars of the Roses—and even beyond—are the subject of this book. It is a study in what the medieval historian Patrick Geary calls "ethnogenesis," the building of imagined political community around patterns of migration and ethnic identification (9; see also Anderson, *Imagined Communities*).

To limit the scope of our investigations, we examine the emergence of various discursive traditions about the most ancient history of Britain that served to legitimate the political ambitions of contending institutional forces during periods of social stress: conquest, colonization, rebellion, civil war, genocide. The chapters that follow examine three periods of cultural crisis: the Norman colonization of England during the eleventh and twelfth centuries, the Wars of the Roses in the fifteenth century, and the rise and resurgence of fascism in twentieth-century Europe. We focus on four English chronicles written during the Norman period—William of Malmesbury's *Gesta Regum Anglorum*, Geoffrey of Monmouth's *Historia Regum Britanniæ*, Wace's *Roman de Brut*, and Laȝamon's *Brut*, all of which contain significant Arthurian sections. We examine John Hardyng's *Chronicle* and Sir Thomas Malory's *Morte Darthur*—both produced during the tumult of the Wars of the Roses—and, finally, we look at two relatively contemporary texts, Jean-Michel Angebert's *The Occult and the Third Reich: The Mystical Origins of Nazism and the Search for the Holy Grail* and Trevor Ravenscroft's *Spear of Destiny: The Occult Power Behind the Spear which Pierced the Side of Christ*, both of which offer to tell the history of Adolph Hitler's acquisition of the Holy Grail. We have chosen these texts because each reveals tensions between the claims history makes about objectivity or referentiality and particular social, political, and ideological agendas. We suggest that, at these historical moments of great stress, the turn to antiquarianism, the move to bypass the traumas of the recent past in favor of archaic origins, offers a unique opportunity for the literary and cultural theorist to interrogate the aims and uses of history itself, to ask questions about the claims history makes to relating "what really happened."

Although the great Arthurian romances of the High Middle Ages, from Chrétien de Troyes to Sir Thomas Malory, have always received their fair share of both scholarly and critical attention, the medieval chronicles of England have, until very recently, languished in relative obscurity, usually—with the possible exception of the *Historia Regum Britanniæ*—meriting only a cursory glance in the histories and anthologies of Arthurian literature. Research on Arthurian romance has far outstripped attention to the histories. A few book-length studies have been devoted to individual historical texts,[6] while older studies that have taken the chronicle tradition as their subject, like Robert Huntington Fletcher's *Arthurian Material in the Chronicles*, serve as surveys of the material. Many of the key texts have remained relatively inaccessible except to scholars.[7] Only in recent years have complete and reliable translations of some of these medieval histories been produced. Perhaps as a result of this activity, there has recently been a revival of interest in chronicle history, as evidenced by studies by Monika Otter, Siân Echard, Michelle R. Warren, and Patricia Clare Ingham. While Malory's *Morte d'Arthur* has long been studied as literature and its textual history endlessly debated, Hardyng's *Chronicle* has never had a modern critical edition; only the later, shorter version is accessible and that only in an edition published in 1812.[8]

Doubtless the reasons for this inattention on the part of literary critics are many. The medieval chronicles we examine belong to periods not well represented in the great tradition of canonical English literature. A time during which elite culture in England was French, the Norman period in England, until very recently, was most often seen by scholars and teachers of English literature as a vast lacuna between *Beowulf* and Chaucer, while the fifteenth century has been noted mostly for the dullness of its literary output.[9] Doubtless the nineteenth century's instantiation of the hegemony of "national" literatures (Davis, "National Writing," 611) ensured that, at least in literary studies, the cultural and linguistic heterogeneity of England during these periods would be lost in the compartmentalization of "national" languages. But, from the perspective of a historian, even a cursory examination of these periods reveals that in addition to being times of conquest and colonization, both periods saw massive transformations in social, legal, political, and cultural organization. Those transformations both reflect and are reflected in the issues raised by the Arthurian chronicle histories produced during the Norman occupation and those of the fifteenth century that largely copied their predecessors. These transformations may provide the basis for a cultural poetics within which to reevaluate these works' aesthetics. Analyses of radical shifts in administration, law, political organization, inheritance patterns, kinship structures, and gender relations during these periods of social and political crisis—as well as resistance to these changes—may reveal something about the cultural purposes these histories served, their aesthetic and social value for their audiences, and the kind of reception these works received.

If literary critics find medieval chronicle histories too episodic—even by the rather loose standards of the romance—and unadorned to be good literature, historians judge them too fabulous to be good history. Writes David Dumville, "The fact is that there is no historical evidence about Arthur; we must reject him from our histories and, above all, from the titles of our books" (*Histories and Pseudo-histories*, 188), while J.N.L. Myres argues that "No figure on the borderline of history and mythology has wasted more of the historian's time" (16). These texts were doomed to remain disciplinary orphans so long as analysis of them was informed by a theory of genre as a formal, ahistorical system of classification in which history and fiction were conceived of as entirely separate entities belonging to disciplines with largely incompatible goals. But the genre theory articulated by proponents of the new historicism attempts to describe a "poetics of culture"[10] that reconceives of genres—poetry, romance, chronicle, history—not as fixed categories belonging to some preexistent reality, but as agents of social and cultural behavior, as producers—as well as products—of social meanings, while historians like Hayden White have articulated a "narrativist-rhetorical conception of historiography" (Zagorin, 263). Within such a cultural poetics (or cultural history), confusion about the genre of the chronicles under consideration ceases to be the result of defects judged from some ahistorical and timeless set of Aristotelian classifications. Rather, it becomes both a reflection of the social transformations that produced these texts and an aesthetic response to social, political, and cultural conditions; they shape social behavior even as they are being shaped by the social forces that produce them.[11]

Because they have been unable to fix these chronicles as either poetry or history, scholars have been reluctant to pin an argument about the origins of the Arthurian legends onto these narratives. It has been easier to look for origins in the obscure Celtic traditions of Gildas, Nennius, and Aneirin. Our question, however, is not where did Arthur originate, or who was the historical Arthur. We do not seek a "historical truth" about Arthur. Rather we are asking why the Arthurian material suddenly sprang up virtually full-grown during the twelfth century in Norman England. Why this time and this place? One answer is that the Norman Conquest was a period of colonization that brought into close and often violent contact three disparate cultures—the Celts, the Saxons, and the Normans. Arthur seems to emerge out of the social chaos of colonization as a kind of social signifier capable of providing an ideological synthesis that covered over the conflicts and contradictions that marked this uneasy confluence of cultures. At the same time, these chronicles bring into relief the disparate uses to which colonizer and colonized put the raw material of these legends.[12]

For this reason, our analysis of the cultural purposes Arthurian materials may have served for its audiences necessarily engages postcolonial theories of cultural dispossession. Recently medieval scholars in several disciplines have begun to bring the tools of contemporary postcolonial theory to bear on the histories and texts of the Middle Ages, including its Arthurian materials.[13] Our reading of Arthur as a social signifier of colonialism engages with theoretical work that challenges the presentist biases of postcolonial theory, unpacking those discourses of and about the Middle Ages that "attempt to give a hegemonic 'normality' to the uneven development and the differential, often disadvantaged histories of nations, races, communities, peoples," to adapt Homi Bhabha's frequently cited definition of postcolonial criticism.[14] In this we join the project for a postcolonial medieval studies (defined not temporally by the time "after" colonization but as the "discourse of oppositionality which colonialism brings into being") outlined by Jeffrey Cohen ("Introduction," 3).

But medievalists cannot, and indeed have not, been content simply to adopt postcolonial theories uncritically. Rather such a program requires we reformulate the key words of postcolonial theory, in order to destabilize hegemonic Western identities, to displace the domination of medieval Christianity, and to decenter universalizing Western narratives that contrast a civilized Europe with primitive "others," "the people without history," to use Eric Wolf's terminology (Cohen, "Introduction," 3, 6–7). A few points of revision will be salient to our postcolonial analysis of Arthurian histories.

1. Postcolonial discourse does not begin in the postwar period of "decolonization," just as colonization did not begin in the nineteenth century, or the eighteenth, or even in 1492 with Christopher Columbus's voyages. Conquest and colonization were a fact of life in the Middle Ages (and no doubt much earlier), and they engendered many of the forms of resistance described by postcolonialist theorists. Indeed Patrick Geary's descriptions in *The Myth of Nations* of the process in late antiquity and the early Middle Ages should remind us of the antiquity of the practices of colonialism and their resistance. At the same time, such practices are historically specific so that an investigation of medieval colonialism will not follow the same paths as an investigation of nineteenth-century colonial practice.

2. In contrast to the orientalism described by Said, colonization is often described by medieval writers as moving from the settled East to the barbaric West (from Troy, for instance, to England), as we will argue in chapter 5. In the Middle Ages, Europe was on the periphery of the world system, not at its center; we explore the effect that geographical marginality has on the colonial impulse.

3. For this reason, the East (which for most medieval writers means the Islamic East) is not the only—or even the best—source of the atavistic "other," the exotic primitive, that has become the privileged site of analysis for postcolonial theorists. Europe itself, especially on its fringes, was populated by groups (both real and imaginary) that could be characterized as "barbaric."[15]

4. Colonization was not just something Europeans did to non-Europeans. The Crusades, which is often the focus of attention for medievalists working in postcolonialism (see, for instance, Heng, "Cannibalism," and the essays in Cohen, *Postcolonial Middle Ages*), represent only one manifestation of European expansionism during this period. Conquest of other European territories was common as well. In speaking of the British Isles, we will use the term "insular colonization" to describe the conquest and colonization of the various peoples who occupied the island during the Middle Ages. We prefer this term over the more common "internal colonization" (see Hechter) or Ingham's "internal primitives" (*Sovereign Fantasies*, 11) with its suggestion of a preexistent geographic integrity.

5. Our analysis of Arthurian histories resists the emerging con-

sensus among postcolonial medievalists about the existence of the nation in the Middle Ages.[16] It is overwhelmingly tempting to read the modern nation back into the Middle Ages (especially given the nineteenth century's use of the Middle Ages to create nationalism; see Geary, 15–40). Most medievalists who argue for the presence of national identity in the Middle Ages base their claim on a critique of Benedict Anderson's notion of the "imagined community," which they argue existed in the Middle Ages as well (Ingham, *Sovereign Fantasies,* 7–9). But Anderson does not simply define the nation as an imagined community. If that were the sole criteria then it would be possible to argue that the nation existed in the Middle Ages or at any other time for that matter. But Anderson also argues that the nation must be imagined in a particular way and that is what makes it a new phenomenon (post-Enlightenment). To be sure, Anderson's claim rests on a very superficial reading of medieval history, as his critics suggest, and the gaps in his account need to be filled in. However, we want to expand on his suggestion that there are many styles of imagining political communities and explore at least a few alternative styles (see especially chapters 4–6).

6. Absent a political organization like the modern nation, both conquerors and conquered used history in their struggle to understand what constituted their differences (and similarities) from other political communities. How was membership in a political community conferred? What were the functions of genealogy, intermarriage, religion, common language, shared geographical territory? History as a narrative structure develops as a means of understanding who is one of us and who is the "other," who is in and who is out.

Because warfare and conquest, genealogy and marriage are primary concerns in the types of histories created by a politics of feudo-dynasticism, gender will be a subtext running throughout our argument. The forging of "imagined communities" structured around the conquest of new territories and legitimate inheritance requires very specific types of men and women, masculinities and femininities. Anxieties about female sexuality—in particular its consequences for the peaceful transfer of property from father to legitimate son—fuel both rape fantasies and the institutions designed to control women and their sexuality. Fantasy, law, and custom work unevenly to produce certain kinds of femininity and condemn others. We will examine these issues more fully in chapters 2 and 4. But we are also interested in the kinds of masculinity produced within the warrior culture represented by these histories. These issues we will examine more fully in chapters 6 and 7.

Central to our postcolonial reading of Arthurian histories, then, is uncovering the ideological work of these histories by redrawing the traditional disciplinary and generic boundaries between literature and history. This rethinking will proceed along two fronts: a theoretical consideration of the narrative structures of historical discourse (to which we will turn in a moment) and an analysis of the uneasy tensions between the historicization of romance and the romanticization of history.[17] This tension is what, finally, connects the disparate texts under investigation. The histories we examine in chapters 2 through 5 are chronicles in the sense that Hayden White defines them, texts in which "events in the historical field are narrated in temporal order of occurrence" (*Metahistory*, 5). For White, chronicles are generally not emplotted, that is, they do not identify the material being narrated as belonging to a particular kind of story (7). But the chronicles by William of Malmesbury, Geoffrey of Monmouth, Wace, Laȝamon, and Hardyng that we examine do emplot the events they narrate—they by and large emplot them as romance (Shichtman, "Gawain in Wace," 108). But genre, as we suggest, is rarely so straightforward. As early as the twelfth century, Arthurian romances appeared side by side with these chronicle histories. While medieval readers could certainly discern the difference between history and fiction, the generic boundaries between the two were much more fluid than they are for modern readers schooled in the *disciplines* of history and literature, and they answer not to some kind of transhistorical laws of genre, but to the social conditions of their production. The development of romances about King Arthur could not fail to have a subversive effect on chronicle histories of King Arthur. The effect of the dialogic interanimation of romance and history by the late Middle Ages was, as Lee Patterson has noted, "that Arthurian romance, often used for purposes of political authentication, defines for itself a complicated relationship to the question of its own authenticity" (*Negotiating the Past*, 207). We examine this relationship in chapter 6. For William Caxton, the printing of Malory's *Morte Darthur*, a text that melds chronicle and romance, functions simultaneously to mediate between feuding factions engaged in the Wars of the Roses and between the structures of patronage and newly emerging systems of print capitalism. It also participates in forging the "imagined community" Benedict Anderson has argued enabled the development of nationalism. Despite the triumph of positivistic historiography in the nineteenth century, the subversive relationships between Arthurian materials, chronicle history, and myths of origins haunt the production of twentieth-century histories at its margins. Jean-Michel Angebert's *The Occult and the Third Reich* and Trevor Ravenscroft's *Spear of Destiny*, the subject of our last chapter, offer purportedly "historical" evidence of the search for and acquisition of the Holy Grail by the Third Reich. For Angebert and Ravenscroft romanticism's fascist potential becomes not only realized but historicized as well.

"The certainty of the things which they did not see": Theoretical Background

For the most part, modern historians have been skeptical about the integrity of the histories written during the Middle Ages, preferring to rely on supposedly more "objective" archival material. The dismissal of medieval histories is the result of a historical method—often unacknowledged, sometimes even unrecognized—that we would like to challenge, a method that demands historical writing strive for a kind of scientific objectivity and exactitude, that it reveal "what really happened." This perspective is perhaps best embodied by the following remarks by the renowned medieval historian Johann Huizinga: "a history adequate to our civilization can only be a scientific history. The instrument of modern Western civilization for the intellectual understanding of the world is critical science. We cannot sacrifice the demand for scientific certainty without injury to the conscience of our civilization. Mythical and fictitious representations of the past may have a literary value as forms of play, but for us they are not history" (8–9).[18] Antonia Gransden in her monumental two-volume survey, *Historical Writing in England*, while claiming to recognize the inability of historical discourse to convey precisely the "truth" about the past, nevertheless is quick to suggest that the efforts of a medieval historian—William of Malmesbury—be taken less than seriously because "[o]ne slender fact or unauthenticated rumor could rouse the storyteller in him" (176). Similarly Jacques Le Goff confesses that he once erred in believing "[t]he ancient historian seemed . . . condemned to a discouraging choice between two alternatives: either he could limit himself to what meager spoils were provided by the legacy of a past ill-equipped to perpetuate itself, and consequently succumb to the emasculating attractions of pure erudition, or else he could yield to the charms of an always risky reconstruction" (vii). But Le Goff takes pride in following the example of Jules

Michelet, the nineteenth-century French historian whose search for the "truth" led to medieval documents found in archives—"was not scientific history born between the mid-seventeenth and mid-nineteenth centuries from the study of medieval charters and scripts?" (viii)—rather than to those narratives acknowledged by the Middle Ages as histories.

But contemporary historiographical theory prompts us to ask rather different questions of medieval histories. To admit that history cannot give us any privileged access to "what really happened" is to belabor the obvious; the point has been made repeatedly in the last decades. Claude Lévi-Strauss has noted that the past can never be experienced in any unmediated way. Even if we could have access to "what really happened," the raw, unprocessed data of the past, we would be unable to process it: "The historian and the agent of history choose, sever, and carve [historical events] up, for a truly total history would confront them with chaos.... Insofar as history aspires to meaning, it is doomed to select regions, periods, groups of men [sic] and individuals in these groups and to make them stand out as discontinuous figures against a continuity barely good enough to be used as a backdrop. A truly total history would cancel itself out—its products would be nought.... History is therefore never history, but always history for."[19] Donald Spence's analysis of the exchange between analyst and analysand in psychoanalysis, though it deals with reconstructions of the past of a very different kind, illustrates Lévi-Strauss's point nicely. Freud, he argues, undoubtedly influenced by the positivistic historiography of his time, insisted that the work performed in analysis should create an unmediated access to the patient's past transparently, as if glimpsed though the window of a moving train (24–25). According to Spence, however, "The model of the patient as unbiased reporter and the analyst as unbiased listener suggests a kind of naive realism that is hard to imagine, harder to practice, and runs counter to everything we have learned about the way we come to understand the world" (25). This "naive realism" characterizes how we often think of history as well, as a collection of facts, dates, and events that refer transparently to some preexistent reality, compiled by an unbiased historian attending to the facts with an "evenly hovering attention" (25). If the historian is assumed, "by virtue of his free-associating stance, to have privileged access to the past, and if the story we hear is assumed to be the same story he is telling, then it is tempting to conclude that we are hearing a piece of history, an account of the 'way things were'" (27). But what we have come to understand about the world is that this "historical truth" is always formulated within a narrative logic that demands that the teller and audience conspire to produce a coherent, completed text agreeable to and, in various ways, responsive to the needs of both. The raw data that we call evidence in history must always be shaped into a narrative, and that narrative will always exist in tension with the "facts."[20] The difficulties do not lie in choosing between the two, in preferring facts to pure fiction or vice versa. Rather the two exist together, playing off one another, the facts always being shaped into coherent and convincing narratives that reflect as much the interests of the writer and his audience as allegiance to objectivity.

By opposing historical truth—"what really happened"—to narrative truth, defined as the coherent and consistent narratives historians make about "what really happened" (the criteria we use to decide when a certain experience has been captured to our satisfaction), we want to call attention to the fact that we can never have unmediated access to the past. Historical events come into being already fully textualized, their cultural meanings already the subject of disputation, struggle, and conflict. After all, history comes to us largely through documents; we almost never have access to the events themselves. (This point is, if anything, more obviously true when we are studying medieval history.) The events of the past are always already bound up in textuality, in the struggle among competing discourses to define the meaning of events (and of course to call something an event is already to assign it narrative coherence—a beginning, middle, and end—and perhaps even to emplot it, to use White's terminology). Even as they are occurring, historical events—battles, coronations, marriages, revolutions, conquests, rebellions, treaties, and palace coups—are invested with contested meanings through all sorts of semiotic practices and utterances: rituals, ceremonies, rationalizations, speeches, pamphlets, sermons, tax rolls, charters. The historian must make order out of the chaos produced by these discourses; she must "choose, sever, and carve up" these texts to produce meaningful narratives. All history, far from being simply a record of "what really happened," may be conceived of as a series of narratives (White, *Tropics of Discourse*, 19, and *Metahistory*; Partner, *Serious Entertainments*), tropes (Certeau, *Writing of History*), or discursive practices (Foucault, *History of Sexuality*) that fabricate a past from which we would like to be descended.[21] If all historical writing is subject to the same forces that give form to all narrative then, as Hayden White suggests, "historical inquiry is born less of the necessity to establish that certain events occurred than of the desire to determine what certain events might mean for a given group, society, or culture's conception of its present tasks and future prospects" ("Historical Pluralism," 487). This assumption, which challenges contemporary disciplinary configurations—the boundary between history and literature, between fact and fiction—provides the theoretical basis for our argument in this book.

Predictably, this "narrativist-rhetorical conception of historiography" (Zagorin, 263) has met with resistance and outright hostility from some historians. According to Zagorin, this attempt to "aestheticize" history by privileging literary tropes and verbal structures "trivializes history and renders it void of any intellectual responsibility," severing it "from its formerly accepted grounding in conditions of truth and reality" (264, 266). The postmodern view of history, according to its critics, ignores those features of historical writing that many historians view as essential to the discipline. Three of those features must inform our discussion.

1. History, unlike literature, presumes a difference between "fact or truth and fictionality.... Unlike the work of literature, the historical work does not contain an invented or imaginary world. It presents itself as consisting, to a great degree, of facts and true or probable statements about the past" (Zagorin, 272).

2. Postmodern history's obsession with style over substance flies in the face of traditional history's insistence on the transparency of its language, on its ability to refer unproblematically to a reality outside of itself. As Zagorin conceives it, "In historiography, the attempt by language to draw attention to itself would commonly be regarded as highly inappropriate and an obtrusive breach of the rules of historical writing. In history language is very largely subservient to the historian's effort to convey in the fullest, clearest, and most sensitive way an understanding or knowledge of something in the past" (270).

3. Finally, Zagorin argues, historians are constrained, in ways that poets and novelists are not, by "the nature and limitations of their evidence.... While it is for them to determine that something is evidence and what it is evidence for, when they have done so the evidence exerts a continuous force upon them. They are not free to ignore it or make of it whatever they please. Its pressure acts as a major determinant in giving shape to the historical work" (270).

King Arthur and the Myth of History explores these features of historical writing—the relationship between fact and fiction, the referentiality of its language, and the nature of its evidence—through its analysis of Arthurian history. But it will be useful at the outset to say a few words in response to Zagorin's charges as a means of assessing the theoretical stakes in the postmodern view of history. It is not enough simply to dismiss the claim that history is "grounded in conditions of truth and reality" as naive and to substitute for it the more sophisticated counterclaim that all history is text without further exploring the consequences of that claim. As a genre, historical writing is nothing without its claims of truth and reference to an independent reality.[22] Because there are no formal features that can reliably distinguish history from fiction, history's claim to relate "what really happened" is fundamental to it. As readers, we could not recognize a history without it. It does no good to argue, as Monika Otter does, that historians can occasionally "disengage" from their truth claims for literary effect; the medieval historians she examines, "while being mostly 'engaged,' can also temporarily, or partially, 'disengage' themselves—with the result that, at least for a short time, referentiality is called into question, truth claims are suspended, and fictionality becomes a possibility" (12). Of course, the historian is free to call into question her own truth claims, even to undermine them in the name of irony, but in doing so, she risks being understood by audiences to be doing something entirely different from history. At the moment the historian abandons the claim to be relating "what really happened," she ceases to be read as a historian, according to the conventions of the speech genre.[23] This is certainly true for modern readers of history; it may well have been true—with some modifications—for medieval readers.

However, as postmodern critiques of history have pointed out, truth claims are just that: claims. They are rhetorical procedures. While he does not say so, even Zagorin recognizes this in the multiple hedges that surround his claim that history is about fact; for him, history *presents* itself as offering *"facts and true or probable* statements about the past." Just because someone claims to be speaking the truth, of course, does not necessarily mean that she is. And the verification of truth claims is almost never as simple as checking a statement against some readily accessible slice of reality. For instance, when Geoffrey of Monmouth claims that the information he presents in his *Historia Regum Britanniæ* came from a "britannici sermonis librum uetustissimum" (ed. Wright, 1) [a very ancient book written in the British language (trans. Thorpe, 51)] given to him by Walter, the archdeacon of Oxford, the veracity of this claim can never be established by reference to an actually existing book. But neither does the absence of that book invalidate the claim. The book may certainly be a fabrication on Geoffrey's part, a means of giving authority to his fiction by claiming to cite sources, or it may have actually once existed but been lost or destroyed (as so many medieval texts have been). There is no way, in this instance, to distinguish between a true claim and a merely rhetorical one. We would venture to guess that only a minuscule portion of all history—if any—is subject to direct verification by comparison to a reality independent of texts. For this reason, it is necessary to understand how readers make distinctions between valid and invalid truth claims; in other words, how they distinguish between fact and fiction, how they make language refer to something outside itself, and how they determine what counts as convincing evidence for truth claims.

Common sense tells us that fictions are made while facts are discovered and therefore indisputable. "The facts speak for themselves" and "You can't dispute the facts" are clichés and, as clichés, they "mask their own ... complicity in perpetuating certain preferred interpretations of the world, in particular the belief that there is a preexistent 'reality' that the objective observer encounters, discovers, and then records as facts" (Finke, *Feminist Theory*, 19). But as the work of writers like Bruno Latour and Steve Woolgar in the cultural studies of science suggests, these clichés may be true in very different ways from our common sense understanding of them. According to Latour and Woolgar, in the sciences, an utterance becomes a fact when it has been cut off from the circumstances of its production, its making (106).[24] A fact is an utterance whose history has been erased. The past controversies, struggles, conflicts, debates, alliances, negotiations, and trials of strength that went into its making have all been rendered invisible. In this sense a fact speaks for itself because it needs no one to speak for it; attribution or authorship would undermine an utterance's status as a fact. We can of course dispute the facts; historians do it all the time. They do so by restoring to the fact the history of its production, opening up the black box that contains it.[25] Scratch the surface of a historical fact and you will begin to untangle the network of alliances of people (eyewitnesses, historical actors, scholars, readers, teachers, students) and of things (books, manuscripts, articles, archives, letters, diaries, buildings, artifacts) that hold it together. We tend to think of these networks as "evidence," but it is worth pointing out that, for most historical controversies, "evidence" gives us no privileged glimpse of reality; it is not a little slice of reality. Twentieth-century readers of medieval history have no access to, say, the Battle of Hastings, but only to a field of discourse—both medieval and modern—about it: eyewitness accounts, chronicles, tapestries, histories, poems. Debate about a historical fact will occur when another network of alliances (consisting again of both people and things) stands against the network that holds the fact together. Each network will attempt to assemble more and better allies, isolating dissenters. At some point, it may simply become too costly (in whatever terms cost is defined) to stand against such a vast and complex network and that network becomes a fact: "you can't argue with the facts." If the dissenters overwhelm the original network, then what was once a "fact" becomes a quaint remnant of past ignorance or superstition. A third possibility is that the equal strengths of both networks will keep the controversy alive indefinitely. Geoffrey allies himself both with the archdeacon of Oxford and with a *librum uetustissimum* to strengthen his role as mouthpiece for British history. A dissenter who successfully severs that link will have an easier time dismissing Geoffrey as a writer of romance.[26] For Latour, the ability or failure to resist "trials of strength" (the attempt of one network to sever the ties between a spokesperson and the network it claims to speak for)[27] determines whether a person or claim is deemed objective or subjective: "Being objective means that no matter how great the efforts of the disbeliever to sever the links between you and what you speak for, the link resists. Being subjective means that when you talk *in the name* of people or things, the listeners understand that you represent only yourself" (Latour, 78).

Some have argued that it is the task of the historian (and certainly of the historiographer) constantly to be opening up black boxes, to be examining the processes by which networks resist or fail trials of strength (Ankersmit, 289). That will be our purpose in exploring Arthurian history. However, we do not stand outside of the discursive processes we describe. We do not claim to do away with facts altogether; that is not our understanding of Latour's critique. It would be virtually impossible to say anything about any subject without some facts. But, like Latour, we hope to focus attention on the processes by which a fact is made to appear finished, fait accompli in the literal sense of that phrase. We hope to unpack the complex but invisible networks that hold the "fact" in place.

Despite modern assessments of the "naivete" of medieval histories, writers of these texts could certainly recognize that the information they hoped to communicate was being undermined by their very method of communication. They realized that words were not a precise enough medium to transfer historical truth, that in transmission historical "truth" became literary discourse—narrative. As early as the seventh century, Isidore of Seville, influenced by the work of Latin grammarians, observed that "Historia est narratio rei gestae per quam ea quae in praeterito facta sunt, dignoscuntur" [History is the narration of events by which those things which were done in the past are sorted out] (Chenu, 167). Isidore's use of "dignoscuntur" suggests that, for him, history's primary function is not merely to report events; it must make meaning of them as well. He understood that history was a representation of reality, not reality itself. Amidst the intellectual upheavals of the twelfth century, Hugh of St. Victor reasserted Isidore's position, arguing for a narrative view of history: "Historia est rerum gestarum narratio" [History is the narration of events] (Chenu, 167).

This characterization of history as a *narrative* of events inevitably raises questions about the relationship between the historian's language and the "events" or reality toward which that language is supposed to point. Could the reader of medieval history expect a correspondence between the historian's account and the events themselves? Was the historian's narrative a transparent medium through which readers might view the past? Walter Map seems to anticipate such an empirical history that at least desires to eliminate textuality. For him, the history of modernity seems to hold out the possibility of an unmediated understanding of the past: "Nostra dico tempora modernitatem hanc, horum scilicet centum annorum curriculum, cuius adhuc nunc ultime partes extant, cuius tocius in his que notabilia sunt satis est recens et manifesta memoria, cum adhuc aliqui supersint centennes, et infiniti filii qui ex patrum et suorum relacionibus certissime teneant que non uiderunt" [And by our times I mean this modern period, the course of these last hundred years, at the end of which we now are, and of all of whose notable events memory is fresh and clear enough; for there are still some centenarians alive, and there are very many sons who possess, by the narration of their fathers and grandfathers, the certainty of the things which they did not see] (122–25).[28] But even as he asserts the possibility that the eyewitness account offers direct access to the reality of the past, he denies it in "the certainty of the things which they did not see." The reality of the past recedes in the face of narratives about it. Map's understanding even of the events of the recent past depends not on his direct access to those events, but to the network of allies he assembles—centenarians, their many sons, the narratives produced by those sons' fathers and grandfathers—to support his claim.

Map's dismantling of his own empiricist claims suggests that history, like any narrative, is also a vehicle for eloquence, for embellishment. Medieval historians did seem to entertain the possibility that their narratives' connection with reality was largely *rhetorical*. As Otter points out, history was throughout the Middle Ages conceived not, as it is in the late twentieth century, as "an empirical study of evidence," but as a branch of rhetoric (9; see also Partner, "The New Cornificius," and Robertson, 42–47). In the writings of many medieval historians, the result of this awareness was a subversion of history as a conveyer of absolute, objective "truth." Of course, medieval writers were often deeply suspicious of rhetoric, believing that language, "treacherously feeding a taste for odd pleasures and spurious achievements," might prove to be a vehicle for deception rather than truth, though this is a fear hardly unique to the Middle Ages; vestiges of that attitude survive in our own distrust of "rhetoric" (Partner, "The New Cornificius," 22–23). However the situation was rather more complicated in those histories produced in the Middle Ages because the reality toward which the historian's narrative was supposed to point was not always an empirical one (as it presumably is for the modern historian); often it was an invisible one. "For medieval historians . . . the whole purpose of history became an anti-rhetorical effort to penetrate the surface of experience, . . . to the stable center of Divine purpose. Serious reality was no longer on earth at all, but only in the immaterial realm which alone gave meaning to human history, and could be traced in microcosm in the individual soul" (48).[29] The insistence that reality is located in an invisible realm of spirit is perhaps what modern readers find most unsatisfying about medieval history (and modern versions of medieval history like those we will examine in our final chapter). Partner, for instance, argues that this program was finally "unworkable" because "it confused the relation of language to serious reality, while rhetorical language and dramatic or play reality continued in effortless union" (48). To represent this *invisibilia*, medieval history had to rely as much on figures, tropes, allusions, and allegory as any imaginative literature, so that its language came to be virtually indistinguishable from the playful language of literature. For this reason, we may learn more about the ways in which the consumers of medieval histories not only read, but *used* these histories if we approach them armed not only with the tools of contemporary historiography, but with those of literary theory as well.

Clearly, however, it is not sufficient simply to state the negative case, that medieval histories undermine objectivity as a value toward which historical narrative should strive. We must be prepared to offer something in its place besides absolute relativism. For this we turn to Lévi-Strauss's comment that history is always "history for": history for someone and for some purpose. Who were the medieval histories of Arthur written for and how did these audiences anticipate using these texts? While Gabrielle Spiegel has argued that in thirteenth-century France the revival of secular historiography, especially in the vernacular, was promoted by an aristocracy anxious about the erosion of its power in the face of a resurgent monarchy, in twelfth-century England it was stimulated by a revival of interest in the writing of history among its Norman rulers (Spiegel, 2–4; Gransden, 186–88). It is perhaps not all that surprising that the Norman kings were more eager than their Continental counterparts to promote the writing of secular history. After all, unlike the Capetian kings, the Normans ruled England by violent conquest rather than legitimate succession. For more than a century after William's victory at the Battle of Hastings, Norman kings had to fight numerous challenges to their legitimacy. The Wars of the Roses, during which both Hardyng and Malory wrote (and during which Caxton published the *Morte Darthur*), was also marked by violent usurpation and rebellion. During both of these periods of social unrest, secular histories may have offered an ideological legitimation these rulers sorely lacked; to possess a lineage, however suspect, was almost as useful as a good army in staking a political claim to a crown.[30] Certainly these histories were not the only, or even the most significant, means by which usurping monarchs could justify their violence. They may, however, have worked in concert with other symbolic gestures. The repetition within Arthurian histories of certain rituals, the Norman practice of wearing the crown on particular feast days, for instance, may have been attempts to reinforce the symbolic meanings of kingship rituals promoted by the Norman kings which, as Koziol has argued, often proved unpredictable and disastrous (136–41).

The histories themselves, however, like the rituals Koziol examines, are hardly monologic; rather they are dialogically agitated sites of ideological conflict in which various factions contend to define what constitutes a legitimate exercise of power, which acts of violence will be sanctioned and which condemned. We argue that Arthurian histories are, first and foremost, about power. As Stephen Knight claims, "Arthur has always been a figure of authority and many versions of the legend have consistently realised the contemporary ways of becoming, and the contemporary problem of remaining, great" (xiv). Arthurian histories "are potent ideological documents through which both the fears and the hopes of the dominant class are realised" (xiv). We would only add that these documents also encode the fears and hopes of subordinated groups, as well as those who hope one day to be dominant.[31] Neither the exercise of power nor its accompanying ideologies are seamless or monolithic. Both are riven by conflict, struggles, contradiction, gaps, and silences. The ruling class cannot effectively silence all opposition. It cannot even ensure that all of its members will have the same interests. Even under the most totalitarian of regimes, language—utterances, texts, and discourses—will be dialogic in the sense that the Russian cultural theorist M. M. Bakhtin uses the term, as the "intense interaction and struggle between one's own and another's word, . . . in which [these words] oppose . . . or interanimate one another" (*Dialogic Imagination*, 354). That is why the control of various forms of language, usually through censorship, is a priority for most totalitarian regimes.[32] Ideologies are not the results of an already finished struggle, but the *sites* of social contest. Drawing upon theorists who have written about power,[33] our analysis attempts to unpack the various threads of this complex dialogue about power in Arthurian histories.

Because the dominant class cannot exercise power by violence alone, it will usually attempt to legitimate its rule by the formation of "imagined communities." We take this term from Benedict Anderson, who uses it to describe the imagined community of the nation. For Anderson, a nation is "imagined because the members of even the smallest nation will never know most of their fellow-members, meet them, or even hear of them." It is a community because "regardless of the actual inequality and exploitation that may prevail in each, the nation is always conceived as a deep, horizontal comradeship" (*Imagined Communities*, 6–7). But the nation is only one kind of imagined community and, as Anderson argues, one of relatively recent invention. All communities, he argues, are imagined; they are distinguished only by the style in which they are imagined. Historical narratives become a means by which writers can create imagined communities of all kinds, and Arthurian history, with its elaborate mythology, provides rich and compelling material with which to fashion imagined communities, material that, as we will argue in our final chapter, cannot be monopolized by any one nation, even that which presumably gave it birth.

Before turning to Geoffrey of Monmouth, who must really be credited, if not with inventing the historical Arthur, at least with gathering together the various and scattered threads of the legend and weaving them into a coherent narrative, it will be useful to examine our three major themes—the tension in historical writing between "what really happened" and the need to shape an inchoate past into comprehensible narratives, the legitimate exercise of power, and the formation of imagined communities—in the work of a medieval historian who is generally accorded more credibility as a historian than Geoffrey. William of Malmesbury's *Gesta Regum Anglorum* [*Chronicle of the Kings of England*] provides a useful foil for Geoffrey's Latin history as well as for the vernacular translations that followed it. In the remainder of this chapter we will focus on the methodologies of writing postcolonial history from two perspectives. The first is William of Malmesbury's "self-fashioning," his construction of himself as a historian—and by extension his construction of a definition of what a historian does—within the framework of the power struggles that occupied twelfth-century English society, even the relatively sheltered monastic society in which William lived and worked. This self-fashioning has, for the most part, been taken at face value by nineteenth- and twentieth-century editors, translators, and historians. The second perspective explores the imagined communities William's history forges, along with the ideological commitments that both produced his text and are reproduced within it.

William of Malmesbury: The Historian History Makes

William of Malmesbury, who has been called a "professional historian" by Rodney Thomson (*William of Malmesbury*, 8) and a "modern historian's historian" by Beryl Smalley (90), makes a good test case for our argument about how the Middle Ages might have perceived historical writing if only because he has so often been accepted and judged by the standards of modern positivistic historical scholarship we described above. Thomson, for instance, emphasizes his scholarly detachment: he "liked to date his authors, in relation to each other and to major rulers and events. He quite explicitly preferred the earliest source of a story, unless there were reason to do otherwise, in which case he explained why. He liked to know who copied from whom, and had little time for mere plagiarizers"(*William of Malmesbury*, 8). Monika Otter declares his "scientific, 'modern' methodology" one of his greatest achievements (97–98). But these same critics condemn him by the very same standard, noting his "credulity, carelessness, willful mishandling of evidence, and meandering irrelevance" (Thomson, *William of Malmesbury*, 11). Both praise and criticism impose contemporary standards of historical accuracy on William's *Chronicle* while failing to understand William's text as both a product and a producer of the massive transformations in social, legal, political, and cultural organization brought on by the Norman Conquest. To be sure, the temptation to judge William's history by modern standards of historical accuracy is encouraged by William's own statements in the *Chronicle*. He ends his preface with a brief but suggestive note on methodology: "habiturus, ut spero, apud posteros post decessum amoris et livoris, si non eloquentiæ titulum, saltem industriæ testimonium" (ed. Stubbs, 1:3) [Trusting that I shall gain with posterity, when love and hatred shall be no more, if not a reputation for eloquence, at least credit for diligence (trans. Giles, 4)]. His self-conscious, and self-effacing, concerns with the production of an "objective" history, one that would grant access—through "diligence"—to the events of the past, have led contemporary historians such as Antonia Gransden to observe, "As a historian William deserves his reputation for two reasons: he occupies an important place in the development of historical method, and his works are repositories of information and views of value to the historian today" (167).

The prologues that preface each of the five books of the *Chronicle* offer a fascinating glimpse of the creation of the historian not as the autonomous and self-sufficient origin of his own writing, but as the production of the process Louis Montrose calls "subjectivization." Montrose argues that individuals are endowed with subjectivity by certain cultural practices that create the capacity for agency; at the same time they position individuals within social networks and subject them to cultural codes that ultimately exceed their comprehension and control (21). Throughout the *Chronicle*, William most often identifies these cultural practices of self-fashioning with struggles over the possibility of "objective" truth offered both by authorities—those authors who have preceded him—and firsthand experience. In the prologue to the first book he remarks on the paucity of reliable sources—especially after the death of Bede—claiming "sciat me nihil de retroactis præter cohærentiam annorum pro vero pacisci; fides dictorum penes auctores erit" (ed. Stubbs, 1:3) [I vouch nothing of the truth of long past transactions but the consonance of the times; the veracity of the relations must rest with its authors (trans. Giles, 4)]. At the same time he attacks contemporary historians—his peers—for their failure to detach themselves from their materials.

Although he credits the veracity of his text partially to his having witnessed the events he records—"Quicquid vero de recentioribus ætatibus apposui, vel ipse vidi, vel a viris fide dignis audivi" (ed. Stubbs, 1:3) [Whatever I have recorded of later times, I have either myself seen, or heard from credible authority (trans. Giles, 4)]—William maintains that proximity to a historical event by no means ensures objectivity. Even eyewitnesses can lie if lying is to their advantage. At the beginning of Book 3, he offers a stinging rebuke of fellow historians, both Norman and English, writing in the dialogically agitated environment of postconquest England, for their handling of the Norman invasion and the reign of William the Conqueror. "De Willelmo rege scripserunt, diversis incitati causis, et Normanni et Angli: illi ad nimias efferati sunt laudes, bona malaque juxta in cælum prædicantes; isti, pro gentilibus inimicitiis, foedis dominum suum proscidere convitiis" (ed. Stubbs, 2:283) [Normans and English, incited by different motives, have written of king William: the former have praised him to excess; extolling to the utmost both his good and his bad actions: while the latter, out of national hatred [literally—"out of the hatred of the people"], have laden their conqueror with undeserved reproach (trans. Giles, 258)]. However, William's critique of his competitors' partisan handling of the Norman conquest suggests the extent to which he is begging the question of what constitutes "credible" authority in an eyewitness. The narrative through which he constitutes his own credibility offers only his own mixed heritage—his position as a *mestiza*[34]—as a warrant for his "disinterestedness." "Ego autem, quia utriusque gentis sanguinem traho, dicendi tale temperamentum servabo: bene gesta, quantum cognoscere potui, sine fuco palam efferam; perperam acta, quantum sufficiat scientiæ, leviter et quasi transeunter attingam; ut nec mendax culpetur historia, nec illum nota inuram censoria cujus cuncta pene, etsi non laudari, excusari certe possunt opera" (ed. Stubbs, 2:283) [For my part, as the blood of either people flows in my veins, I shall steer a middle course: where I am certified of his good deeds, I shall openly proclaim them; his bad conduct I shall touch upon lightly and sparingly, though not so as to conceal it; so that neither shall my narrative be condemned as false, nor will I brand that man with ignominious censure, almost the whole of whose actions may reasonably be excused, if not commended (trans. Giles, 258)]. Because he is *both* Norman and Saxon, he assures his readers, he is able to avoid both the extreme praise and the extreme censure that mark the more biased eyewitness accounts of either Norman or Saxon historians. William's concerns about the manipulation of the record of the past prompt him to describe his writing as steering a middle course between "Scylla and Charybdis," necessary so that the "truth" will not suffer (trans. Giles, 326).

Contemporary historiographers have tended to emphasize his statements about historical method, condemning him where he fails to achieve it, while, until very recently, downplaying his considerable emphasis on the language of history (see Ward, Otter). Nevertheless, William's claims to the "objectivity" of his historical writing, to his history as "truth," deconstruct even as he offers them. Tensions continually arise between the demands of historical "fact" and those of storytelling, with William more often coming down on the side of a good story rather than that of fact. Speaking of his attraction to history as a discipline, William suggests that

> Et multis quidem litteris impendi operam, sed aliis aliam. Logicam enim, quæ armat eloquium, solo libavi auditu: physicam, quæ medetur valitudini corporum, aliquanto pressius concepi: jam vero ethicæ partes medullitus rimatus, illius majestati assurgo, quod per se studentibus pateat, et animos ad bene vivendum componat: historiam præcipue, quæ, jocunda quadam gestorum notitia mores condiens, ad bona sequenda vel mala cavenda legentes exemplis irritat. (ed. Stubbs, 1:103)

> [I gave, indeed, my attention to various branches of literature, but in different degrees. Logic, for instance, which gives arms to eloquence, I contented myself with barely hearing. Medicine, which ministers to the health of the body, I studied with somewhat more attention. But now, having scrupulously examined the several branches of Ethics, I bow down to its majesty, because it spontaneously unveils itself to those who study it and directs their minds to moral practice; History more especially, which by an agreeable recapitulation of past events, excites its readers, by example, to frame their lives to the pursuit of good, or to aversion of evil.](trans. Giles, 93–94)

As he prioritizes the disciplines, he carefully links history with ethics so that it emerges as the first among all disciplines because, by the example of an "agreeable" narrative and not because it relates "what really happened," it impels its readers to pursue the good and avoid evil. Indeed, narrative coherence emerges in William's metahistory as an important property of good history; it is the impetus for his own work.

> Ita prætermissis a tempore Bedæ ducentis et viginti et tribus annis, quos iste nulla memoria dignatus est, absque litterarum patrocinio claudicat cursus temporum in medio; unde mihi, tum propter patriæ caritatem, tum propter adhortantium auctoritatem, voluntati fuit interruptam temporum seriem sarcire, et exarata barbarice Romano sale condire. (ed. Stubbs, 1:2)

> [Thus from the time of Bede there is a period of two hundred and twenty-three years left unnoticed in his history; so that the regular

series of time, unsupported by a connected relation, halts in the middle. This circumstance has induced me, as well out of love to my country [*patriæ*], as respect for the authority of those who have enjoined on me the undertaking, to fill up the chasm and to season the crude materials with Roman art.] (trans. Giles, 3–4)[35]

William's Latin "interruptam temporum seriem sarcire" literally means "to mend the interrupted sequence of time," which suggests, more strongly than Giles's translation, the desire for narrative closure.[36] William produces his history, he says, not so much to correct previous errors as to restore coherence to a "halting" narrative, to create a finished story (even if the subject of William's history, the lineage of Britain's monarchs, could never truly be finished).

History, for William, requires not merely diligence but also eloquence. He has nothing but praise for Bede, "vir maxime doctus et minime superbus" [a man of singular learning and modesty] who wrote "plano et suavi sermone" [in a clear and captivating style](ed. Stubbs, 1:1; trans. Giles, 2). He more frequently attacks other historians for the vulgarity of their language, their inability to produce a pleasingly eloquent literary text, than for the accuracy of their materials. Elward, who translated the *Anglo-Saxon Chronicle* into Latin is "diligent," but lacks style; his language "disgusts" William (trans. Giles, 2). In fact, he calls upon "divinus favor" [Divine favour] to "arriserit, et me præter scopulos confragosi sermonis evexerit, ad quos Elwardus, dum tinnula et emendicata verba venatur, miserabiliter impegit" (ed. Stubbs, 1:3) [smile on my undertaking, and carry me safely by those rocks of rugged diction, on which Elward, in his search after sounding and farfetched phrases, so unhappily suffered shipwreck (trans. Giles, 4)]. Eadmer, on the other hand, who wrote a more contemporary history of the years from 1066 to 1122 (*Historia Novorum*), is credited with "sobria sermonis festivitate" (ed. Stubbs, 1:1–2) [a chastened elegance of style (trans. Giles, 2)]. Historical writing since Bede has suffered because of the literary weaknesses of historians not because of their purported inaccuracies:

> Sepulta est cum eo gestorum omnis pene notitia usque ad nostra tempora. Adeo nullus Anglorum studiorum ejus æmulus, nullus gloriarum ejus sequax fuit, qui omissæ monetæ lineam persequeretur: pauci quos æquus amavit Jesus, quamvis litteris non ignobiliter informati, tota vita ingratum consumpserunt silentium; alii, vix primis labris illas gustantes, ignavum confoverunt otium. Ita

cum semper pigro succederet pigrior, multi tempore in tota insula studiorum detepuit fervor. Magnum ignaviæ testimonium dabunt versus epitaphii, pudendi prorsus, et tanti viri mausoleo indigni. (ed. Stubbs, 1:66–67)

[With this man was buried almost all knowledge of history down to our times, inasmuch as there has been no Englishman either emulous of his pursuits, or a follower of his graces, who could continue the thread of his discourse, now broken short. Some few indeed, "whom the mild Jesus loved" though well skilled in literature, have yet observed an ungracious silence throughout their lives; others scarcely tasting of the stream, have fostered a criminal indolence. Thus to the slothful succeeded the others more slothful still, and the warmth of science for a long time decreased throughout the island. The verses of his epitaph will afford sufficient specimen of this indolence; they are contemptible, and unworthy of the tomb of so great a man.] (trans. Giles, 60–61)

For William the composition of an epitaph and the writing of chronicle history require the same skills; both must be judged not only by their "truth" but by their beauty as well. For William, as for his contemporaries, rhetorical eloquence was essential to good history. To accept William's statements about method without interrogation, then, fails to account for the range of issues voiced in the metahistorical narrative that pervades the *Chronicle of the Kings of England*.

Even as he attempted to reproduce the past through a more or less "scientific" method of historical investigation, even as he bemoaned the failings of lesser historians and the gullibility of a populace inclined to believe, as he notes of the Britons, "fallacious fables" (trans. Giles, 11),[37] his efforts were undermined by the cultural imperatives—social, political, and economic—informing his narrative. Nowhere is this truer than in William's narratives relating to King Arthur, brief though they may be. Although William insists he is offering "veracious histories" of the Arthurian period, he offers instead a text pervaded by the social and political instabilities of twelfth-century England and by the patronage system that encouraged his authorship ("the authority of those who have enjoined on me the undertaking"; trans. Giles, 4).

Thomson maintains that "The monk William . . . was by choice a careerless man. About his self-ideal there is likewise no doubt: his hero was Bede, a model of detached and selfless devotion to Christian learning, to the recovery and promotion of the legacy of the past" (*William of Malmesbury,* 9). Thomson's account of William's motives accepts at face value William's own fashioning of his image as a devotee of learning for its own sake and for the greater glory of God, who modeled himself on the equally selfless devotion of his predecessor Bede, and who sought no reward for his labors except the opportunity to continue them. We would like to suggest, however, that the love of learning that Thomson attributes to William would have been costly in England during the first part of the twelfth century. The monastic community of which William was a member supported his labors. Although it may not be possible to locate ways that William of Malmesbury directly profited as an individual from the *Chronicle of the Kings of England,* as, say, Geoffrey of Monmouth or Wace were to profit from their histories in the next generation (see chapters 2 and 3), the text itself locates William within an elaborate patronage network in which various forms of capital, often exchanged under the pretense of gift-giving, freely circulated. A letter to King David of Scotland, prefacing Troyes, Bibliothèque Municipale, MS 294, notes "Quanuis enim amplissimus fructus bonorum operum sit pura conscientia, nonnichil tamen aduocatio et fauor principum nutrit and fouet ingenia: uester precipue, cuius mens benigna, manus munifica, regalis uita sine querela predicatur" [for though the most abundant reward of good works is a clear conscience, the support and favour of princes does much to feed and foster gifted men: and your favour in particular, whose beneficent purpose, generous hand, and kingly way of life are extolled with no dissident voice] (ed. and trans. Mynors, 4–5).

The most obvious example of William's participation in the Norman-dominated patronage networks of his day is his dedication of the *Chronicle* to Robert, earl of Gloucester, who was also, ironically, the dedicatee of Geoffrey of Monmouth's *Historia Regum Britanniæ* (see chapter 2). It is hard not to read some kind of expectation of reward, however veiled, into William's fulsome praise of Robert: "Nullum enim magis decet bonarum artium fautorem esse quam te, cui adhæsit magnanimitas avi, munificentia patrui, prudentia patris; . . . Quid quod etiam notitia tua dignaris litteratos, quos vel invidia famæ vel tenuitas fortunæ fecit obscuros" (ed. Stubbs, 2:356) [None, surely, can be a more suitable patron of the liberal arts than yourself, in whom are combined the magnanimity of your grandfather [William the Conqueror], the munificence of your uncle, the circumspection of your father [Henry I]. . . . You condescend to honour with your notice those literary characters who are kept in obscurity, either by the malevolence of fame, or the slenderness of their fortune (trans. Giles, 2)].[38] Thomson has suggested, however, that Henry's queen, Matilda, and not his illegitimate son, might have been the book's original patron: "the recently printed dedicatory letters prefacing the *Gesta* in Troyes, Bibliothèque Municipale MS 294 (*bis*) clearly shows that the production of this work was a task originally laid upon the whole Malmesbury community by Queen Matilda of England (d. 1118)" (*William of Malmesbury*, 15). He cites a letter to her daughter (Matilda), at least part of which was written by William himself, that explains that some of the *Chronicle* was written while the queen was alive: "Sed uix imperatis institeramus cum illam repente Fortuna, profectibus Angliae inuidens, immortalitatis, ut speramus, sedibus, dedicauit. Quo merore consternati, decreuimus stili abiurare studium, cum uideremus exisse de medio hortatricem studiorum. Enimuero procedente tempore rupere silentium tum amicorum petitio, tum rei utilitas...." [Scarcely however had we started on our task when on a sudden Fortune, grudging the success achieved by England, removed her, as we trust, to the realm of immortality. Prostrated by grief, we decided to abandon the attempt to write, seeing that the lady who had encouraged our endeavors had been taken from our midst. Then, as time went on, our silence was broken, partly by requests from our friends, partly by the value of the project....] (ed. and trans. Mynors, 8–9). Thomson also suggests that William's "grand tour," the extensive literary travels required to research his history, which seems to have been sponsored by his abbey of Malmesbury, was perhaps also funded by Queen Matilda.

Thomson's suggestion that William may have received royal patronage for the *Chronicle* might be read in the context of the veiled criticisms that emerge in William's portrait of Matilda, where he even admits generally that no one can be content simply with "the precious fruits of a good conscience," but that desire for reward is a natural outgrowth of accomplishment. He writes:

> Inde, liberalitate ipsius per orbem sata, turmatim huc adventabant scholastici tum cantibus tum versibus famosi; . . . Nec in his solum expensas conferebat, sed etiam omni generi hominum, præsertim advenarum: qui, muneribus acceptis, famam ejus longe per terras venditarent. Est enim cupiditas gloriæ ita innata mentibus hominum, ut vix aliquis, bonæ conscientiæ pretiosis contentus fructibus, si quid bene fecerit, non dulce habeat efferri in vulgus: unde aiunt, et constat, dominæ esse surreptum, ut extraneos quos posset præmiis delineret;

ceteros promiissis, aliquando efficacibus, aliquando et sæpius inanibus, suspenderet. Eo effectum est ut prodige donantium non effugeret vitium, multimodas colonis suis deferens calumpnias, inferens injurias, auferens substantias; quo bonæ largitricis nacta famam, suorum parvi pensaret contumeliam. (ed. Stubbs, 2:494)

[Her generosity becoming universally known, crowds of scholars, equally famed for verse and for singing, came over; . . . Nor on these only did she lavish money, but on all sorts of men, especially foreigners [*advenarum*], that through her presents they might proclaim her celebrity abroad; for the desire of fame is so rooted in the human mind, that scarcely is any one contented with the precious fruits of a good conscience, but is fondly anxious, if he does anything laudable, to have it generally known. Hence it was justly observed, the disposition crept upon the queen to reward all the foreigners [*extraneos*] she could, while the others were kept in suspense, sometimes with effectual, but oftener with empty promises. Hence, too, it arose that she fell into the error of prodigal givers; bringing many claims on her tenantry, exposing them to injuries, and taking away their property; by which obtaining the credit of a liberal benefactress, she little regarded their sarcasms.] (trans. Giles, 494)

The passage, which begins with praise for Matilda's patronage, ends up strongly criticizing her for favoring her foreign clients (presumably Norman or French) over her own countrymen (presumably Saxon). William describes the uncertainties of the Norman system of patronage, which we will examine more closely in chapter 2, uncertainties that he himself must have experienced. This brief portrait covers virtually all the significant features of Norman patronage. The patron must be generous (*liberalitate*); she must give freely, even lavishly (although she can be chastised for giving prodigally, usually when she is giving to someone else). What she desires in return is that "they might proclaim her celebrity abroad." This perhaps explains why Matilda favored foreign clients over domestic ones; the return on her investment is greater. William's description of Matilda's patronage stresses less the rewards of patronage than the uncertainties that haunt those dependent on it (which during this period was almost everyone): they are left hanging, strung along with promises of rewards that may never materialize.

Certainly there is nothing in the record to suggest that William himself ever directly profited from the patronage of the royal family—whether through monetary rewards or offices—which is why Thomson's portrait of the selfless antiquarian toiling away for the sheer joy of it seems so convincing. However, William's virtual obsession with the endowments of monasteries suggests that William perhaps did not need or want capital or advancement for himself; he simply needed appropriate funds to be given to his monastery so that he could keep on doing what he loved—traveling, reading, and writing. He needed the institutional support the monastery could provide—a different (and more indirect) kind of reward from that usually associated with patronage networks, which as we shall see in chapter 2 tend to be individualistic and diffuse. William's criticism that Matilda's support of foreign clients has injured her own tenants, taking away their property, would support such a reading of William's plea for patronage.

Thus, even as William condemns other historians for being compromised by their partisanship of particular political, ideological, or economic factions, one of the major themes of William's *Chronicle* is the conflict over royal patronage of monasteries, especially the conflict surrounding William's own house of Malmesbury. Throughout the *Chronicle*, William devotes a disproportionate amount of space to a discussion of particular acts of patronage to monasteries and the persistent conflicts among the kings of England, various bishops, and monasteries over the royal patronage of monastic houses. He praises the patronage of the Saxon king Kenwalk, "qui ita fuit munificus ut nihil patrimoniorum cognatis negaret" (ed. Stubbs, 1:29) [who was of a character so munificent that he never refused to give any part of his patrimony to his relations (trans. Giles, 28)], for advancing the fortunes of Malmesbury, "in quo tereni incolatus prætendimus militiam" (ed. Stubbs, 1:30) [where I carry on my earthly warfare (trans. Giles, 28)], and criticizes the Mercian king Offa's rapacity— "prædia publicus expilator abrasit" (ed. Stubbs, 1:86) [a downright public pilferer (trans. Giles, 78)]—in seizing its wealth and property, which was only restored later by his son Egfert. He also condemns the avarice of Bishop Ealstan for seizing Malmesbury for his own use and King Edwy for turning it into "stabulum clericorum" (ed. Stubbs, 1:163) [a sty for secular canons (trans. Giles, 146)]. Of these seizures he writes: "Sentimus ad hunc diem impudentiæ illius calumniam, licet locus idem statim, eo mortuo, omnem illam eluctatus fuerit violentiam, usque ad nostrum tempus, quando in idem discrimen recidit" (ed. Stubbs, 1:109) [We feel the mischief of this shameful conduct even to the present day, although the monastery has baffled all similar violence from the time of his death until now, when it has fallen again into like difficulty (trans. Giles, 98)]. He blames such conflicts for the monastery's state of ruin, especially following the seizure of Malmesbury by Roger, bishop of Salisbury, Henry I's chancellor and regent, for his own use in 1118 (trans. Giles, 508). Presumably royal patrons endowed monasteries as a means of accruing spiritual capital (in the thirteenth century nearly a quarter of all monasteries enjoyed royal patronage), but they also represented a substantial capital investment that would make them appetizing targets for both ambitious kings and bishops looking to finance their expenditures and increase their influence. Even good patrons cannot escape the temptation: "Ita sacra fames avaritiæ mortalia pectora exedit; ita magnificos, et illustres in ceteris, viros in Tartara trudit" (ed. Stubbs, 1:109) [Thus the accursed passion of avarice corrupts the human soul and forces men, though great and illustrious in other respects, into hell (trans. Giles, 98)].

The *Chronicle*'s narratives about Arthur are products of this dialogically agitated environment in which William wrote, an environment of uneven, unsettled, and conflicted cultural, political, ideological, linguistic, and economic agendas. With these narratives, William negotiates the highly ambiguous patronage networks created by the imposition of a Norman cultural hegemony over a culturally heterogeneous island. The Norman barons were troubled by the general circulation of stories proclaiming the second coming of Arthur, a messianic figure who would, as he had done previously, drive invaders from England. The threat posed by a "Celtic" revival had become serious enough by the reign of Henry II that it had to be countered by dramatic action. Between 1190 and 1191, under orders issued by Henry before his death according to Giraldus Cambrensis, the abbot of Glastonbury Abbey ordered excavations to uncover the graves of Arthur and Guinevere.[39] The "discovery" of these graves provided symbolic evidence that might help to undermine Celtic enthusiasms for rebellion that plagued Henry's reign (it may also have increased the tourist trade at Glastonbury Abbey as well). Definitive "proof" was produced to demonstrate that England's once great king had no future whatsoever. The Norman aristocracy, which controlled the affairs of monasteries such as Malmesbury during William's day, had not yet come upon such a stroke of propagandistic genius. For this aristocracy, William the "objective," "detached" historian seems to offer comfort. But William's narrative also produces anxiety, its literariness deconstructing the certainty of "scientific" history. Early in the *Chronicle*, William writes, "Hic est Artur de quo Britonum nugæ hodieque delirant; dignus plane quem non fallaces somniarent fabulæ, sed veraces prædicarent historiæ, quippe qui labantem patriam diu sustinuerit, infractasque civium mentes ad bellum acuerit; postremo, in obsessione Badonici montis, fretus imagine Dominicæ matris, quam armis suis insuerat, nongentos hostium solus adorsus incredibili cæde profligarit" (ed. Stubbs, 1:11) [It is of this Arthur that the Britons fondly tell so many fables, even to the present day: a man worthy to be celebrated, not by idle fictions but by authentic history. He long upheld the sinking state and roused the broken spirit of his countrymen to war. Finally, at the siege of Mount Badon, relying on an image of the Virgin, which he had affixed to his armor, he engaged nine hundred of the enemy, single-handed, and dispersed them with incredible slaughter (trans. Giles, 11)]. For William, the fables the Britons so fondly tell must be even more ludicrous than the suggestion that one man, single-handedly, could crush an army of nine hundred—an item he offers as "authentic history." No doubt the idle fictions William dismisses had something to do with Arthur's return; such tales removed Arthur from the register of the historic and made him immortal, mythological. On the one hand, then, William's narrative repudiates efforts to deny historical logic, repudiates the notion, threatening to the Norman aristocracy, of any once and future king. On the other hand, William's narrative serves to moralize the cause of the oppressed—Arthur fights with the picture of Mary attached to his shield—and to remind both the oppressed and their oppressors of historical precedents for successful rebellions.

William's second invocation of Arthurian history is similarly ambiguous. In this section of William's *Chronicle*, the authority of historical evidence is undermined, suggesting simultaneously that Arthur is dead and buried and that he may still be alive. This section also includes what may be read as a warning to ungenerous patrons of the dangers inherent in not circulating capital magnanimously and locally. William writes:

> Tunc in provincia Walarum, quæ Ros vocatur, inventum est sepulchrum Walwen, qui fuit haud degener Arturis ex sorore nepos. Regnavit in ea parte Britanniæ quæ adhuc Walweitha vocatur: miles virtute nominatissimus, sed a fratre et nepote Hengestii, . . . regno expulsus, prius multo eorum detrimento exilium compensans suum; communicans merito laudi avunculi, quod ruentis patriæ casum in plures annos distulerint. Sed Arturis sepulcrum nusquam visitur, unde antiquitas næniarum adhuc cum venturum fabulatur. Ceterum, alterius bustum, ut præmisi, tempore Willelmi regis repertum est super oram maris, quatuordecim pedes longum; ubi a quibusdam as-

seritur ab hostibus vulneratus, et naufragio ejectus; a quibusdam dicitur a civibus in publico epulo interfectus. Veritatis ergo notitia labat in dubio, licet neuter eorum defuerit famæ suæ patrocinio. (ed. Stubbs, 2:342)

[At that time in the province of Wales, called Ros, was found the sepulchre of Walwin, the noble nephew of Arthur; he reigned, a most renowned knight, in that part of Britain which is still named Walwerth; but was driven from his kingdom by the brother and nephew of Hengist . . . though not without first making them pay dearly for his expulsion. He deservedly shared, with his uncle, the praise of retarding, for many years the calamity of his falling country [patriæ]. The sepulchre of Arthur is nowhere to be seen, whence ancient ballads fable that he is still to come. But the tomb of the other, as I have suggested, was found in the time of king William, on the sea-coast, fourteen feet long; there, as some relate, he was wounded by his enemies, and suffered shipwreck; others say, he was killed by his subjects at a public entertainment. The truth consequently is doubtful; though neither of these men was inferior to the reputation they have acquired.] (trans. Giles, 315)

William's ambivalence concerning the site of Arthur's grave both honors and subverts the agendas of official Norman culture. William offers the objectivity of history as a corrective to the ancient ballads fabling Arthur's return. But lacking an eyewitness report confirming the presence of a sepulcher, despite his dismissal of these claims as mere fable, he leaves room for the further spread of such ballads. Similarly, Arthur and Walwin are portrayed as fighting for a doomed cause, "the calamity of [a] falling country." But they make their oppressors "pay dearly." Walwin's fourteen-foot sepulcher testifies to his having been, quite literally, larger than life. Though Walwin's death is verifiable, though he can no longer discomfort invaders, his fantastic sepulcher associates him with a kind of magic and magnificence that contains disruptive ideological potential.

But perhaps William's most intriguing strategy in this portion of the history may involve shifting the association of official Norman culture from Hengist, and the enemies of Britain, to Walwin and those who deserve praise as defenders of the island. As adapted by the Norman rulers of England in narratives like William's, Arthurian legends, from the start, served as a crucial avenue for the kind of cultural recovery described by Anne McClintock in *Imperial Leather*. In such narratives, "colonized people do not inhabit history proper but exist in a permanently anterior time within the geographic space of the modern empire as anachronistic humans, atavistic, irrational, bereft of human agency—the living embodiment of the archaic 'primitive'" (40). William's Norman patrons would not have been averse to appropriating the Arthurian mystique when it served their purposes, as the work of Geoffrey of Monmouth and Wace, or even that of Marie de France, demonstrates. Like Arthur, Walwin is a "renowned knight," a man not "inferior to the reputation [he has] acquired," who may have died in war, wounded by foes and shipwrecked. But William also offers the possibility that Walwin died ignominiously, murdered by those he governed. By fashioning himself as the detached chronicler who assembles conflicting data and presents them without privileging one version, William can simultaneously flatter patrons like the earl of Gloucester, suggesting that they possess a nobility equal to that of figures from Britain's antique past, and at the same time criticize them, insinuating that they need to be warned about the volatility of a frustrated citizenry.

William of Malmesbury's reputation in medieval studies as an objective historian—who sometimes fails to be objective—perpetuates the ideologies and mythologies of positivistic history by privileging those items that conform to twentieth-century ideas of what history should be while dismissing others—often more interesting and revealing of medieval ideas about historiography—that strain credulity. In the following chapters, we attempt to characterize medieval historiography in its own terms by investigating the ways in which Arthurian legends—stories considered fictional by twentieth-century readers—circulated as history in both Latin and vernacular traditions.

2

Profiting from the Past

History as Symbolic Capital

The *Peterborough Chronicle*, the late continuation of the *Anglo-Saxon Chronicle*, provides graphic descriptions from an English perspective, the perspective of the colonized, of the depredations of the Norman barons during the political "anarchy" that accompanied the reign of King Stephen, who succeeded his uncle Henry I in 1136. The ensuing civil warfare led to a fragmentation of society that ended, according to the anonymous chronicler, in suffering, disorder, and economic ruin. The entry for 1137 begins by describing the physical violence directed against "the people":

> namen hi þa men þe hi wenden ðat ani god hefden, bathe be nihtes 7 be dæies, carlmen 7 wimmen, 7 diden heom in prisun 7 pined heom efter gold 7 syluer untellendlice pining; for ne uuæren næure nan martyrs swa pined alse hi wæron. Me henged up bi the fet 7 smoked heom mid ful smoke. Me henged bi the þumbes other bi the hefed 7 hengen bryniges on her fet. Me dide cnotted strenges abuton here hæued 7 uurythen it ðat it gæde to þe hærnes. Hi diden heom in quarterne þar nadres 7 snakes 7 pades wæron inne, 7 drapen heom swa.... In mani of þe castles wæron lof 7 grin: ðat wæron rachenteges ðat twa other thre men hadde onoh to bæron onne, þat was sua maced, ðat is, fæstned to an beom—7 diden an scærp iren abuton þa mannes throte 7 his hals, ðat he ne myhte nowiderwardes, ne sitten ne lien ne slepen, oc bæron al ðat iren. Mani þusen hi drapen mid hungær. (ed. Clark, 55–56)

> [They took the people they believed had any goods, both by day and by night, men and women, and put them in prison; they were after gold and silver, and tortured them with unspeakable tortures, for

never were martyrs tortured as they were. Men hung them by the feet and smoked them with foul smoke. Men hung them by the thumbs, others by the head, and hung byrnies on their feet. Men put knotted strings about their heads and twisted them so that they went to the brain. They put them in prisons with adders, snakes, and toads therein, and killed them thus.... In many castles were lof and grin, that is, chains that two or three men had enough to do to bear one, so made that it is fastened to a beam and a sharp iron done on around a man's throat and his neck, that he might not move from there any way, neither sit nor lie nor sleep, but bear all the iron. Many thousands they killed with hunger.] (trans. Savage, 265)

The entry continues by turning to the economic and social chaos that accompanied this violence. Narratively, the violence performed on the bodies of the English people has its echo in the violence performed on the land, the "body" of the state:

Hi læiden gældes on the tunes æure um wile, 7 clepeden it "tenserie." Ða þe uurecce men ne hadden nammore to gyuen, þa ræueden hi 7 brendon alle the tunes, ðat wel þu myhtes faren al a dæis fare, sculdest thu neure finden man in tune sittende ne land tiled. Ða was corn dære, 7 flesc 7 cæse 7 butere, for nan ne wæs o þe land. Wrecce men sturuen of hungær.... ne forbaren hi nouther circe ne cyrceiærd, oc namen al þe god ðat þarinne was 7 brenden sythen þe cyrce 7 al tegædere. Ne hi ne forbaren biscopes land ne abbotes ne preostes, ac ræueden munekes 7 clerekes.... Ðe biscopes 7 lered men heom cursede æure, oc was heom naht þarof, for hi uueron al forcursæd 7 forsuoren 7 forloren. (ed. Clark, 56)

[They laid taxes on the towns all the while, and called it "tenserie," protection money; when poor men had no more to give, they plundered and burned all the towns, so that though you might well fare all day, never would you find a man staying in a town, nor land tilled. Then was corn dear, and meat, and cheese and butter, for there was none in the land. Poor men died of hunger.... they spared neither church nor churchyard, but seized all the goods therein, and later burned the church and all together. Nor did they spare in the land either abbots or priests, but plundered monks and clerics.... Bishops and clergy cursed them ever, but it was nothing to them, for they were all utterly cursed, forsworn and lost.] (trans. Savage, 268)

We invoke the *Peterborough Chronicle*'s litany of horrors not because it represents an "objective" historical account of the activities of the Norman aristocracy during the mid-twelfth century, but because it provides an interesting—although certainly not disinterested—narrative vividly conveying the sense of political and social upheaval that many of the chronicler's countrymen must have shared. It suggests that the state apparatus—the systems of finance, justice, and administration—put in place during Henry's reign seemed to be unraveling and with it the grudging civil peace that marked the first decades of the twelfth century, revealing the strains and conflicts created by the imposition of Norman feudalism on England after the conquest.[1] The chronicler offers, as an explanation for the rampant disorder he documents, the rationalization that "Crist slep 7 his halechen" (ed. Clark, 56) [Christ and his saints slept (trans. Savage, 268)]. Ideologically he could perceive of such disorder only as a fate to be endured, punishment for some terrible sin. Stephen was foolish and mild, the barons traitors and forsworn.

The chronicler glosses over the political, constitutional, economic, and social transformations created by Stephen's reign. He shows little interest in the dynastic crises precipitated by the conquest that came to a head with the death of Henry I when succession was put in doubt. Such temporal issues were not supposed to interest the medieval historian, who busied himself with the ultimately timeless concerns of salvation history and the individual's pursuit of perfection.[2] But these social crises and transformations concern us here. The growth of monarchical and state power, and the consolidation of feudal prerogatives under Henry, followed by the disorder and chaos created by the civil war between Stephen and Henry's daughter Matilda provide the material conditions under which the first postconquest Arthurian histories were produced and enable us to interrogate the interests served by the creation of a legendary king from Britain's antique past.

In 1138, only two years after Stephen's coronation, Geoffrey of Monmouth's *Historia Regum Britanniæ* first appeared.[3] Written by a canon of Oxford, the *Historia*'s account of a Celtic chieftain named Arthur would become the basis of one of Britain's most enduring culture heroes and the subject of countless medieval romances. But Geoffrey's legendary kings of Britain were not yet romance heroes.[4] They are conceived of as historical monarchs whom Geoffrey used to fabricate a myth of origin for a British monarchy (see Patterson, *Negotiating the Past*, 199–204). They create the illusion of a more or less unbroken line of succession that culminates in the emergence of Arthur out of the social chaos of the Saxon invasions. This teleological account of history feeds a nostalgia for an originary wholeness, a past from which Geoffrey's patrons could legitimate their own rule and consolidate their interests. By identifying themselves with *British* rather than Norman or Saxon kings, the first Norman rulers of England were able to counter the fragmentation and decentralization that marked feudalism in France and that remained an obstacle to the establishment of a centralized administrative bureaucracy (see Crane, 14–24). In this chapter we explore the specific anxieties that impelled Geoffrey of Monmouth, a cleric possibly of British ancestry, to create such a historical origin for his Norman patrons. Our claim is not that Geoffrey was the first historian to mention Arthur; rather we argue that he created him by being the first to shape scattered and enigmatic references in Latin and perhaps in Welsh or Breton into a coherent narrative, a story with a beginning, middle, and end. Our interest, then, is less in reconstructing a textual pedigree for a historical Arthur than in examining the textual Arthur as a social signifier, whose function was to smooth over the ideological conflicts created by the Norman colonization of England and the uneasy and unequal cohabitation of three distinct cultures—Norman, Saxon, and Celt.[5]

"Idle Fictions" and "Authentic History"

As we suggest in chapter 1, medieval scholars in the twentieth century have tended to understand and value the *Historia Regum Britanniæ* based on the functions we have assigned to it as the progenitor of the characters who appear in literally thousands of Arthurian narratives—histories, chronicles, romances, poems, paintings, novels, films, even comic books. We generally read it proleptically from our own time, with the benefit of hindsight. Perhaps we cannot read it in any other way.[6] Yet, what we shall call Geoffrey's "performance of history" may reveal as much to us about medieval attitudes toward history as the most serious and sober, the most trustworthy, of Geoffrey's contemporaries, historians like William of Malmesbury.

Why, for instance, might the Norman conquerors of England choose to legitimate their rule by linking themselves through these histories to a specifically *British* past? Clearly the historians involved all understood the danger of this move at the same time they were promoting it. The very same stories about Arthur that glorified their Norman patrons could be (and were) used by the Welsh to foment rebellion against them. These anxieties seem central to twelfth-century debates about the truth of Arthurian narratives. William of Malmesbury contrasts the "idle fictions" of the foolish Britons with "authentic histories," as does Giraldus Cambrensis. Geoffrey trades on this contrast between vernacular Celtic "storytelling" and the learned Latin histories produced by those in power by choosing to write in Latin, a choice that, William of Newburgh notes, gives his text "the colour of an honest history" (see Chambers, 107).[7]

The issue of the "truth" or "falsity" of Geoffrey's *Historia* has dominated discussions of this first complete chronicle account of King Arthur since its first appearance in the mid-twelfth century. During the Middle Ages, the work was described by "serious" historians, like William of Newburgh, as a well-crafted fiction, but a pack of lies nonetheless.[8] The well-known anecdote related by Giraldus Cambrensis in *Itinerarium Cambri* perhaps more wittily expresses the doubts of other twelfth-century historians about the veracity of the *Historia Regum Britanniæ*. He writes of a possessed man who could discern the truth or falsity of a book, even though he was illiterate:

> It is worth relating that in our days there lived in the neighbourhood of the City of Legions a certain Welshman called Meilyr who could explain the occult and foretell the future.... Although he was completely illiterate, if he looked at a book which was incorrect, which contained some false statement, or which aimed at deceiving the reader, he immediately put his finger on the offending passage. If you asked him how he knew this, he said that the devil first pointed out the place with its finger.... When he was harassed beyond endurance by these unclean spirits, Saint John's Gospel was placed on his lap, and then they all vanished immediately, flying away like so many birds. If the Gospel were afterwards removed and the *History of the Kings of Britain* by Geoffrey of Monmouth put there in its place, just to see what would happen, the demons would alight all over his body, staying there longer than usual and being even more demanding. (Gerald of Wales, 117–18)

It is worth pointing out, however, that Giraldus's attack on Geoffrey's veracity takes the form not of the methodical investigation and exposure of the *Historia*'s errors that the modern positivist scholar might expect, but, in most medieval fashion, of a trial by ordeal, however ironically he conceives of it. The body of the illiterate becomes the sign that guarantees the truthfulness of the book of God's Word and the falsity of Geoffrey's, just as in the *Peterborough Chronicle*'s account of Stephen's reign, the body of "the people" becomes God's most visible sign of social disorder. Giraldus is far less concerned with "objective" reporting than with what we might call "poetic justice," which his audience would have understood as divine providence. Medieval history, in both its "serious" and "fabulous" forms, invested its world with the power to reveal truths through symbols that were not strictly literal but poetic, or more accurately, that confounded the literal and the metaphoric.[9]

Such an orientation may suggest why Geoffrey's *Historia* was, despite the fulminations of a William of Newburgh, so well received as a historical document. J. C. Crick points to the existence of 215 extant manuscript copies of the *Historia*, including fifty-eight texts from the twelfth century alone (Crick, 3:196–217; Reeve). Even more convincing evidence of the *Historia*'s significance is the fact that there are few medieval historians after 1150, Giraldus Cambrensis included, who do not show extensive traces of Geoffrey's influence. Down to the sixteenth century Geoffrey's history found its way not only into works that modern scholars would call fiction—medieval romances, and Renaissance plays like *Gorbeduc* and *Lear*—but also into the works of serious English chroniclers.[10] Although there are few manuscripts of the *Historia* after 1500, evidence suggests that materials relating to Geoffrey's account of Arthur continued to circulate among historians, courtiers, politicians, and poets side by side with what we might consider more sober history in an uneasy and conflicted cohabitation well into the seventeenth century.[11] If the historical narrative provided by the *Historia* is not in some strictly objective sense of the word "true," that is, if it does not tell us "what really happened" in the Celtic prehistory of Britain, it clearly spoke to something that resonated for Geoffrey's twelfth-century contemporaries and for historians up until the English Civil War. It provided a narrative of cultural identity and origins that proved to be remarkably long lived not only in British culture, but in European culture as well.[12] This is not to suggest that Geoffrey's *Historia* was uncritically accepted by all. However, the strength of the humanist critique of Galfridian history perhaps gains from hindsight. This skepticism did not immediately sweep away Arthurian history as a vestige of medieval ignorance, for it still had important political functions to serve.[13] Until the end of the seventeenth century the *Historia* (along with its many redactions) provided a readily available account of British origins that did not represent the British simply as barbarians colonized first by the Romans, then the Saxons and Normans. Furthermore, it provided legitimation for and mystification of monarchical rule. Henry VII and James I, for instance, to buttress their claims to the throne, commissioned genealogies linking them to the kings of Geoffrey's *Historia* (Parry and Caldwell, 89). Geoffrey's history seems to have lost its appeal as an appropriable source of information only in the seventeenth century after the divine right of kings had been thoroughly discredited by two decades of civil war.

Modern historians and literary historians focus on questions about the book's literal truth that are quite different from those its original audience asked; they carefully investigate Geoffrey's sources, the possible existence of the mysterious book given him by Walter, archdeacon of Oxford, and the nature of the "historical Arthur" that the *Historia* refracts. Most argue that Geoffrey's book is best read as a fictional narrative rather than a historical one. Antonia Gransden dismisses it as "intellectually dishonest" (1:203). N. Wright, in pointing to the unlikelihood that the *Historia* was derived, as Geoffrey maintains, from an ancient Celtic text, insists that "few modern critics believe Geoffrey's assertions" (Geoffrey, ed. Wright, vii).[14] But it was Geoffrey's ability to seize upon his audience's interests, in the guise of history, that made his work so enormously popular. An emphasis upon sources and the veracity of sources—upon historical facts—reflects a much more rigid separation of historical truth and poetic fiction than the twelfth-century audience of the *Historia*, even its critics, would have understood.

From the opening series of dedications, Geoffrey, like William of Malmesbury, begins a continuous self-commentary on the nature of historical writing; he "performs" history in much the same way his character Merlin performs various astonishing feats for the court.[15] In these passages Geoffrey's scholarly voice emerges most clearly, establishing for his audience his credibility to undertake the task of writing a history of the kings of Britain. Employing a discursive strategy widely incorporated by scholars even today—and therefore an immediately recognizable and conventional marker of historicity—Geoffrey cites his sources, explains why they are inadequate, and claims that he will rectify their inadequacies. The central feature of Geoffrey's dedication is his assertion that he received the information for his work from Walter, archdeacon of Oxford, in a "Britannici sermonis librum uetustissimum" (ed. Wright, 1) [very ancient book written in the British language (trans. Thorpe, 51)]. This new scholarly find, a heretofore unknown manuscript in a foreign language, whether it actually existed or not, and whether Geoffrey claims it seriously or ironically, is a performance designed to establish the authority of the *Historia*.

Even Geoffrey's commentaries on historical style serve as markers of his credibility. Geoffrey, in fact, points to the *Historia*'s absence of style as proof of its legitimacy. This absence, he claims, offers the reader unmediated access to the events of the distant past. From the very beginning, Geoffrey informs his readers:

> Rogatu itaque illius ductus, tametsi infra alienos ortulos falerata uerba non collegerim, agresti tamen stilo propriisque calamis contentus codicem illum in Latinum sermonem transferre curaui. Nam si ampullosis dictionibus paginam illinissem, tedium legentibus ingererem, dum magis in exponendis uerbis quam in historia intelligenda ipsos commorari oporteret. (ed. Wright, 1)

> [At Walter's request I have taken the trouble to translate this book into Latin, although, indeed, I have been content with my own expressions and my own homely style and I have gathered no gaudy flowers of speech in other men's gardens. If I had adorned my page with high-flown rhetorical figures, I should have bored my readers, for they would have been forced to spend more time in discovering the meaning of my words than in following the story.] (trans. Thorpe, 51)

This strategy too is performative. Geoffrey's assertions about historical style deconstruct even as he deploys them.[16] His insistence that historical writing must be devoid of flowery metaphor is subverted by the metaphoric language—"gather[ing] gaudy flowers of speech in other men's gardens"—that makes the assertion. Geoffrey's performance is at once self-effacing and promotional. It disavows, as Robertson has argued (45), the tradition of classical rhetoric that Geoffrey's university education—his position as *magister*—would have trained him for, at the same time that it claims authority and credibility from his status as a translator, as one who transforms British "idle fictions" into "authentic history" written in Latin.

Geoffrey, then, went to great lengths to provide the illusion that his work was a rendering of "historical truth," rather than "narrative truth."[17] At the heart of Geoffrey's performance of history is the representation of the historian offering unmediated access to the past. His choice to write his history in Latin (which given his education was most likely not a choice at all) is an integral part of that performance. His claim (whether true or not) to translate from the language of the twice-conquered Britains into the international language of power and authority gives force to his claims to historical accuracy.

However, if history, as Claude Lévi-Strauss suggests, "is partial in the sense of being biased even when it claims not to be" (*Savage Mind*, 257–58), then the audience and the audience's expectations have as much force in forming a historical document as the "objective facts" that are supposed to give that document its shape. Nowhere is this more true than in the darkest recesses of unrecorded prehistory. Geoffrey's subject was the most ancient history of Britain, its Celtic prehistory before the coming of either the Saxons or the Normans. The narratives to which he would have access and from which he compiled his own narrative—Gildas's *De Excidio Britanniae* and Bede's *Historia Ecclesiastica* are both mentioned—offer a sparse and often enigmatic record. Geoffrey of Monmouth gave his readers exactly what they wanted and expected. Unlike Gildas, he refrained from excessive moralizing, and he dramatically expanded upon much of the information provided by Bede. He fills the gaps left in the writings of his predecessors, transforming their "free associations" into a narrative, written not only in very good medieval Latin, but also incorporating medieval literary conventions with such ease that they were hardly noticeable.

Contemporary scholars are inclined to focus on the *Historia* as revolutionary because it is the first text to offer a complete history of Arthur's reign. Without the *Historia*, such snippets as we have of Arthur in other early histories would hardly have coalesced into a satisfying narrative, let alone a cultural, and indeed almost national, mythology. But were the *Historia* a completely groundbreaking document, it would have been viewed during the Middle Ages with a much healthier degree of skepticism. As H. R. Jauss and Thomas Kuhn both suggest, texts that cause a shift in "horizons of expectation" are virtually certain to be dismissed by their initial audiences. Geoffrey slowly draws his readers into his revision of history. Even as he takes stylistic and factual liberties with received materials, Geoffrey remains close enough to his sources, at times even quoting them directly, to convince his audience that nothing really unusual is happening. Chronological markers, which establish a time frame in relation to biblical time, make the text seem, as Susan Schwartz has remarked, "steeped in the traditions of Christian historiography" (34). The impression one receives from the beginning of the *Historia* is that it is a traditional piece of medieval history. As R. W. Leckie Jr. maintains, Geoffrey's "approach is seemingly orthodox, the events endowed with surpassing verisimilitude. In the absence of controlling data it was inordinately difficult to catch him in a lie" (40).

However, the success of the *Historia*, we would claim, was based not so much on the credibility of his sources as on Geoffrey's ability to extend the limits of historical discourse, on his ability to fuse and confuse historical truth and narrative truth and to provide his readers with a past, with a myth of origin. When Geoffrey reaches his section on the Saxon invasions and the kingship of Vortigern, he offers not only new historical material but a new manner of presentation that includes authorial intrusions, extensive descriptions, and psychological analyses. With his prophecies of Merlin, Geoffrey redefines the nature of material meriting inclusion in "historical" writing.[18] By this time, however, Geoffrey's original readers, no doubt, were drawn in by the compelling narrative, more interested in Geoffrey's story than in whether it conveyed objective "facts" or looked like the histories with which they were familiar. These two narrative moments—the Saxon invasions and the appearance of Merlin—that begin the Arthurian history signal the shift in Geoffrey's narrative from a conventional medieval chronicle history to history encoded as romance (Shichtman, "Gawain in Wace," 103–19).

The question, finally, that suggests itself is not whether Geoffrey's sources are trustworthy, but what the source is of his interest in this ancient prehistory. For whom is Geoffrey writing? Geoffrey's own answer is characteristically enigmatic.

> Cvm mecum multa et de multis sepius animo reuoluens in hystoriam regum Britannie inciderem, in mirum contuli quod infra mentionem quam de eis Gildas & Beda luculento tractatu fecerant nichil de regibus qui ante incarnationem Christi inhabitauerant, nichil etiam de Arturo ceterisque compluribus qui post incarnationem successerunt repperissem, cum et gesta eorum digna eternitate laudis constarent et a multis populis quasi inscripta iocunde et memoriter predicarentur. (ed. Wright, 1)

> [Whenever I have chanced to think about the history of the kings of Britain, on those occasions when I have been turning over a great many such matters in my mind, it has seemed a remarkable thing to me that, apart from such mention of them as Gildas and Bede had each made in a brilliant book on the subject, I have not been able to discover anything at all on the kings who lived here before the Incarnation of Christ, or indeed about Arthur and all the others who fol-

lowed on after the Incarnation. Yet the deeds of these men were such that they deserve to be praised for all time. What is more, these deeds were handed joyfully down in oral tradition, just as if they had been committed to writing, by many peoples who had only their memory to rely on.] (trans. Thorpe, 51)

If, as Hayden White suggests, history is a collection of narratives we tell to construct a past from which we would like to be descended, then reconstructing Geoffrey's purpose would seem to require that we consider whose past Geoffrey is setting out to construct. The simple answer might be to note that Geoffrey may have been at least partly Celtic by birth and thus a member of a British race twice conquered, once by the Saxons and again by the Normans. That he called himself Geoffrey of Monmouth suggests that he had some connection with Monmouth, birth being the most likely. Several geographic references to Caerleon-on-Usk, which is only twenty miles from Monmouth, reinforce the belief that Geoffrey's knowledge of Wales was firsthand. Geoffrey's connections to Wales suggest that he may have been writing a history to glorify his own doubly oppressed people, to create for them a past that "deserve[d] to be praised for all time."[19]

We might, however, entertain the possibility that Geoffrey was constructing a past for a "we" more heterogeneous than the pronoun can suggest. T. D. Crawford has suggested that Geoffrey, even if he was Celtic by birth and even if he was conscious of his British origins, was thoroughly Norman in his upbringing and tastes. Most likely his "mother tongue" was Anglo-Norman rather than Breton or Welsh and, if he knew any Welsh, he would have learned it as an adult, along with English (157). Geoffrey praises the Bretons, but not the Welsh, with whom the Normans were frequently at war.[20] Michelle Warren usefully describes the *Historia* as "border writing," a text conceived "at the edges of regional differences," which represents "the formation of spatial, ethnic, linguistic, and temporal boundaries" (*History on the Edge*, 2). Geoffrey's epithet Monemutensis locates him in the periphery, in the Welsh marches created by Norman colonization, but his position as clerk of Oxford and his name on several of Stephen's charters locates him firmly at the center of Norman power (25). And indeed, in the *Historia*, his most lavish praise is reserved for his Norman patrons. Fiona Tolhurst demonstrates the numerous and flattering parallels Geoffrey's text draws between the Normans and the early Britons (76–84; see also Gransden, 201). These parallels suggest that one function of the *Historia* was to legitimate and naturalize the Norman occupation of England by linking it to Britain's earliest prehistory. A closer examination of the opening series of dedications to the Norman magnates Robert, earl of Gloucester, and Waleran, count of Meulan, however, best reveals the complex, dialogically agitated political environment in which Geoffrey wrote.

Patronage and Symbolic Capital

Of the 215 complete manuscripts of the *Historia Regum Britanniæ*, the majority are dedicated to Robert of Gloucester (who is also the dedicatee of William of Malmesbury's *Gesta Regum Anglorum;* Crick, 4:119–20). Cambridge, University Library, MS Ii.i.14 (1706), which is the basis of Acton Griscom's edition, and eight other manuscripts, however, are dedicated both to Robert and to Waleran, count of Meulan. Only one, Bern, Burgerbibliothek, MS 568, the basis of Neil Wright's edition, is dedicated both to Robert and to King Stephen (Crick, 4:116–17; Geoffrey, ed. Wright, 1).[21] Geoffrey's dedications make it clear that he desired patronage from his Norman overlords and hoped that his history would win him advancement and perhaps even royal favor, given the prominence of his dedicatees. Robert of Gloucester was Henry I's illegitimate son, and Count Waleran was the head of the powerful Beaumont family that, under Henry and his successor Stephen, enjoyed royal favor and controlled extensive landholdings in both Normandy and England.

However, by the time the *Historia* appeared, a dedication to both Robert and Count Waleran (or alternatively to Robert and Stephen) must have seemed either awkward or, more likely, a way of hedging his bets. When Henry I, the last of the Conqueror's sons, died in 1135 without a male heir, he designated his daughter Matilda as his heir. She was at the time married to Geoffrey, count of Anjou (the Angevins were traditionally enemies of the dukes of Normandy, so the marriage represented a political alliance), and her son Henry was still an infant. Upon the death of Henry I, Stephen of Blois, Henry's nephew and a grandson of the Conqueror, moved quickly to seize the throne. With the help of his half brother, Henry of Blois, who was bishop of Winchester and abbot of Glastonbury, Stephen was crowned on December 22, 1135 in Winchester.[22] During the two decades of his reign, Matilda waged an on-and-off civil war to regain her throne, something that she nearly succeeded at for a brief period in 1141. Stephen's reign, then, was marked by almost continual internecine warfare—the "anarchy" so vividly depicted by the *Peterborough Chronicle*. The Norman aristocracy used the conflict between Stephen and Matilda, playing their loyalties off against each side, to aggrandize their own positions of power and influence at the expense of the crown and "the people." That Geoffrey could dedicate his *Historia* to these men—the one an illegitimate son of Henry and the chief prosecutor of his daughter Matilda's claims to the throne, the other a loyal supporter of King Stephen—and that Geoffrey could then in various manuscripts change the subjects of these dedications to suit the occasion without changing the language, demonstrates the nature of the *normal* procedures, established through nearly a century of Norman occupation, that dictated the relationships of wealth, power, and influence under the monarch, and the mechanisms for distributing what Pierre Bourdieu has called symbolic capital (178).

The language of the dedications merits some attention for what it can tell us about the operations of patronage relationships in twelfth-century England. Geoffrey asks that through Robert's patronage, his book will be

ut sic doctore te monitore corrigatur quod non ex Galfridi Monemutensis fonticulo censeatur exortum set sale Minerue tue conditum illius dictatur editio quem henricus illustris rex Anglorum generauit quem philosophia liberalibus artibus erudiuit quem innata probitas in milicia militibus prefecit; unde Brittannia insula tibi nunc temporibus nostris acsi alterum Henricum adepta interno congratulatur affectu. (ed. Wright, xiii)

[emended by your knowledge and your advice so that it must no longer be considered as the product of Geoffrey of Monmouth's small talent. Rather, with the support of your wit and wisdom, let it be accepted as the work of one descended from Henry, the famous King of the English; of one whom learning has nurtured in the liberal arts and whom his innate talent in military affairs has put in charge of our soldiers, with the result that now, in our lifetime, our island of Britain hails you with heartfelt affection, as if it had been granted a second Henry.] (trans. Thorpe, 51–52)

To a modern audience inured to the market relations involved in twentieth-century publishing, this fulsome dedication must seem sycophantic in the extreme.[23] Its sincerity must seem even more strained when the second dedicatee, Waleran, count of Meulan (or alternately Robert of Gloucester), is praised in exactly the same terms as "altera regni nostri columpna" (ed. Wright, xiii, 1) [a second pillar of our kingdom (trans. Thorpe,

52)]. Waleran, like Robert, is praised for his military prowess and his learning:

> ut in militaribus clareres exercitiis ad castra regum direxit ubi commilitones tuos audacter supergressus & terror hostium existere & protectio tuorum esse paternis auspiciis addidicisti. Fidelis itaque protectio tuorum existens me tuum uatem codicemque ad oblectamentum tui editum sub tutela tua recipias ut sub tegmine tam patul arboris recubans calamum musae tue coram inuidis atque improbis tuto modulamine resonare queam. (ed. Wright, xiv, 1–2)

> [so that you might become famous in the military affairs of our army, she [Mother Philosophy] has led you to the camp of kings, and there, having surpassed your fellow-warriors in bravery, you have learnt, under your father's guidance, to be a terror to your enemies and a protection to your own folk. Faithful defender as you are of those dependent on you, accept under your patronage this book which is published for your pleasure. Accept me, too, as your writer, so that, reclining in the shade of a tree which spreads so wide, and sheltered from envious and malicious enemies, I may be able in peaceful harmony to make music on the reed-pipe of a muse who really belongs to you.] (trans. Thorpe, 52)

These twin dedications gloss over the political turmoil and divided loyalties of Stephen and Matilda's struggle over the throne, collapsing them into and resolving them by means of the dyadic relation between patron and client, liege lord and vassal. One would hardly guess from the dedications that these two "pillar[s] of our kingdom" were locked in a deadly civil war that was, as the *Peterborough Chronicle* suggests, tearing the kingdom apart.

The rhetoric of the dedications reveals a structure of patron–client relationships in twelfth-century England that accords well with what anthropologists, like Mauss (*The Gift*) and Bourdieu (*Theory of Practice*), and sociologists, like Eisenstadt and Roniger (*Patrons, Clients, and Friends*), who study patron–client networks have learned about them.[24] The patronage networks that marked feudal relationships dominated by the exchange of gifts were still the primary means by which those outside of the aristocracy negotiated their relations with it. The anonymous author of the *Gesta Stephani* frequently iterates the importance of Stephen's patronage. For instance, having accepted Stephen as their king, his barons enact the rituals of feudalism, including the receiving of gifts: "Omnes fere primi totius regni læte eum et ueneranter recepere, plurimisque ab eo muneribus donati, sed et terris amplificati, liberali cum iureiurando, præmisso hominio, eius sese seruitio ex toto manciparunt" [almost all of the chief men of the kingdom accepted him gladly and respectfully, and having received many gifts from him gladly and respectfully and likewise enlargement of their lands, they devoted themselves wholly to his service by a voluntary oath, after paying homage] (8). Social relations in twelfth-century England were marked by an economy of expenditure rather than by an economy of accumulation characteristic of commodity exchange. Status was achieved not by accumulating and hoarding vast amounts of wealth, but by "having the gift" of that wealth.[25]

Patron–client relationships, Eisenstadt and Roniger argue, are particularistic and diffuse, rather than legal or contractual. They are less formal than legal ties and highly interpersonal, established between individuals or networks of individuals rather than between organized corporate groups. Lewis Hyde has shown that gift giving draws individuals together, establishing personal bonds between them, while commodity exchange is possible precisely when such bonds are absent, when individuals are alienated from one another (56–57; see also Eisenstadt and Roniger, 48–49). Gift relations are usually delimited by a system of finely articulated symbolic and institutional terms, involving elaborate rituals, codes, and rules. These rules are almost always unspoken or spoken only in an elaborately codified language (such as that used by Geoffrey in his dedications) that functions to disguise as personal and private what, in a commodity exchange, would be seen as economic or political transactions. This suggests why so much of the contemporary political climate must be erased in Geoffrey's appeals to Stephen, Robert, and Waleran; it has simply been privatized.

Patron–client relations are entered into voluntarily; as a result, they are highly unstable relationships and can be terminated voluntarily by either party. For this reason, it was not unusual for a client to seek out more than one patron or even to incur obligations on both sides of a conflict between patrons. We find unconvincing Michelle Warren's argument that Geoffrey's appeals to individuals on both sides of the conflict between Stephen and Matilda "authors (and authorizes) the reconciliation that he eventually witnessed in 1153 when Stephen recognized Henry's grandson as his heir" (*History on the Edge*, 29). Geoffrey's appeal to more than one patron was a common feature of the patronage relationships that organized political relationships well into the early modern period, providing clients, who usually had less power in the exchange, with a means of profiting from the competition among patrons for a clientele.[26] Geoffrey's dedications can be used interchangeably precisely because the highly codified formal language of his appeals did not need to be tailored to fit specific individuals or political situations.

The relationships between a client and his patrons are furthermore marked by extreme inequality. The distance between Geoffrey and Robert of Gloucester (or Stephen) in this dedication is measured by the distance between Geoffrey's "small talent" and Robert's supposed reputation as a "second Henry." In the case of such extreme inequality, the client can act effectively only if he can exploit the competition among patrons to secure a clientele. Geoffrey literally constructs relationships with his patrons by offering them the "gift" of his book. Such gifts call for reciprocity. Geoffrey calls on Robert to "support" his work, but the nature of that support is unspecified; his dedication to Waleran is a bit more specific, suggesting that he desires from him protection from "envious and malicious enemies." Sometimes clients will attempt to mitigate that inequality by casting their gift of symbolic capital as the greater, reversing the situation and projecting dependency onto the patron (see Finke, "Spenser for Hire," 219). But we see no evidence in Geoffrey's dedications that he is attempting to "overturn these inequalities" or "expose the malleability of relations of domination" as Warren suggests (*History on the Edge*, 28).

Because they are based on the exchange of gifts, patron–client relationships are not simple one-time exchanges; rather they entail long-term obligations and credit. There is no evidence that Geoffrey received any immediate benefit as a result of any of his dedications. But by 1151 (after Robert of Gloucester's death) he had been given the relatively minor episcopacy of St. Asaph, so eventually he was able to capitalize on his relationships—however nebulous and undefined—with his Norman patrons, even if Welsh insurrections prevented him from ever visiting his see before his death.

The most important feature of patron–client relationships, however, is that they involve exchanges of different types of resources. These resources may be economic and material (the fief or benefice); often they are political and military (support, loyalty); but they are also quite often intangible, but no less vital resources like power, influence, prestige, and status. In *Outline of a Theory of Practice*, Bourdieu uses the term "symbolic capital" to refer to the means by which the wealthy convert some of their disproportionate wealth into forms of prestige, status, and social control through acts that are understood as voluntary acts of generosity. This symbolic capital would be transferable into labor and services that, in turn, would generate even more material wealth (178).[27]

In praising Stephen, Robert, and Waleran for strength and wisdom, Geoffrey hopes to receive not only wealth or economic gain, but more intangible symbolic capital like power, influence, or prestige. According to Bourdieu, in a precapitalist economy, economic consideration must be extended to all the goods, material and symbolic, without distinction, that present themselves as rare and worthy of being sought after: "which may be fair words or smiles, handshakes or shrugs, compliments or attention, challenges or insults, honors or honours, powers or pleasures, gossip or scientific information, distinction or distinctions" (178). There is no necessity to distinguish here between military, cultural, economic, political, and spiritual resources. All are able to circulate freely within the social formation of feudalism.

A closer examination of the climactic Arthurian section of the *Historia* may enable us to explore more precisely the nature of the symbolic capital Geoffrey's patrons might have received from the book, as well as that which Geoffrey may have hoped to gain from their favorable reception. The last two sections of this chapter will explore how Geoffrey's text reflects the needs, desires, and anxieties of both patrons and client in the shifting, unstable, and complex set of power relations that constituted the Norman aristocracy under Stephen's rule.

Gender, Genealogy, and Imagined Communities

The symbolic capital that Geoffrey's patrons might have looked for from the *Historia* must be understood in terms of the political anarchy of Stephen's reign and Geoffrey's attempts to appeal to both sides in the conflict. Gransden has argued that Stephen's reign was characterized by a tremendous revival of interest in history, but she offers no explanation, except personal taste, for this interest (186). If a history could function as a species of symbolic capital, however, then what it might offer that both Stephen's and Matilda's supporters needed was a narrative of legitimacy. It could offer a connection with the island's past greatness that would buttress their disputed claims to the throne and, more importantly, "naturalize" Norman rule, promoting a fantasy of insular wholeness (Ingham,

Sovereign Fantasies, 9–10; Warren, *History on the Edge*, 25–59) appropriate to the centralization that was the hallmark of Norman political organization.

The letter prefacing the Troyes manuscript of William of Malmesbury's *Gesta Regum Anglorum* provides a revealing illustration of the exchange of symbolic capital at work in the writing of history (Troyes, Bibliothèque Municipale, MS 294). The passage describes how the *Gesta* came to be written at the request of Henry I's queen, Matilda:

> Thus on one occasion we were engaged in conversation with her on the subject of St. Aldhelm, whose kinswoman she claimed with proper pride to be, and she asked for information about his family. When told in reply that his lineage was the same as that of the kings of the West Saxons, she asked us to set out his whole family history in a short essay for her benefit, claiming that she was unworthy to receive the tribute of a volume on traditional lines on the history of the English kings. In our humble position we could not refuse a request backed by such imperious authority. We therefore arranged for the drawing up of a brief list of the English kings, both names and dates. She was then attracted by the project of a somewhat fuller narrative, and with that charm which was one of her strong points she easily induced us to contemplate a full history of her predecessors. So we came "to set on foot a greater enterprise" about our kings, one that would (as she put it) make them better known, bring her credit and be both useful and honourable to our foundation. (trans. Mynors, 9)

Here set out explicitly is the exchange of symbolic capital: credit for the queen, "utilitati et famae" for Malmesbury. Of particular interest in this passage is the fascinating glimpse into the strategies employed by potential clients to inflate the size of the commission by inflating the size of the patron's ego. At first unworthy for an enterprise as great as a full-fledged history, by the end of the passage, the queen is urging on a "greater enterprise," a full history of her ancestors that will link her with the glories of England's past.

History, in Geoffrey's hands, becomes a tool for working out the relations among various kinds of political communities, both imagined and face-to-face in the absence of discrete, independent sovereign nation-states. Britain, Geoffrey tells us at the beginning of the *Historia*, is inhabited by diverse peoples.

Postremo quinque inhabitatur populis: Normannis uidelicet atque Britannis, Saxonibus, Pictis et Scotis. Ex quibus Britones olim ante ceteros a mari esque ad mare insederunt donec ultione diuina propter ipsorum superueniente superbiam Pictis et Saxonibus cesserunt. (ed. Wright, 2)

[Lastly, Britain is inhabited by five races of people, the Norman-French, the Britons, the Saxons, the Picts, and the Scots. Of these the Britains once occupied the land from sea to sea, before the others came. Then the vengeance of God overtook them because of their arrogance and they submitted to the Picts and the Saxons.] (trans. Thorpe, 54)

In this passage, Geoffrey contrasts a fantasy of a time long past (*olim*) of insular unity with the recent history of complex and conflicted relations among groups with many competing loyalties. His use of *uidelicet* (of course, naturally) following "the Normans" perhaps hints of a future return to this previous state of wholeness. But in the meantime, how do these groups constitute themselves imaginatively as communities? How do they differentiate themselves as a group from the others, and how do they manage their interactions with one another? If, as Ingham has argued, "medieval community is imagined not through homogeneous stories of a singular 'people,' but through narratives of sovereignty as a negotiation of differences, of ethnicity, region, language, class, and gender" (*Sovereign Fantasies*, 9), it is important, on the one hand, to understand the function of "homogeneous stories of a singular people" in managing the complex and frequently rancorous differences among ethnicity, region, language, class, and gender that troubled twelfth-century England. On the other hand, we must understand how practices associated with region, ethnicity, class, and gender interact within the kinds of homogeneous origin stories Geoffrey's history represents to produce these five "races" (*populis*) he describes. Genealogy is a central practice that both obscures and negotiates the differences among various kinds of imagined British and English communities in the *Historia*.

Interest in genealogy in the twelfth century, as Howard Bloch has shown, was fueled by the shift in the methods by which aristocratic families in both France and England calculated kinship, a shift that coincided with attempts by both the monarchies and the church to centralize and extend their political power (Duby, *Knight*, 64–75, and Herlihy, 79–111). Prior to the twelfth century, aristocratic families were, in Bloch's terms, "a loosely defined grouping of relatives and retainers, 'friends' and neighbors [who] gravitated around the residence of a lord who was, above all, a patron, a distributor of land and gifts, the spoils of war or exchange" (65). Kinship was calculated horizontally, and little distinction was made between the lineage of the husband and that of the wife. This simple, yet highly unstable and always shifting set of patronage and kinship relationships, increasingly after the twelfth century, came to be replaced by a strategy that Bloch has called "the biopolitics of lineage" (65). To limit its size and the dilution of feudal holdings through partition, the aristocracy began to calculate lineage vertically, based on descent from a single male founder, to practice strict primogeniture, and to privilege blood ties over marriage ties. The family estate had to be passed on from eldest son to eldest son in an unbroken chain. Such a kinship system requires a narrative that enables a family to trace its ancestry back to an original founder; that is, it requires written genealogical history like Geoffrey's *Historia*.[28] As Frances Ingledew has argued, "British history is . . . systematically genealogized for the first time at the same moment it is first systematically imperialized" (678). To effect the transition from the dukes of Normandy to the kings of England, the claimants to the throne needed a lineage, preferably one of ancient origins. They needed a history that elided, as much as possible, the conflicted relationships among the five *populis* of England.

But they also needed to explain those conflicts. By the twelfth century, genealogical history provided one ideological practice that could bind individuals together as members of a particular kind of imagined community, one linked through lineal descent. But the fantasy of a single genealogical line is balanced, in Geoffrey's *Historia,* as in almost all genealogical narrative, by a paradoxical movement in the other direction toward filiation and discontinuity that threatens the autonomy and coherence of a single "people." Ingledew's linkage of imperialism and genealogy becomes ironic on closer inspection, as the expansionism that fuels twelfth-century imperialism undermines the very premises of lineal descent. The assimilationist strategies of imperialism that stress similarities run almost directly counter to those required to forge imagined communities that require differentiation. For this reason, the *Historia* must continually strike a balance between continuity and discontinuity, center and periphery, endogamy and exogamy, genealogy and filiation.

There is no better illustration of the complexities involved in imagining medieval communities than the situation that created the so-called Norman Conquest. From our vantage point, the Norman Conquest looked like a conquest—the forcible replacement of one ruling "people" by another. And such a view is no doubt fueled by historical accounts like that of Robert of Gloucester in the thirteenth century, which figure class differences in terms of ethnic differences (see discussion, chapter 4).

> Of þe Normans beþ heyemen þat beþ of Englonde,
> And þe lowemen of Saxons, as ich vnderstonde.
> (cited in Turville-Petre, 18)

Yet, at the time, the change may not have seemed quite so radical. The Norman claim to the throne rested on an exogamous marriage between Ethelred the Unready and Emma, who was the sister of Duke William's grandfather. This marriage may have introduced Norman culture into England long before the events of 1066. Edward the Confessor, Ethelred's son and the last "Saxon" king, was raised in Normandy and was thoroughly Norman in his tastes and attitudes. Childless, he promised the throne to his distant Norman cousin, William, on his death. It may well be that what was different after 1066 was not the ethnic makeup of the island or even the ethnic identifications of its people. Rather what changed was its political organization, the structure of power and the networks through which it ran. We must be careful not to confuse ethnic identity with the distribution of political power throughout society.

This example suggests the significance of marriage to the formation of imagined communities in the Middle Ages. With its emphasis on strict primogeniture, the narrative of lineage would seem to be a decidedly masculine affair, with little room for the stories of women who were, after all, simply vessels for the transmission of lineage. But the anxieties spawned by genealogy tend to bring gender to the foreground. Geoffrey's *Historia* seems unable not to mention women. It is populated by all sorts of women, whose stories weave their way through the battles, trades, and negotiations: Lavinia, Lavinia's niece who was Brutus's mother, Ignoge who was Brutus's wife, Estrildis, Gwendolen, Cordelia, Goneril, Regan, the daughter of Elsingius the king of Norway, the daughter of Duke Segnius the leader of the Allobroges, Tonuuena who was Belinus's and Brennius's mother, Genvissa, Helen who was the mother of Constantine, Renwein, Ygerna, Guinevere, Anna, Helena, and several unnamed queens, wives, and daughters. One explanation for the visibility of women in the *Historia* has been offered by Gransden, who argues that it was a mark of Geoffrey's partisan support for Matilda's claim, as evidenced by his dedication of the

Historia to Matilda's half brother. The presence of so many prominent women in the *Historia*—and Geoffrey's praise of those women—serves to create a precedent for the woman ruler (207–8; see also Tolhurst). This explanation seems reasonable but incomplete; without contradicting it, we would like to explore more fully the complex role gender plays in the biopolitics of lineage created during the twelfth century and the ways in which Geoffrey manages the anxieties created by women's necessary participation in genealogy.

The biopolitics of lineage required a marital strategy based on monogamy, exogamy, and the repression of pleasure (Duby, *Knight,* 30–31). Women's sexuality had to be strictly controlled in order to assure the legitimacy of any heir. An aristocratic woman had to be a virgin upon marriage and after marriage could have no sexual partners except her husband. Duby describes in eight words what the aristocratic classes of twelfth-century Europe considered womanly perfection: *pia filia, morigera conjunx, domina clemens, utilis mater.* "Until she married she was a dutiful daughter [*pia*]; she accepted the husband chosen for her. Her destiny being that of a wife, she then becomes what all wives should be: meek, obedient, *morigera.* But she was also a *domina,* or a mistress of a household, endowed with considerable power.... But ... she was relegated to an ancillary position, like the Virgin standing beside Christ as he sat in the seat of judgment; and there she was *clemens,* indulgent, introducing a little kindness into the seigniorial office.... Did motherhood, then, give her some authority at last? No, as a mother she had to be *utilis.* 'Useful' to whom? To other men, to her own sons" (234). Most of Geoffrey's portraits of women accord well with this characterization. In the *Historia,* women are dutiful daughters, like Cordelia. They are gifts, given with other kinds of gifts to men in strategic marriages, pawns in the gender politics of feudo-dynasticism. Brutus, for instance, is advised to ask for Pandrasus's daughter, Ignoge: "cum ea aurum & argentum, naues, et frumentum et quodcunque itineri uestro necessarium erit" (ed. Wright, 7) [With her you should ask for gold and silver, ships and grain, and everything else that you will need for your journey (trans. Thorpe, 63)]. Throughout the *Historia* the political marriage is a recurring motif; the "love match" has no place in this narrative. Women—given in marriage to strangers—are required to smooth over the conflicts between various political communities. Genvissa, for instance, is required to mediate the dispute between her husband, Arvirargus, and her father, Claudius, the former the British king and the latter the Roman emperor. Exogamy, in the *Historia*, becomes a means by which imagined communities negotiate their differences with one another.

Finally, women are mothers. Tonuuena's appeal to her son Brennius characterizes this role:

> Memento, fili, memento uberum istorum que suxisti matrisque tue uteri quo te opifex rerum in hominem ex non homine creauit, unde te in mundum produxit angustiis mea uiscera cruciantibus. Anxietatum igitur quas pro te passa sum reminiscens petitioni mee acquiesce fratrique tuo ueniam concede atque inceptam iram compesce. (ed. Wright, 28)

> [Remember, my son, remember these breasts which you once sucked! Remember the womb of your mother in which the Creator of all things fashioned you as a man-child from that stuff that was not yet human, bringing you forth into the world while the birth-pangs tore at her vitals because of you. Remember all the care and anxiety which I endured for your sake and then grant me my request. Forgive your brother.] (trans. Thorpe, 95–96)

Her pleas prevent a civil war between Brennius and his brother, Belinus.

Up until the reign of Vortigern and the arrival of the Saxons, then, Geoffrey's treatment of women is nothing if not conventional; most of the women, with a few notable exceptions (Cordelia, for instance, reigns as a queen) conform to gender roles that serve the needs of a biopolitics of lineage. But with the arrival of Hengest and Horsa as colonizing barbarians, there is a subtle shift in the narrative representation of women. Hengest's daughter Renwein is Geoffrey's first female villain.[29] What makes her story different from previous narratives about women in the *Historia* is that she assumes the narrative position of the "evil woman," who initiates tragedy by plotting against the men around her. Exotic, alien, and dangerous, she is endowed with faintly mysterious powers, embodying twelfth-century anxieties about women's role in completing the circuit of uneasy exchanges that mark the colonial encounters of the Norman ruling class.

Most recent writing on postcolonialism by medievalists has focused on medieval Europe's encounters with the East—depicting Jews and Saracens as the exotic, atavistic "other" of European expansionism.[30] Geraldine Heng, for instance, writing about Geoffrey, situates the *Historia* in the shadow of the First Crusade as a means of "negotiating the shock of communal trauma in the period of European and Norman history preceding the *Historia*'s appearance" ("Cannibalism," 99–102). And there is no question that Christian monarchs and nobles from the eleventh century on pursued what can only be described as aggressively imperialistic and militaristic policies against the Muslims to the east. Yet, as Janet Abu-Lughod has argued, throughout most of the Middle Ages, Europe lagged far behind the Middle East, India, and China in terms of cultural development. Medieval *mappaemundi* confirm this sense of Europe's marginality. Jerusalem was considered the center of the earth, "the navel of the region and of the whole earth" (Akbari, 21; Higgins, 34; see also chapter 5), while Europe was very much at the periphery of the world system—an upstart. And England was the periphery of a periphery (Abu-Lughod, 8–14). Occupying one of the northernmost outposts of civilization in the twelfth century, Normans did not need to travel all the way to Jerusalem to encounter the alien "other" (although they did do that as well). They were surrounded on all sides by groups they had either colonized or were trying to assimilate—Welsh, Scots, Irish, Saxons—whose cultures provided ample opportunity to explore the atavistic "other"[31] and to validate the stereotypes of otherness that a dominant culture requires to contain a subaltern people. We might bring the lens of postcolonial theory, then, to bear on the colonization of various ethnic groups in England throughout the Middle Ages. Arthurian narrative seems to provide medieval writers with a space to explore the cultural traumas of colonization, while at the same time projecting them into the fantasy frame of romance. In the *Historia*, the arrival of Hengest and Horsa stages a cultural encounter between the Christianized and cultured Britons and their pagan and primitive "other." Renwein becomes the mediator—the go-between—in this encounter.

As the exoticized other, Renwein disrupts the normal procedures through which women are exchanged as gifts between men.[32] Her beauty injects desire into what should be primarily a political transaction—the cementing of a political alliance—introducing what is essentially a romance motif into a text that has up until this moment been resolutely unromantic. But that motif is not seamlessly incorporated into the *Historia*; rather it generates contradiction, conflict, and a change in narrative style. The clash of generic expectations between the narrative of political and military history and that of romance strikingly and economically conveys the disastrous consequences of Vortigern's rashness. Upon seeing Renwein, Vortigern "est tantum eius decorem & incaluit" (ed. Wright, 67) [is greatly struck with her beauty and was filled with desire for her (trans. Thorpe, 159)]. His desire gets the better of his political judgment, placing him at a disadvantage in his political dealings with the Saxon chieftain Hengest. There is even a slight suggestion that Renwein lures him with instruments more artificial than her beauty. At their first meeting Vortigern "autem diuerso genere potus inebriatus intrante Sathana in corde suo amauit puellam & postulauit eam a patre suo" (ed. Wright, 67) [was tipsy from the mixture of drinks which he had consumed. Satan entered his heart, so that he fell in love with Renwein and asked her father to give her to him (trans. Thorpe, 160)]. This scene subtly suggests that Vortigern falls prey to some kind of erotic magic, that he is drugged both by his lust for Renwein and the mixture of unspecified intoxicants she offers him.[33]

Renwein's knowledge of potions and poisons links her with Merlin. Like the wise man, she is an exotic outsider—an alien—who can apparently call upon magic potions to negotiate her relationship with the men who otherwise possess and control her. The results of this subversion of power are made clear by Geoffrey, whose authorial voice intrudes judgmentally, repeating himself, "Intrauerat, inquam, Sathanas in corde suo quia christianus cum esset cum pagana coire desiderabat" (ed. Wright, 67) [I say that Satan entered his heart because, despite the fact that he was a Christian, he was determined to make love with this pagan woman (trans. Thorpe, 160)], and psychologizing its participants—Vortigern is recognized as having a "leuitate animi" (ed. Wright, 67) [unbalanced nature (trans. Thorpe, 160)].

Vortigern's marriage to Renwein may represent some anxieties about exogamy as a political strategy in the biopolitics of imperialism (Warren, *History on the Edge*, 47–48). It suggests the fear that one's wealth might pass into the hands of strangers or foreigners, either through death or, more likely, through an unequal gift exchange in which the wife's "people" are valued and rewarded at the expense of the husband's.[34] For the "gift" of his daughter, Hengest exacts from Vortigern the province of Kent, dispossessing the king's British client, Earl Gorangonus, who ruled that territory. Fearing the contaminating influence of these pagan outsiders—the corruption of blood, of religion, and, ultimately, of property—Vortigern's subjects turn against him:

> Quod cum uidissent Britones, timentes audatiam eorum dixerunt regi ut ipsos ex finibus regni sui expelleret. Non enim debebant pagani christianis communicare nec intromitti quia christiana lex

prohibebat. Insuper tanta multitudo advenerat ita ut ciuibus terrori essent. Iam nesciebatur quis paganus esset, quis christianus, quia pagani filias et consanguineas eorum sibi associauerant. Talia obicientes dissaudebant regi retinere illos ne in proditione aliqua ciues supergrederentur. At Vortegirnus diffugiebat consilio eorum adquiescere quia super omnes gentes propter coniugem suam ipsos diligebat. Quod cum uidissent Britones, deseruerunt ilco Vortegirnum. (ed. Wright, 68)

[When the Britons saw this, they were afraid that the Saxons would rebel. They told the King that he should banish the newcomers from the lands over which he ruled, for pagans ought not to be in close communication with Christians, nor be allowed to infiltrate in this way, for Christian faith forbade it. What was more, so large a force had now come that the inhabitants were terrified by them. Already no one could tell who was pagan and who was Christian, for the pagans were associating with their daughters and their female relations. By making such objections as these they urged the King not to let the Saxons stay any longer, for they feared that their fellow-countrymen would be crushed in some treasonable revolt. Vortigern was completely opposed to accepting his people's advice, for, because of his wife, he loved the Saxons above all other folk. Once the Britons understood this, they immediately deserted Vortigern.](trans. Thorpe, 161)

Renwein represents not only a threat to the normal operations of patronage and gift giving. She also represents the threat of miscegenation, the darker side of exogamy.[35] Particularly anxiety-inducing in this passage is the contact between Christian and pagan and the fear that that contact would obliterate differences.

The "evil woman" refuses to be merely a silent sign of exchange—a gift—but becomes instead a producer of her own signs (Lévi-Strauss, *Elementary Structures,* 496). Renwein undermines primogeniture, the very heart of the biopolitics of lineage. In poisoning Vortigern's son, Vortimer, she disrupts the orderly transmission of property from father to son. At a time when multiple marriages must have been the rule rather than the exception, anxieties about the security of the eldest son when the father or mother remarried must have been common. Similar anxieties haunt the story of Arthur's conception, although in this case (at least in Geoffrey's account) Ygerna is not cast in the role of the "evil woman." The role of schemer is displaced onto and smoothed over by Merlin who serves his king—and history—well by providing the "medicaminibus" [drugs] that enable Utherpendragon to satisfy his lust (ed. Wright, 97; trans. Thorpe, 207).[36] Subsequent writers down to Malory would worry about how to reconcile the time of Arthur's conception with the time at which Ygerna's "marital obligations" to her husband Gorlois end.[37] Geoffrey's unwillingness to address this issue is indicative, we believe, of the desire to present his patrons with a history that would conform to their ambitions, one in particular that could raise no questions about Arthur's legitimacy.

Once Arthur's birth has been explained, women seem much less central to the narrative. In the rare instances they appear, they are either victims of male lust (Helena, the niece of King Hoel, abducted and killed by the Mont Saint Michel giant) or gifts given in marriage (Guinevere). The "evil woman" plot recedes, only to be hinted at in the story of Mordred, during which Geoffrey tells us that this treacherous tyrant "proditionem insignitum esse reginamque Ganhumeram uiolato iure priorum nuptiarum eidem nephanda uenere copulatam fuisse" (ed. Wright, 129) [was living adulterously and out of wedlock with Queen Guinevere, who had broken the vows of her earlier marriage (trans. Thorpe, 257)]. Geoffrey is silent about Guinevere's role in this betrayal, refusing to tell us whether she had "broken the vows of her earlier marriage" willingly or unwillingly; he refuses to name her explicitly as an "evil woman": "Nec hoc quidem, consul auguste, Galfridus Monumontensis tacebit" (ed. Wright, 129) [About this particular matter, most noble Duke, Geoffrey of Monmouth prefers to say nothing (trans. Thorpe, 257)]. His silence both accuses and covers over the accusation. Though Geoffrey refuses to exonerate Guinevere, he seems to fear that outright condemnation will expose too starkly the corruption inherent in the biopolitics of lineage, thus tainting his own gift. This is the only passage outside of the dedication in which Geoffrey refers directly to his patron, the duke of Gloucester. Geoffrey's refusal either to name or exonerate Guinevere as a coconspirator and the symbolic capital his story offers his patron are linked in this passage. He seems to remind Gloucester that the gifts of lineage—whether brides or family histories—are never wholly unambiguous, but such ambiguities that arise are within the power of the historian and the reader, the client and the patron, to neutralize.

Magic and the Management of Intellectual Property

If the *Historia Regum Britanniæ* served to calm the anxieties of its principal patrons concerning issues of origin, what compensatory symbolic capital might Geoffrey have looked forward to if these patrons favorably received his gift of the book? We think it was not simply direct payment, in the form of either money or office. This kind of direct commodity exchange would not be consistent with a gift economy. But presumably an author would desire for his book to be read as widely as possible, especially a work that does not appear to have been directly commissioned. A patron could—and often did—circulate a manuscript to a small circle of retainers. The evidence suggests that Gloucester may have done just that. There was a twelfth-century copy of the *Historia* at Margam, a Cistercian abbey under the patronage of the duke of Gloucester, probably donated by the duke himself. He also gave a copy to Walter Espec who lent it, in turn, to Ralph Fitz Gilbert. His wife, Constance, passed it on to Geoffrey Gaimer, author of *L'Estoire des Engleis*, asking him to translate it into Norman French (Gransden, 208–9). But this sort of limited distribution surely is not what Geoffrey sought from a magnate as powerful as the duke of Gloucester.[38] Surely a lesser patron could have performed the same service. Geoffrey's dedication to Count Waleran, with its arboreal metaphor requesting shelter from envious and malicious enemies, makes it clear that he chiefly desired protection. What sort of protection did Geoffrey need for his work? Who would these envious and malicious enemies have been? To investigate these questions, we turn to the introduction, in book six, of Merlin Ambrosius, the magician who engineers the villain Vortigern's downfall, Utherpendragon's rise to power, and the tryst with Ygerna that produces Arthur. The marvelous feats attributed to Merlin in the *Historia* provide a fascinating example of the necessarily elaborate codes and rituals required for disguising the exchange of symbolic capital within patronage networks.[39] The depiction of Merlin also illustrates some of the anxieties the clients of powerful patrons may have had about the fruits of their intellectual labors.

The introduction of Merlin into his Arthurian history marks a second narrative shift within the *Historia* through which we might explore the limits of history as symbolic capital. Even by twelfth-century standards of historical scholarship, Merlin's presence calls into question the historicity of Geoffrey's text, as witnessed by William of Newburgh's attack on the *Historia*:

Et hunc quidem Merlinum patre incubo daemone ex femina natum fabulatur, cui propterea tanquam patrissanti excellentissimam atque latissimam tribuit praescientiam futurorum, cum profecto et veris rationibus et sacris literis doceamur daemones a luce Dei seclusos futura nequaquam contemplando praescire, sed quosdam futuros eventus ex signis sibi quam nobis notioribus conjuciendo magis quam cognoscendo colligere.

[His story is that this Merlin was born of a woman and sired by a demonic incubus; accordingly he ascribes to him a most outstanding and extensive foreknowledge of the future, on the grounds that he took after his father. In fact we are instructed by both true reasoning and the sacred writings that demons are shut out from God's light, and are wholly unable to have prior knowledge of the future by mentally observing it, though they apprehend certain future events by guesswork rather than knowledge, through signs better known to them than to us.] (28–31)

There is very little evidence of such fantastic figures elsewhere in the *Historia*, and Merlin certainly does not have the highly developed role he will have in the later chronicles and romances. Geoffrey seems to limit Merlin's role to the rise of Utherpendragon and the begetting of Arthur; he then disappears from the narrative. Yet Merlin's function is vital to the biopolitics of lineage Geoffrey is celebrating. He ensures that Arthur becomes the culminating figure of the lineage of the British kings.

Howard Bloch has called Merlin "the patron saint of letters in the Arthurian world, . . . as powerful an image of the writer as the Middle Ages produced" (1–2). As such, it does not seem far-fetched to suggest that Geoffrey used Merlin to understand and represent in fantasy his own cultural position as a writer and intellectual, a *magister*. Merlin provided the figure of a powerful, yet marginal, outsider who allows himself to become the client of great men without ceding any of his own power. He represents a power to govern significantly different from physical domination—the brute force—embodied in the kings of England Merlin serves and Geoffrey praises in his dedication to his patrons. Merlin's power is based on his *ingenium*—his technical mastery and his mastery of signs. He alone consistently embodies the link between power and knowledge that Geoffrey's dedications attribute to his patrons in praising not just their military prowess but their wisdom as well. We would like to suggest that Merlin illuminates Geoffrey's own anxieties about competition among *curiales* for patronage by focusing attention on the circulation of intellectual property within the Norman political and economic spheres.

The systems of justice, finance, and administration created by Henry I required a cadre of bureaucrats to staff them who could gain access both to information and to new technologies required for governing. The years between 1066 and 1300 saw the growth of a government bureaucracy that required specific skills in literacy, numeracy, mathematics, accounting, logic, and financial and legal record keeping that were not generally part of the training of the ruling warrior class. The so-called new men, or *curiales*—men educated in the schools in France and occasionally at home in England—who provided these services often came from outside the aristocracy and negotiated their relations to their Norman masters through patronage.[40] While the mechanisms for rewarding warriors were well established, methods for compensating *ingenium* (intelligence or craft) were less highly developed. Informal patronage networks offered little or no protection for the products of intellectual creativity—no trade secret, patent, or copyright laws. Under such conditions, information and technologies once made available would immediately lose any economic value they may have possessed, thus stifling technological advances within the culture.

Social structures, then, had to be developed within informal patronage networks to govern the creation and dissemination of ideas. Intellectual property is the term used by legal scholars to refer to structures designed to regulate the value attributed to such intangibles as technological innovation, invention, and authorship and to distinguish it from the tangible products or devices produced by that knowledge (Long, 846). However, because intellectual property has several characteristics that make it notoriously difficult to protect, it has been called the "law's stepchild" (Wincor, 11). The most salient of these characteristics is that ideas, while often costly to develop, become valueless to their creator once they are revealed. This characteristic makes it difficult for innovators to capitalize on their ideas since investors cannot know the value of information until they have sampled it, but once they have done so, the incentive to buy is gone (Suchman, 1267–69).

Merlin's sudden appearance in the *Historia* offers a spectacular example of one way of resolving this problem, creating a de facto protection for ideas and technologies where no legal mechanisms existed—magic. Our analysis therefore extends Bloch's perception of Merlin as the personification of the knowledge required to govern and argues that Merlin's magic points to the anxieties of Geoffrey's contemporaries about the circulation of intellectual property—the products of intellectual labor—within the economy of feudal patronage.

This analysis of intellectual property does not distinguish writing or "authorship" from other forms of intellectual property because we do not believe the distinction was as sharp in the twelfth century as it is in the twentieth. Nor are we arguing for a twentieth-century notion of authorship, which we believe follows from copyright laws, just as the ownership of other forms of intellectual property follows from patent and trade secret laws. Rather we argue that, even in the absence of such legal protection, individuals will desire to protect the fruits of their intellectual labors. That medieval authors may have thought about these issues seems clear from comments like those made by Marie de France, writing only a generation later at the court of Stephen's successor, Henry II, in the epilogue to her *Fables*:

> Al fine ment de cest escrit,
> Que en romanz ai treité e dit
> Me numerai pur remembrance:
> Marie ai num, si sui de France.
> Put cel estre que clerc plusur
> Prendreient sur eus mun labur.
> Ne voil que nul sur li le die!
> E il fet que fol ki sei ublie!
>
> [To end these tales I've here narrated
> And into romance tongue translated
> I've given my name for memory:
> I am from France, my name's Marie.
> And it may hap that many a clerk
> Will claim as his what is my work.
> But such pronouncements I want not.] (256–77)⁴¹

Such self-interest need not be calculated to be present. Individuals may desire to profit from their intellectual labors without being able consciously to articulate that desire as Marie has done. Magic may offer one means by which to realize that desire without articulating it; patronage, we would suggest, offers another. In the case of Merlin, we might ask these questions: Are the "drugs" through which Merlin transforms Uther medicines or magic potions? Is his removal of Stonehenge from Ireland a feat of magic or engineering skill? If one does not know how a technology works, does it not seem like magic? To what extent might this confusion have aided individuals—like Merlin—who wished to protect the products of their genius? These are issues we want to examine further in our analysis of intellectual property.

Merlin's encounters in the *Historia* are always framed as contests—battles of wits in which Merlin must outmaneuver malicious or envious competitors. In these encounters, magic affords Merlin the kind of protection from competitors that Geoffrey seeks from his patrons. In this regard, the confrontation between the boy Merlin and Vortigern's court magicians is instructive. When Vortigern's attempts to build an impregnable tower repeatedly fail, he calls on his magicians to explain why. The magicians insist that Vortigern must find a boy who has no father, kill him, and sprinkle his blood on the mortar and stones. Merlin is this fatherless boy. When brought to Vortigern, Merlin challenges the magicians, asserting that they have lied to the king, and initiating a conflict with them, clearly labeled as a battle of wits, not strength. This is the first time in the *Historia* in which a conflict is framed as an intellectual challenge rather than a physical one. It is Merlin's knowledge that saves him, not martial skills. After Merlin reveals the reason for the builders' failure to erect the tower, he launches into a long series of prophecies that reveal just enough so that "suorum astantes in admirationem commouit" [he filled all those present with amazement]—but not too much; the "ambiguitate uerborum" [equivocal meaning of his words] conceals as much as it reveals (ed. Wright, 84; trans. Thorpe, 186). His ability to use information to his advantage without revealing so much that he loses his monopoly on knowledge is what makes him such a phenomenon. Even Vortigern "uero pre ceteris admirans et sensum iuuenis et uaticinia collaudat. Neminem enim presens etas produxerat qui ora sua in hunc modum coram ipso soluisset" (ed. Wright, 84) [spoke highly of the young man's wit and his oracular pronouncements, for that particular period in history had produced no one who was ready to speak his mind in this way in front of the King (trans. Thorpe, 186)]. After vanquishing his rival magicians, Merlin becomes chief councilor to the king, a position he will continue to hold despite dramatic changes in administration.

An understanding of magic as an instrument of economic protection—whether it is intentional on the part of the magician or not—may shed new light on some of the more bizarre incidents in the *Historia* criticized by "serious" historians like William of Newburgh. Writing about intellectual property and magic in preliterate cultures, Mark Suchman has argued that "because human memory is limited, we must embody our ideas in 'hosts' in order to transmit or store them. Although such hosts are often physical models or written records, they can also be oral descriptions, practical demonstrations, or even cultural myths" (1269). Magic, he argues, may function as one of these hosts: "Because the value of magic derives purely from social construction, adding magical components to a new technology costs relatively little. . . . At the same time, magic may be much easier to monopolize than the physical process it accompanies" (1273). A precapitalist "inventor," someone like Merlin for instance, who has discovered some new technique that has economic value can use it to earn material and social rewards, but only if he can monopolize it. Unfortunately, the odds of keeping such a discovery secret are slight, particularly if the benefits promised by that technology are great and the technique itself so simple anyone could replicate it as effectively as the inventor. Magic, however, can solve this problem. The inventor can claim that the technology only works through some talisman or spell that he alone possesses: "Such enchantment costs relatively little, since the talisman may be valueless prior to its association with the new technology; yet the magicked process is far easier to monopolize than the simple technology alone" (1274). The possession of such a talisman or spell does not necessarily eliminate competition, but it does give the inventor a monopoly over at least "one specific set of technical manipulations" (1275).

In book eight, Merlin is dispatched with Utherpendragon to Ireland to bring back the Giants' Ring (Stonehenge) and erect it in Britain. This imperialistic venture requires Merlin's technical expertise.[42] When the Britons reach the stones Merlin taunts them as they gaze on the Ring in wonder. He must set his competitors up to fail in order to highlight his artifice, his own unique mastery of technologies: "'Utimini uiribus uestris, iuuenes, ut in deponendo lapides istos sciatis utrum ingenium uirtuti an uirtus ingenio cedat.' Ad imperium igitur eius indulserunt unanimiter multimodis machinationibus aggressi sunt choream deponere. Alii funes, alii restes, alli scalas parauerunt ut quod affectabant perficerent; nec ullatenus perficere ualuerunt" (ed. Wright, 91) ["Try your strength, young men," said he, "and see whether skill can do more than brute strength, or strength more than skill, when it comes to dismantling these stones!" At his bidding they all set to with every conceivable kind of mechanism and strove their hardest to take the Ring down. They rigged up hawsers and ropes and they propped up scaling-ladders, each preparing what he thought most useful but none of these things advanced them an inch (trans. Thorpe, 197)]. Merlin contrasts his competitors' brute strength with his own intellectual mastery. Only when all the known engineering technologies fail does Merlin intervene with his "magic": "Denique, cum queque necessaria apposuisset, leuius quam credi potest lapides deposuit" (ed. Wright, 92) [He placed in position all the gear which he considered necessary and dismantled the stones more easily than you could even believe (trans. Thorpe, 198)]. Merlin thus proves "ingeniumque virtuti preualere" (ed. Wright, 92) [that his artistry was worth more than any brute strength (trans. Thorpe, 198)].

The Latin word Geoffrey uses to describe Merlin's skills is *ingenium*. This word has a somewhat ambiguous history in the Middle Ages. Robert Hanning associates *ingenium* with the emergence in the twelfth century of something like a concept of the self, in which the individual's wit and skill could replace mastery of a received tradition as a measure of accomplishment. We might also associate it with the emergence of a literate class of royal *curiales* who made their living not by their martial prowess, but by their wits. Hanning points to Peter Abelard as an embodiment of this new way of thinking about genius: "Having announced, after attending Anselm of Laon's lectures on the scriptures and the standard commentaries that he did not see the need for such extensive training in how to read either text or commentary, Abelard accepts a challenge from some of Anselm's students to lecture on an obscure biblical passage and its gloss, despite his lack of formal training regarded as essential for public exposition" (*The Individual*, 28–29). Note that in this narrative as well Abelard's demonstration of his *ingenium* is framed as a public contest, a competition in which he can prove the truth of his words, "non esse mee consuetudinis per usus proficere sed per ingenium" (cited in Hanning, *The Individual*, 29). Abelard's opposition of *usus* and *ingenium* rejects the "entire system of training" used to arrive at the truth of the Scriptures and substitutes "his own impulse to control the system through the power of the mind, rather than be controlled by it" (29). Merlin's *ingenium* provides the host for a new technology—the mysterious "gear"—that remains mysterious and so offers a virtual monopoly to the court magician. He may be the king's client, but his knowledge enables him to maintain a reciprocal power in their relationship. Merlin alone understands the certain secret rites and various properties associated with Stonehenge (which remain a mystery even today). He alone can tap the Ring's powers. Merlin's *ingenium* gives him influence he would otherwise have been unable to claim as a fatherless child, someone of questionable birth. Merlin is thus able to negotiate his patronage relationship with a number of kings through his monopoly on magic and prophecy.[43] The "new men" central to the public policy of the first Norman monarchs, who increasingly came to provide the administrative skill required by secular government, would also increasingly need to rely on their *ingenium* rather than martial skill for advancement.

As Abelard was to discover, however, *ingenium* is an ambiguous commodity. He was assailed by those jealous of him and became obsessed with their intrigues. As Hanning notes, "that he was the object of envy by lesser men, the conversion of whose envy into hostility was the cause of his suffering, springs precisely from, and confirms his inner consciousness of his *ingenium* as the property which defines him and sets him apart" (*The Individual*, 31). Furthermore *ingenium* was not regarded unproblematically as artistry, talent, or genius. It was also associated with deviousness, artifice, and fraud. Geoffrey glosses over the limitations of Merlin's *ingenium*, just as he glosses over the limits of his own. The magician does not remain in the narrative long enough to have his abilities challenged by an even more talented rival—as will happen in a number of later romances. He is removed from history before age robs him of his genius, before patrons begin to think his miracles mere tricks. With Merlin, Geoffrey allows the possessor of intellectual property a monopoly so absolute and so valuable that it almost equalizes the relationship between client and patron; he grants the possessor of *ingenium* the history he desires for himself. The reality, the truth, of Merlin's accomplishments is, of course, every bit as suspect as the reality, the truth, of Geoffrey's accomplishments. "Serious" historians—who reckon *ingenium* a liability—are kind to neither Merlin nor Geoffrey, faulting them for deviousness and fraud for exercising the genius that brought them success.

For Geoffrey of Monmouth, the writing of history was performance, an ingenious manipulation of language to create a past that would ease the anxieties of a powerful ruling class concerned with discovering origins so that claims of lineage might be upheld. At the same time, it was an entry in a competition—waged against the evil and malicious—the stakes of which, though they were never specified, were believed enormous. As the circulation of symbolic capital in twelfth-century England is evaluated, it seems Geoffrey's patrons received much more than they gave in return. In exchange for relatively minor ecclesiastical promotion, Geoffrey of Monmouth provided them with a powerful myth of origin—that of King Arthur. In this, we would argue, he was not all that different from his contemporaries, like William of Malmesbury or the anonymous author of the *Gesta Stephani,* or later translators like Wace or Laʒamon, whose vernacular *Bruts* we will examine in the next chapters.

3

The Romance of Empire

Vernacular History and the Structuration of Power

Orderic Vitalis, a chronicler writing during the reign of Henry I, provides a starting point for our investigations into the vernacular *Bruts*. He writes that "In the year 1127, on one day and at one hour appointed, a general massacre of the Normans was to take place throughout England" (cited in Thierry, 362). The Saxon rebellion Orderic Vitalis describes—engineered with the assistance of those traditional Norman antagonists, the Welsh and the Scots—was discovered by Richard le Noir, bishop of Ely, during confession. The bishop, apparently indifferent to the sanctity of the confessional, leaked this information to his Norman overlords. While a substantial part of the conspiracy's leadership escaped Norman vengeance by running to Wales, many followers were caught, tortured, and executed. Nearly seven hundred years later, in 1825, the French historian Augustin Thierry pondered the meaning of this rebellion from the perspective of nineteenth-century nationalism:

> This event happened sixty-six years after the last defeat of the insurgent Saxons in the Isle of Ely, and seventy-two after the battle of Hastings. Whether it be that the chroniclers have not told us all, or that after a time the broken thread which had attached Saxons to Saxons, and made them a nation, was never again joined, we find in subsequent periods no project of deliverance conceived with common accord by a great mass of men, in a manner at all national. The old English cry, No Normans! here ceases to resound in history; and later insurrections have other rallying cries, more vague, more political, more social, in their appearance. In the fourteenth century, the insurgent peasants of England cried *No gentlemen!* In the seventeenth, the towns and fields rung with *No tyrant king! no haughty nobles! no hollow-hearted bishops!* Yet can the historian discern, in still

more recent occurrences, the living marks of the native hatred between the two races—the one powerful and the other crushed, the one opulent and the other poor—of the conquerors and the subjugated of England. (Thierry, 363–64)

Once the last traces of the Saxon hegemony had been replaced by the emergent Norman culture, those at the margins of the new hegemony appear to be effectively silenced.[1] Histories, both medieval and modern, chronicling the reigns of Stephen, Henry II, and Richard have astonishingly little to say about the Saxon population of England. If Saxons, as a recognizable ethnic community, exerted influence upon the policies of these kings, their efforts have been all but erased. History is generally written by its winners; it records their perspective and serves their interests.[2]

To understand history, as Thierry does, as a struggle between those who rule and those who are subjugated over who will determine "what really happened" in the past, we must understand the "fundamental asymmetry" between two groups who do not share equal access to the means of preserving their narratives about the past. If we are to uncover the histories of the subjugated rather than the conquerors, the poor rather than the opulent, and the crushed rather than the powerful, we must look to the gaps and silences, the discontinuities and "broken threads" that mark the texts that record history. This chapter and the next trace the interplay between ruling class history and that which might represent the marginalized, subjugated, and conquered—history's losers—in vernacular translations of Geoffrey's Arthurian histories attributed to Wace and Laȝamon.

Slavoj Žižek, drawing upon Walter Benjamin's "Theses on the Philosophy of History," marks the fundamental asymmetry between the powerful and marginalized by distinguishing two different modes of temporality: to the ruling class and its official histories belongs the "empty, homogeneous time" of continuity, while the subjugated (or the historical materialist who speaks for this group) make due with the "filled" time of discontinuity.[3] In explaining the continuous time of official history, Žižek could easily be describing the *form* of the Arthurian history as it was pioneered by Geoffrey: "by conceiving history as a closed, homogeneous, rectilinear, continuous course of events, the traditional historiographic gaze is a priori, formally, the gaze of 'those who have won': it sees history as a closed continuity of 'progression' leading to the reign of those who rule today. It leaves out of consideration what *failed* in history, what has to be denied so that the continuity of 'what really happened' could establish itself" (138). The interest in vernacular history among the Norman rulers of the twelfth and thirteenth centuries, as we argued in chapter 2, was fueled by shifts in the kinship structure of the aristocracy that required that the family estate be passed on from eldest son to eldest son in an unbroken chain. The family must at least be able to construct a credible fiction that it can trace its ancestry back to an originary founder. In other words, the ruling Norman class needed to be able to demonstrate a continuous and progressive history that culminated logically in its own rule. The narrative produced by Geoffrey of Monmouth could serve this function, but it was written in Latin. This means that the Norman patrons of the *Historia Regum Britanniæ* would probably not have been able to read it. However learned someone like Robert of Gloucester may have been, his education probably would not have included sophisticated Latin prose.[4] For these patrons, Geoffrey's book functioned as an artifact, a symbol of their prestige and status. It could, if necessary, be used as documentation of political legitimacy, but such a use would likely require the mediation of a third party, of a cleric capable of reading and interpreting the Latin. Within one generation, the consumers of such works—the Norman aristocracy—demanded histories written in their own vernaculars, in languages they could read for themselves or at the very least have read to them. They demanded an official progressive history in a language they could understand.

In contrast to what Žižek calls the "triumphal procession of victors" offered up by official history, the history of the dispossessed records discontinuous time: "the oppressed appropriates the past to itself in so far as it is 'open,' in so far as the 'yearning for redemption' is already at work in it—that is to say, it appropriates the past in so far as the past already contains—in the form of what failed, of what was extirpated—the dimension of the future" (138). What sets the history of the dispossessed apart, Žižek argues, is "its capacity to *arrest*, to *immobilize* historical movement and to *isolate* the detail from its historical totality" (139). In other words, we need to search for the history of marginalized groups in what Laurie Finke, in another context, has called the "noise" of history, that which has been repressed, omitted, or forgotten in order to create a continuous, progressive, and coherent narrative about the past (Finke, *Feminist Theory,* 22–28).

For the medievalist, this project is made more difficult by the fragmentary nature of the documentary record for this period, which exaggerates the asymmetry between the powerful and the marginalized. This discrepancy between Žižek's chronotopes of domination and resistance[5] might be further illuminated by James Scott's distinction between public and hidden transcripts in situations of unequal power. Scott argues that traditional analyses of power obscure much of its dynamics—and especially the nature of the resistance to it—because they focus only on the public displays and records of power, what he calls the *public transcript* (*Domination and the Arts of Resistance*, 5) and what Žižek refers to as continuous, official history. The public transcript records the interactions between the powerful and their subordinates only as an elaborate public mask. Interactions in the public transcript are designed to legitimate the expectations of those who wield power and, as such, can represent only incompletely the complexities of power relations. Scott argues that public displays of conformity, deference, and docility for the benefit of those in power that are generally cited as evidence of false consciousness or submissiveness on the part of the oppressed often mask covert defiance. In fact, the greater the disparity between dominant and subordinate, "the more the public transcript of subordinates will take on a stereotyped, ritualistic cast. In other words, the more menacing the power, the thicker the mask" (5). Only rarely do the powerless "speak truth to power."

Behind the scenes, however, and away from the surveillance of the dominant, the subordinate display a whole range of discourses and behaviors that contradict their public performance. Because they only rarely emerge in the public record, these events are rarely considered in analyses of subordination. These events and discourses Scott calls the *hidden transcript;* these correspond to Žižek's notion of discontinuous history, the history of what has failed. The hidden transcript might be marked by such everyday acts of resistance as sabotage, foot dragging, desertion, evasion, poaching, or outright disobedience ("what failed," Žižek, 138), as well as by symbolic and discursive gestures like complaints, curses and other rituals of verbal aggression, gossip, rumor, and carnival. By positing this other realm of activity not subject to the surveillance of the dominant, Scott does not mean to suggest that what happens in the public transcript is necessarily false and what happens in the hidden transcript is necessarily true. He is not claiming "the former as a realm of necessity and the latter as a realm of freedom" (*Domination and the Arts of Resistance*, 5). Nor does he suggest that the subordinate have the freedom to say "what they really think" in the hidden transcript. The exercise of power cannot be so simply reduced to a binary equation. Both transcripts are performances; but as performances they are directed toward different audiences and operate under different constraints. These performances produce quite different histories; we might explore this divergence by examining the very different vernacular translations of Geoffrey's *Brut* produced by Wace and Laʒamon.

Wace was an Anglo-Norman cleric writing for an audience of Anglo-Norman aristocrats, painfully aware of his dependence on his patrons. Whatever inequalities existed between Wace and his royal patrons,[6] however, they shared a common language, court culture, and purpose. Wace wrote histories to legitimate the rule of his patrons. His *Roman de Brut* is marked by "a fanatical attention to the details of lineage" (Blacker, 36). It provided an official progressive history—a closed continuity leading to the reign of Wace's Angevin patrons.

> Ki vult oïr e vult saveir
> De rei en rei e d'eir en eir
> Ki cil furent e dunt il vindrent
> Ki Engleterre primes tindrent,
> Quel reis i ad *en ordre* eü,
> Ki anceis e ki puis i fu,
> Maistre Wace l'ad translaté
> Ki en conte la verité. (1–8; emphasis ours)

[Whoever wishes to hear and know about the successive kings and their heirs who once upon a time were the rulers of England—who they were, and whence they came, what was their sequence, who came earlier and who later—Master Wace has translated it and tells it truthfully.] (3)[7]

This introductory passage stresses the sequence of history, its orderly progression from king to king and era to era, presumably to culminate in the reign of his Plantagenet patrons, Henry II and his wife, Eleanor. Indeed what most stands out in Wace's historical writing is the tension between his desire to please his patrons and his claim that what he is reporting is true. In the *Roman de Rou* (which traces the lineage of the dukes of Normandy) he writes:

> suvent aveient des baruns
> e des nobles dames beaus duns,
> pur mettre leur nuns en estoire,
> que tuz tens mais fust de eus memoire.

> [Often barons and noble ladies
> Gave great gifts
> To put their names into an *estoire*
> That for all time they be held in memory.] (Blacker, 40)

Wace dedicates himself to the pursuit of truth (*la verité*) but always with the knowledge that even if he can arrive at anything approaching a truth, his story is always shaped by the desires of his patrons.

Wace, however, does not criticize his patrons as the primary obstacle in establishing "la verité." In the tradition of William of Malmesbury a generation before him and his contemporary Giraldus Cambrensis, he casts the British in the position of liars. The many tales the Bretons tell about King Arthur constitute a bigger challenge for the unbiased historian than the demands of royal patronage:

> Furent les merveilles pruvees
> E les aventures truvees
> Ki d'Arthur sunt tant recuntees
> Ke a fable sunt aturnees.
> Ne tut mençunge, ne tut veir,
> Tut folie ne tut saveir.
> Tant unt li cunteur cunté
> E li fableur tant flablé
> Pur lur cuntes enbeleter,
> Que tut unt fait fable sembler. (9789–98)

[The wondrous events appeared and the adventures were sought out which . . . are so often told about Arthur that they have become the stuff of fiction: not all lies, not all truth, neither total folly nor total wisdom. The raconteurs have told so many yarns, the story-tellers so many stories, to embellish their tales that they have made it all appear fiction.] (247)

This passage teems with words denoting the truth status of various claims about a historical Arthur: "fable," "mençunge," "veir," "folie," "saveir," "cuntes." To produce veracious history, the objective writer must sift among fables, lies, truths, follies, wisdom, and stories produced by the very people who have been dispossessed—colonized—by that history. In the fables of the Britons we can catch a glimpse of the hidden transcript— of what failed in history and what Wace must repress to produce his own "official" version of the past.[8]

Laȝamon, by comparison, has been described by Tatlock as an "obscure cleric living in a rural backwater" (509, 514). The only biographical information we have about this first English translator of Geoffrey's *Historia* is given at the beginning of the two late-thirteenth-century manuscripts that record the poem and even these two tantalizingly sparse accounts are not identical. London, British Library, MS Cotton Caligula A. ix begins

> An preost wes on leoden; Laȝamon wes ihoten.
> he wes Leouenaðes sone; liðe him beo Drihten.
> He wonede at Ernleȝe; at æðelen are chirechen.
> vppen Seuarne staþe; sel þar him þuhte.
> on-fest Radestone; þer he bock radde. (ed. Brook and Leslie, 1–5)

> [There was a priest living here, who was known as Laȝamon;
> He was the son of Liefnoth—the Lord have mercy on him!
> He had a living at Areley, at a lovely church there,
> Upon the River Severn bank—splendid he found it—
> Right beside Redstone, where he recited his Missal [or read books].] (trans. Allen, 1–5)

This passage tells us that Laȝamon was a priest and that he held a living in Areley in the diocese of Worcester on the Welsh border. His father's name identifies him as Anglo-Saxon by birth (Wace appears to have been, like William of Malmesbury, of mixed parentage). His home of Areley locates him geographically at the confluence of the three cultures that coexisted uneasily in thirteenth-century England—Celt, Anglo-Saxon, and Norman. Areley Kings was part of the manor of Martley that, according to Elizabeth Salter, passed in 1196 into the hands of Philip de Aire and in 1200 into the de Frisa or de Frise family. They kept it until 1233 when it passed to the Despensers (Salter, 67).[9] According to Madden, the advowson of Martley had been, since the time of Domesday, in the possession of the abbey of Cormeilles in Normandy. The prior of Newent, which was the English cell of Cormeilles, occasionally presented to the living but, as Allen has argued, Laȝamon most likely had an Anglo-Norman monk as his rector (trans. Allen, xviii).

Yet it seems unlikely that Laȝamon would have produced his translation for Norman monks who could easily have read either Geoffrey's Latin or Wace's Anglo-Norman. Yet he certainly would not have undertaken such a laborious task for the edification of his parishioners nor simply for his own amusement. The time and effort required of the task—Laȝamon claims he traveled "wide ӡond þas leode" (ed. Brook and Leslie, 14) [the length of this whole land] (trans. Allen, 14) to research his book—would require a wealthy patron to bear the costs, most likely someone who understood neither Latin nor Anglo-Norman easily. London, British Library, MS Cotton Otho C. xiii presents a slightly different view of our priest-poet:[10]

> A prest was in londe. Laweman. was hote.
> he was Leucais sone. lef him beo Driste.
> He wonede at Ernleie wid þan gode cniþhte.
> uppen Seuarne. merie þer him þohte.
> faste bi Radistone þer he bokes radde. (ed. Brook and Leslie, 1–5)
>
> [There was a priest living here who was known as Lawman.
> He was Leucais's son, he was dear to the Lord.
> He lived at Areley with this good knight.
> Upon the River Severn bank—merry he found it—
> Right beside Redstone where he read books.] (translation ours)

This portrait of the author as a young priest suggests that Laӡamon was a chaplain to a secular household, to a knight wealthy enough to employ a tutor for his children, but that he was marginalized by his provincial status.[11] He may even have been a client of the family that held the manor of Martley. It seems unlikely, however, that a family as influential in Anglo-Norman politics as the Despensers (if the poem was written after 1233) or even the less prominent de Frises (if it was written before) would commission a book in English rather than Anglo-Norman. As Salter points out, there were many less distinguished landowners in that area who, by the thirteenth century, would be more comfortable in English than Anglo-Norman, any one of whom might have been the "good knight" of the Cotton Otho manuscript (Salter, 67).

Central to postcolonialism is the problem of translating across cultures in a multilingual environment in which languages become a site for political conflict (Niranjana, Evans). Writing in the polyglot climate of postconquest England, neither Wace nor Laӡamon produced translations in the sense that we understand the word. Neither attempted literally to "carry over" the sense of Geoffrey's Latin, or to achieve a formal equivalence between Latin prose and vernacular verse (Le Saux, 25). Rather they produced hybrid texts. They loosely paraphrased their sources, sometimes embellishing the original's sparser accounts, sometimes cutting material or abbreviating it. They added both descriptions and dialogue that significantly lengthen the original. Wace's *Roman de Brut* runs nearly to fifteen thousand lines; Laȝamon's translation, depending on how the lines are counted, is nearly double that (Le Saux, 24). Significantly, both writers chose the vehicle of poetry rather than prose for their histories, which left them with all the attendant problems of versification: which verse form to choose and how to express particular ideas given the limitations imposed by any verse form. Their translations would be tied specifically to the resources of the language in which they chose to write—Anglo-Norman and English. The writers of vernacular insular history were not simply transcribing Geoffrey of Monmouth, they were creating new forms and new genres of historical writing. They were exploring the potential of the vernacular to record significant events and to sort out and preserve the truth of the past. Their texts look and sound different from Latin histories of the period. They serve different functions and circulate among different audiences. This chapter and the next examine these differences more closely as a means of elucidating Žižek's chronotopes of continuous and discontinuous history—the histories of winners and losers—in the vernacular *Bruts*.

Continuous Time: Wace and the Economics of Peace

Of course, the most obvious mark of Wace's presentation of continuous progressive history is his presentation of the sequence of English kings, one following the other, in which the discontinuities created by breaks in lineage (whether through default of an heir or civil conflict) have been covered over by the sheer force of succession, creating a continuity that transcends the vicissitudes of any individual's or family's fortune. But we might also locate those characteristics of "official historiography" Žižek describes in the relationship between the text's aesthetic and social logics.[12] It has become a critical commonplace to argue that Wace "romanticized" Geoffrey of Monmouth's *Historia Regum Britanniæ*. Romance as a popular literary genre was just beginning to emerge at about the same time as vernacular history and it was patronized by the same audiences.[13] It is hardly inconceivable that there might have been some commingling of the two genres, with historians like Wace drawing upon the aesthetic devices of the romance—such as the octosyllabic couplet—to structure their narratives in ways that would entertain as well as edify their aristocratic audiences and legitimate their ambitions. Closer examination of the dialogic "interanimation" of the languages of romance and historiography might tell us a great deal about the processes of imperialism and colonization that have marked the progressive narrative about western civilization since the Middle Ages.

Romance as a genre is organized around "a testing of the identity of heroes (and things)—basically, their fidelity in love and their faithfulness to the demands of the chivalric code" (Bakhtin, *Dialogic Imagination*, 151). Hayden White describes history encoded as romance as "a drama of self-identification symbolized by the hero's transcendence of the world of experience, his victory over it" (*Metahistory*, 8). Its characteristic chronotope, as Bakhtin argues, is "organic and internally consistent" even when it exhibits, as it often does, a "subjective playing with time" (*Dialogic Imagination*, 154–55). Such a narrative of triumph over opposition—in which "heroic deeds are performed by which the heroes *glorify* themselves and *glorify* others (their liege lord, their lady)" (153; emphasis in original)—would appeal to the imperial and cultural ambitions of the Norman aristocracy Wace served.

Some have contended that the romanticization of Wace's history was the result of his having written for an audience that included women—in particular Eleanor of Aquitaine. Critics cite as evidence Laʒamon's claim that the French clerk Wace presented his *Roman de Brut* not to the king but to "the noble Eleanor, King Henry's queen." But there has also been a tendency among critics to argue that the *Roman de Brut*, romanticized by its emphasis on chivalric practice and courtesy, represents an evolutionary, even paradigmatic, shift in the aesthetics of the Arthurian legend. J.S.P. Tatlock claims that in Wace's *Roman de Brut*, one could read how "[t]he expansion and fresh contacts of the Norman state advanced its own civilization beyond the cultural roughness of the Anglo-Normans of the Conquest and just after it. It and its sphere of influence were learning *courtoisie*, the frequency of which word among those who wrote for the Normans is as significant in regard to social aspirations as the frequency of the word 'culture' in some parts of America at the end of the nineteenth century" (465–66). Robert Huntington Fletcher maintains: "[i]n almost every case [Wace] takes pains to expunge from the story certain suggestions of barbarity or lack of chivalrousness on the part of Arthur or his knights which occur (survive?) in Geoffrey's version" (*Arthurian Materials*, 138). We could cite many more recent examples of this tendency to read Wace's interest in chivalry as aesthetic, but two should suffice. Jean Blacker notes that "[w]here Geoffrey underscores Arthur's military might and unified rule in his advice to princes at the drawing board, as it were, Wace highlights Arthur's *curteisies* in his exemplum for courtiers in the drawing room. Each Arthur is a symbol, a vehicle shaped to suit the metaphorical ends of the story in which he appears" (101–2). Martin Shichtman writes that "[i]n the *Roman de Brut* Wace continuously colors received material with the prevailing attitudes of Norman France. He transforms Geoffrey's story ... into a romantic history suited to an audience familiar with the marvelous tales of *conteurs* and partial to narratives concerning chivalry, lady love, and the glorification of the individual" ("Gawain in Wace," 110). In all these assessments of the *Roman de Brut* lurks the suggestion that Wace's emphasis on activities of the court, his celebration of peacetime amusements, is primarily aesthetic, that it represents an apolitical—or depoliticized—social development.

As Walter Benjamin has argued, however, the celebration of great achievements and cultural treasures that marks official historiography can never be viewed with total detachment; they have their own social logic as well: "the cultural treasures [the historian] surveys have an original which he [sic] cannot contemplate without horror. They owe their existence not only to the efforts of the great minds and talents who have created them, but also to the anonymous toil of their contemporaries. There is no document of civilization which is not at the same time a document of barbarism" (256). We would like to argue that Wace's de-emphasis of martial activity was never solely an aesthetic choice and almost certainly had nothing to do with concerns that his audience—male or female—might be squeamish, or offended by depictions of violence. Rather, Wace's reverence for peace reflected the favorable political and economic situation of his benefactors. His frequent allusions to the pleasures of peace arose from his audience's desire to enjoy the fruits of its political dominance. Wace's discourse, therefore, is reflective of a shifting social logic in the Anglo-Norman empire, one in which the profits from peace have, at least for those who have been victorious, begun to surpass the dividends of war.

Wace places the completion date of the *Roman de Brut* in 1155. The date is significant. On December 19, 1154, Henry II and Eleanor of Aquitaine were crowned at Westminster Abbey, putting to a close twenty years of civil war, twenty years of violent anarchy during which, as we have seen in chapter 2, Stephen and Matilda battled for rule of England. A twelfth-century historian like Henry of Huntingdon might well glorify the exploits of a warlike King Stephen in his account of the battle of Lincoln:

Nulla eis quies, nulla respiratio dabatur, nisi in ea parte qua rex fortissimus stabat, horrentibus inimicis incomparabilem ictuum eius inmanitatem. Quod ubi comes Cestrensis comperit, regis inuidens glorie, cum omni pondere armatorum irruit in eum. Tunc apparuit uis regis fulminea, bipenni maxima cedens hos, diruens illos. Tunc nouus oritur clamor, omnes in eum, ipse in omnes. Tandem regia bipennis ex ictuum frequentia confracta est. Ipse gladio abstracto dextra regis digno rem mirabiliter agit, donec et gladius confractus est.

[No pause or respite was given them, except in the area where the mighty king was standing, his enemies trembling at the incomparable ferocity of the blows he struck. When the earl of Chester saw this, he envied the king's glory, and rushed at him with the whole weight of his knights. Whereupon the king's lightning strength showed itself as, wielding his great battle-axe, he slew some and scattered others. Now a new clamor arose—all against him, he against all. Eventually the royal battle-axe was shattered by incessant blows. He drew out his sword, worthy of a king, and performed wonders with his right hand, until the sword, too, was shattered.] (736–39)

He can extol the sheer beauty of physical combat to highlight the power and dominance of the king he serves. For the majority, however, the reality was far grimmer. Even the partisan *Gesta Stephani* is somewhat less enthusiastic about the constant warfare that raged throughout the land during the anarchy of Stephen's civil war. Its author condemns the robbing and burning of churches, monasteries, and nunneries that was endemic, while the *Peterborough Chronicle*, as we saw in the previous chapter, describes the reign of King Stephen almost exclusively as a time of suffering, disorder, and economic ruin. Matilda was as guilty as her cousin of abuses against the people and the church. Both sides relied on mercenaries to fight their wars for them, and these mercenaries had little regard for the land or its citizens. The *Gesta Stephani* refers to the hired soldiers as "profane scoundrels," a "savage crowd of barbarians," who "were affected neither by bowels of compassion nor by feelings of human pity over sufferings so many and so great, but everywhere in the castles they conspired with one mind to commit crime and outrage, were unceasingly occupied in pillaging the goods of the poor, devoted all the zeal of their evil hearts to encouraging hostility on both sides and murdering men in every quarter."[14] Both parties constructed fortifications that were abhorrent to the masses, and both spent lavishly on campaigns that brought nothing but misery to England.

The same Henry of Huntingdon who liberally praised Stephen also welcomed the coming of Henry II as he marched against the incumbent monarch. He writes that "miserabilis Anglia" [Wretched England] greets its new king with these words:

> Dux Henrice, nepos Henrici maxime magni,
> Anglia celsa ruo, nec iam ruo ruina.
> Dicere uix possum "fueram," "sum" namque recessit,
> Si michi que miseris superset uel spes superesset,
> Clamarem, "Miserere, ueni, succurre, resiste!
> Nam sum iure tui iuris, potes, erige lapsam". . . .
> Gemma uirum uir, aue, mea spes dum spes michi, salue!
> Sero uenis, perii; clamas tamen, "Anglia surge,
> Immo resurge, tuam refero tibi, mortua, uitam."

[Duke Henry, greatest descendent of great Henry, I am falling into ruin—I, noble England, am falling, though not yet in complete ruin. I can scarcely say "I had been," for "I am" has departed. If even the hope that remains for the wretched remained for me, I would cry, "Have mercy, come, help, stop! Rightfully I belong to you, so you have the power—raise me from my fall". . . . Hail, jewel of manhood, my hope—while I have hope—greeting! You come too late: I have passed away. But you cry, "England, arise! Or rather, rise again! Dead one, I give you back your life."] (760–61)

The extravagance of Henry of Huntingdon's language—written, it is important to note, after the reported event—must be regarded with reference to the social, political, and economic upheavals endured by England throughout Stephen's reign. The historian's depiction of Henry II as savior seems no metaphor. Henry's arrival brought, in the short term, the expectation of order instead of chaos, of imperialistic expansion instead of civil war. In the long term, Henry II offered England the possibility of wealth and ultimately the prospect of peace.

Even before taking power, Henry began to accumulate the good will and love of subjects frustrated with the destructive excesses of an unstable monarchy. Before taking the crown, Henry succumbed to the arguments of his advisors and put together an army largely devoid of mercenaries. What Henry sacrificed in the immediate military talent mercenary soldiers might have provided his invading force, he more than made up in public relations. Upon coming to power, Henry issued a coronation address, a seemingly innocuous bit of nostalgia that advanced Henry's claim to the monarchy by linking it to the social stability of Henry I's reign: "for the common improvement of my whole realm I have conceded and given and by this my present charter confirmed to God and Holy Church and to all my earls and barons and all my men, all the concessions and gifts and liberties and free customs that King Henry my grandfather gave and conceded to them. Likewise, all evil customs that he wiped out and remitted I remit and concede that they be wiped out by me and my heirs" (Appleby, 40; see also Stubbs, 158).[15] Two weeks after his coronation, Henry met with his advisors at Bermondsey and issued a set of decrees calling for the expulsion of all mercenaries from England, the destruction of potentially rebellious fortifications, and the reinstatement of all fiefs to their condition in 1135.[16] Henry likewise soon after his coronation put into place a plan for succession that he no doubt (mistakenly) believed would circumvent the internecine conflicts that had divided the Anglo-Norman nobility since the conquest. Prior to Henry's reign, kingship in England had been, at least in theory, elective. In fact, when Stephen attempted to name his son Eustice successor to the crown, the English lords, led by Archbishop Theobald, rejected what they regarded as an inferior choice. Within three months of seizing control, Henry made claim to England as his by hereditary right. Henry called together in Wallingford the English lords who had sworn allegiance to him and demanded that they recognize his two-year-old son, William, as his legitimate heir. Henry also demanded that these lords recognize his recently born second son, Henry, as next in line to the throne should William die before coming of age.

Like his grandfather, Henry II signaled his independence from powerful, potentially mutinous, always demanding lords by surrounding himself with a coterie of "new men," bureaucrats to staff the systems of justice, finance, and administration required to govern effectively (see chapter 2 above). These "new men," often drawn from outside the aristocracy—Thomas Becket, for instance, was the son of a London merchant—negotiated their status through patronage networks and owed their position in the court directly to the king instead of to hereditary right.[17] Among this group, apparently, was the cleric Wace. Having spent the early portion of his career writing saints' lives, Wace discovered greater profit could be accrued producing histories to meet the needs and expectations of the new regime. Despite his frequent complaints of poverty and the neglect of patrons, there can be little doubt that Wace was something of an insider, a player—even if a minor one—in the court of Henry II. If Laȝamon's account of the presentation of the *Roman de Brut* is to be believed, Wace enjoyed at least some access to both the king and the queen—a matter concerning which Laȝamon must have felt no small amount of envy, given his genuinely marginalized position. In 1160 Henry commissioned Wace, then a clerk at Caen, to compose a chronicle of the dukes of Normandy, the *Roman de Rou*. In *Chronique ascendante*, Wace provides some corroborating evidence for Laȝamon's assessment of Wace's position at court, alluding to his relationship to Henry and Eleanor:

> Du roi Henri voil faire ceste premiere page,
> qui prist Alianor, dame de haut parage,
> Dex doinst a ambedeuls de bien faire courage!
> Ne me font mie rendre a la court le musage,
> de dons et de pramesses chascun d'euls m'asouage.
>
> [I wish to make this first page about Henry
> Who took Eleanor, lady of noble lineage,
> May God grant each of them courage!
> They never make me waste my time at court
> Each of them soothes me with gifts and promises.] (Blacker, 37)

Even though this commission was ultimately revoked—Jean Blacker discusses the politics of the revocation in *The Faces of Time* (37–44)—by 1169 Wace was awarded the canonry at Bayeux. Wace understood that historical writing was a political gesture, claiming, in his *Roman de Rou*, as his audience "La riche gent, / ki unt les rentes et le argent, / kar pur eus sunt li livre fait / e bon dit fait e bien retrait" (ed. Holden, 1:167) [rich folk who possess revenues and silver, since for them books are made and good works are composed and well set forth (trans. Foulon, 94)]. He also understood the vagaries of life as a royal client; the king's gifts and promises were not always commensurate with the poet's needs: "mes besoing vient souvent qui tost sigle et tost nage / et souvent me fait meitre le denier et le gage" [but need comes soon, sailing swiftly onward / And often makes me put down money and [place] bets] (Blacker, 37–38).

The politics of Wace's romance historiography can be seen in the *Roman de Brut*'s accounts of peacetime activity. We are not suggesting that the *Roman de Brut* is in any way a pacifist text. There were, in fact, good reasons for Wace to continue proclaiming the value of warfare. When a number of his former allies proved reluctant to make the sacrifices demanded by the Bermondsey decrees, Henry did not hesitate to intervene militarily. The most significant resistance to the decrees came from the powerful barons on the Welsh marches. In particular, the rebellion of Hugh Mortemer, whose castles at Wigmore, Cleobury, and Bridgnorth were strategically located on the border between England and Wales, demanded Henry become involved in extended siege warfare—from which the king ultimately emerged victorious. On the other hand, Henry restrained his territorial ambitions after Pope Adrian IV issued a bull confirming the king's legal authority over Ireland and his right to invade the land. Despite the temptation offered by the bull, Henry allowed himself to be dissuaded from aggression by his mother, Matilda, who argued that too many problems remained at home for the king to enter into a costly campaign, though by 1166 Henry would have to move to contain a situation that was quickly threatening to spin out of his control (Mortimer, 143).

Wace's *Roman de Brut* balances the benefits of imperialistic conquest (which we will examine more fully below) with the pleasures of interspersed stretches of peace. In Wace, peace always comes during the reign of a strong monarch who is able to quell, usually violently, any disruptions to the peace. When Arthur's grandfather, Constantine, ruled the realm, he "Tute la terre en amendast" (6456) [would have set right the whole land] (163). It is only during peacetime, however, that the nuances of *courtoisie* can be fully explored. Once Arthur has put right the civil disruption caused by Constantine's death and the ensuing struggle over succession, he can turn his attention to more refined pursuits. He can turn his attention to courting Guenevere who is

> Une cuinte e noble meschine;
> Bele esteit e curteise e gente, ...
> Mult fu de grant afaitement
> E de noble cuntienement,
> Mult fu large e buene parliere. (9646–47, 9653–55)

> [a graceful and noble girl. She was beautiful, courteous, and well born. . . . Her manners were perfect, her behavior noble, and she talked freely and well.] (243)

Guenevere is described in exactly the same abstract terms as the heroine of a romance or the *dompna* of a troubadour lyric; she is the very essence of *courtoisie*, and so becomes a fitting symbol of the cultural aspirations of Arthur's court.

The Arthurian section of the *Roman de Brut* lavishes attention on the dividends of the twelve years of peace that Arthur's successful campaigning wins.

> En Engleterre est revenuz
> E a grant joie est receüz.
> Duze ans puis cel repairement
> Regna Artur paisiblement,
> Ne nuls guerreier ne l'osa
> Ne il altre ne guereia.
> Par sei, senz altre enseinement,
> Emprist si grant afaitement
> E se cuntint tant noblement,
> Tant bel a tant curteisement,
> N'esteit parole de curt d'ume
> Neis de l'empereür de Rome.
> N'oeit parler de chevalier
> Ki alques feïst a preisier,
> Ki de sa maisnee ne fust. (9729–43)

[[H]e came back to England and was welcomed with great joy. For twelve years after his return, Arthur reigned in peace. No one dared to make war on him, nor did he go to war himself. On his own, with no other instruction, he acquired such knightly skill and behaved so nobly, so finely and courteously, that there was no court so talked about, not even that of the Roman emperor. He never heard of a knight who was in any way considered praiseworthy who would not belong to his household, provided that he could get him.] (245)

Wace lingers over the details of the sumptuous feasting, the rituals, the founding of the Round Table, the tournaments, games, and largess with which Arthur's court occupy themselves during this interlude. He even devotes a long passage to the pleasures (and pains) of gambling (10557–88). These passages suggest that Wace's patrons were interested in seeing reflected in their histories the pastimes of the Angevin court enjoying the imperial peace secured by its superior military strength.

But peace provides not only opportunities for the wealthy to amuse themselves. Wace indicates that it is the obligation of the king to provide peace for all the people. The lament of the Scottish ladies (9477 ff.) shows the misery that follows when he fails. Faced with the high costs of continued warfare, the Danish king, Acil, quickly agrees to Arthur's imperialistic demands: "Ne se volt laissier damagier / Ne sa bone terre empeirer, / Sun or ne sun argent despendre, / Sa gent ocire, ses turs rendre. / Tant dist, tant fist, tant purchaça / E tant pramist e tant duna / E tant requist e tant preia, / Al rei Artur se concorda" (9877–84) [He did not want himself harmed or his good land despoiled; he neither wished his gold and silver spent, nor his people killed, nor his towers surrendered. He said, did and strove so much, promised and gave so much, asked and begged so much, that he reached an agreement with king Arthur] (249). Wace demonstrates both the misery of warfare and the need for a strong king to provide peace in his representation of another Arthurian enemy, the French lord Frollo. In Geoffrey's *Historia*, Frollo, after being vanquished by Arthur on the battlefield, retreats with his host into Paris. Geoffrey writes:

> At dum exercitum suum uicinorum auxilio roborare intenderet, uenit ex inprouiso Arturus. ipsumque infra ciuitatem obsedit. Emenso deinde mense, cum Frollo gentem suam fame perire doluisset, mandauit Arturo ut ipsi soli duellium inissent et cui uictoria proueniret alterius regnum optineret. Erat enim ipse magne stature et audacie. atque fortitudinis quibus ultra modum confisus ista mandauerat ut hoc modo aditum salutis haberet. (ed. Wright, 108)

> [Just as Frollo was considering how to strengthen his army by calling upon neighboring peoples, Arthur arrived unexpectedly and besieged him inside the city. A whole month passed. Frollo grieved to see his people dying of hunger, and sent a message to Arthur to say that they should meet in single combat and that whichever was victorious should take the kingdom of the other. Being a man of immense stature, courage and strength, Frollo relied upon these advantages when he sent his message, hoping in this way to find a solution to his problem.] (trans. Thorpe, 224)

Geoffrey's Frollo, though "grieved to see his people dying of hunger" undertakes single combat with Arthur because he is confident he will win, that his courage and strength will be enough to triumph over his enemy.

Wace expands this scene to more than double its length, using it to praise a leader whose concern for the multitude overwhelms his concern even for his own person. He enlarges to nearly twenty lines Geoffrey's observation that Frollo was grieved by his people's suffering. Like the Peterborough chronicler, Wace asks his readers to contemplate in detail the suffering of the civilian population during wartime:

> La ville tindrent bien Franceis,
> E Artur i sist prés d'un meis;
> Grant pople aveit en la cité,
> De viande orent tost chierté;
> Tut le purchaz e tut l'atrait
> Qu'en poi de tens aveient fait
> Orent tost mangié e usé;
> Mult veïssez pople afamé!
> Poi unt vitaille, e grant gent sunt;
> Enfant e femes grant duel funt;
> Si la gent povre en fust creüe
> La cité fust bien tost rendue.
> Mult vunt criant: <<Frolle, que faiz?
> Pur quei ne quers a Artur paiz?>>
> Frolles vit le pople destreit
> Pur la vitaille ki failleit,
> Vit lé genz, ki de faim mureient,
> E vit que rendre se vuleient,
> Vit la cité mise a eissil. (9977–95)

[The French held out well and Arthur sat there nearly a month. There were many people in the city and soon they were short of food; all that they had acquired and collected in a short time was soon eaten and used up. They were starving! There was little food and many people. The women and children wept and wailed; if it had been up to the poor, the city would soon have surrendered. They kept crying: "Frollo, what are you doing? why don't you ask Arthur for peace?" Frollo saw the people distraught for lack of food and men dying of hunger, saw they wished to surrender and saw the city made destitute.] (251)

What is most striking about Wace's depiction of the Paris siege is his emphasis on the distress of the masses—the common people—during times of war. By calling attention to the suffering of the women, the children, and the poor, Wace vividly demonstrates the consequences of aristocratic contention. He also suggests that submission to powerful authority is sometimes in the best interest of a suffering populace, that it is the only means of achieving peace. If the decision were left to the poor, they would choose to surrender their city rather than starve. It is up to Frollo to find a more honorable means of ending the siege.

> Mielz volt sun cors mettre en peril
> E en abandun de murir
> Que plainement Paris guerpir;
> Bien se fiout en sa bunté.
> Al rei Artur ad fors mandé
> Que il dui en l'isle venissent
> E cors a cors se combatissent,
> E li quels d'els l'autre ocirreit
> U qui vif veintre le purreit
> La terre tute a l'altre eüst
> E tute France receüst,
> Si que li poples ne perist
> E que ville n'en destruisist. (9996–10008)

[He preferred to endanger his body and risk his life rather than totally abandon Paris; he relied on his valor. He sent word to king Arthur that the two of them should come to the island and fight in single combat, and whoever killed the other, or could take him alive, would have all the other's land and receive all France, so that the people would not die or the city be destroyed.] (251, 253)

Wace's portrayal of the aristocratic magnanimity of a French overlord may reflect on his patron Henry's Angevin upbringing. Whereas Geoffrey's Frollo offers Arthur the option of single combat hoping to outmaneuver the king, Wace's figure enters into the contest because "Bien se fiout en sa bunté" [he relied on his valor], so that "li poples ne perist / E que ville n'en destruisist" [the people would not die or the city be destroyed]. In the light of the chaos brought on England by the hostilities between Stephen and Matilda, Wace, in representing the misery of the smallest, the weakest, underlines the importance of Henry's new, powerful, centralized monarchy in bringing resolution to such pain.

At the same time, the use of single combat as the device to end the stalemate diverts attention from the consequences of warfare, creating in the midst of the siege something of the festive atmosphere of the tournament: "Dunc veïssiez pople fremir, / Homes e femes fors eissir, / Sur murs saillir e sur maisuns" (10019–21) [You could see the people in tumult, men and women coming out, jumping on walls and houses] (253). The single combat shifts our attention from the fate of a people to the honor of a single aristocratic individual and from the genre of history to that of romance.

Following the conquest and subjugation of France, both Geoffrey and Wace indicate how Arthur apportions the spoils of war among his closest and most powerful followers. Wace, however, departs from Geoffrey's narrative to proclaim the benefits of the newly won peace:

> Quant il out ses baruns feufez
> E fait riches tuz ses privez,
> En avril, quant esté entra.
> En Engleterre trespassa.
> Mult veïssiez a sun repaire
> Humes e femes joie faire;
> Baisent les dames lur mariz
> E les meres baisent lur fiz;
> Filz e filles baisent lur peres
> E de joie plurent les meres;
> Cusines baisent lur cusins
> E les veisines lur veisins.
> Les amies lur amis baisent
> E, quant leus est, de plus s'aaisent;
> Les antes baisent lur nevuz;
> Mult aveit grant joie entre tuz.
> Par rues e par quarefors
> En veïssiez ester plusors
> Pur demander cument lur est
> E que unt fait e de lur cunquest,
> Que unt fait e que unt trové
> E pur quei unt tant demuré. (10171–92)

> Artur enura tuz les suens,
> Mult ama e duna as buens.
> Pur ses richeises demustrer
> E pur faire de sei parler,
> Prist cunseil si li fu loé
> Qu'a la Pentecuste en esté

Feïst sur barnage assembler
E dunc se feïst coruner. (10197–10204)

[When he had given his barons fiefs and made all his friends rich, he crossed to England in April, at the start of the summer. Men and women could be seen celebrating his return: the ladies kissed their husbands and the mothers their sons, sons and daughters kissed their fathers and mothers wept for joy, cousins and neighbors embraced, as did sweethearts who, when opportunity allowed, indulged themselves rather more. Aunts kissed their nephews; for everyone, joy was widespread. In streets and at crossroads many people would congregate to ask the new arrivals how they were and what they had done with their conquests, how they had acted, what they had found and why they had been away so long. . . . Arthur honored all his men, especially cherishing and rewarding the best ones. To display his wealth and spread his fame, he took counsel and was advised to assemble his barons at Pentecost, in summer, and then to be crowned.] (257)

Wace associates peace with the coming of spring, with renewal, rebirth, resurrection. Once again emphasis is directed toward the effects of peace on the general population. The catalogue of those who benefit directly from the conclusion of hostilities includes dames, mothers, sons and daughters, cousins, aunts, ladies, friends. But Wace makes clear that peace is even more to the advantage of the king and his lords. Arthur apportions wealth and property among the deserving, consolidating his own authority by making his vassals happy. Once again, he schedules a great feast to consume—conspicuously—the profits of victory. War holds out the promise for a patron's rewards. But it is during peacetime that those rewards are distributed; it is during peacetime that the system of patronage flourishes. For Wace, client of the rich and powerful, peace is a time of advantage, when warrior-class patrons have the leisure to consider the contributions of their ancestors—and themselves—to the advancement of civilization, a time when warrior-class patrons can expend the capital they have accumulated through plunder on endowing projects having little or no military value, projects like the composition of histories.

As Arthur and his court engage in festivities they are interrupted by an embassy from the Roman emperor, Lucius, demanding that Arthur pay tribute. A council of Arthur's lords is convened to consider an appropriate response. In both the *Historia Regum Britanniæ* and the *Roman de Brut* Cador delivers a wildly militaristic speech advocating an aggressive reaction. Cador's speech eroticizes war; he argues that Arthur's lords have grown soft, effeminized, from a prolonged peace and that only through trial by combat can masculinity be reasserted. In Wace's narrative Gawain follows Cador's speech with a rebuttal:

> Bone est la pais emprés la guerre,
> Plus bele e mieldre en est la terre;
> Mult sunt bones les gaberies
> E bones sunt les drueries.
> Pur amistié e pur amies
> Funt chevaliers chevaleries. (10767–72)

[Peace is good after war and the land is better and lovelier for it. Jokes are excellent and so are love affairs. It's for love and their beloved that knights do knightly deeds.] (271)

Gawain eroticizes peace. The land comes alive and knights turn their thoughts to love and lovemaking. The discourse of combat is transformed into the language of sensual desire. Pleasant words and procreative pleasures take the place of threats, violence, and death. While Cador extols the homosocial world of the battlefield, Gawain represents peace as a time of heterosexual negotiation and exchange. Ultimately both Cador and Gawain join Arthur's expedition of Roman conquest. Nevertheless, as the final spokesman at the council, Gawain reconfigures aristocratic preference, choosing peace as more normative, more fulfilling, and more profitable than war. Cador, a voice of older tradition, speaks the language of a court culture in constant competition with other court cultures; in Cador's universe, plunder is necessary for survival. Gawain is the voice of a new order that has benefited from accrued wealth; he is the advocate of a status quo imposed by a powerful centralized monarchy, a status quo that would be undermined by violent competition among lords.

Wace's *Roman de Brut* was history written for winners, written for an aristocracy with enough capital to commission its production, with enough leisure time to be interested in its accounts. Wace's *Roman de Brut* was written for an audience sufficiently satisfied with its possessions and strong enough not to worry about anyone else coveting those possessions, although this confidence would not survive the death of Henry II and his son John's loss of his patrimony in France. Wace did not advocate peace because his Anglo-Norman readers were cultured. He did not advocate peace because his Anglo-Norman readers were prepared for an aesthetic paradigm shift that demanded that narrative subject matter be reevaluated. Wace wrote about peace because it was to the political and economic advantage of his patrons that nothing disturb the position of domination—of empire—they worked so hard to achieve.

Policing the Boundaries of Empire

Since we are interested primarily in the social functions of Arthurian histories (rather than, say, their literary histories) within the genre of historical writing, we must explore the social conditions under which vernacular *Bruts* were produced at the end of the twelfth century and the beginning of the thirteenth by looking at the interests of their patrons and potential patrons. Twelfth-century patrons of vernacular histories like Henry II or his queen, Eleanor, were responding, in the period during which Wace was writing, to a series of economic and political developments that resulted from the pressures of maintaining an empire that by the late twelfth century stretched from the Pyrenees to Scotland and as far east as Jerusalem.

This empire was amassed during what Robert Bartlett has called the "aristocratic diaspora" of the high Middle Ages, a period of military expansion during which the aristocracy of Western Europe, especially those who occupied the old Carolingian empire, spread out from their homelands into new areas where they settled and augmented their fortunes (*Making of Europe*, 24–56). This acquisitive expansionism coincided with—but was not limited to—the age of the Crusades. It included the attempted conquest of such far-flung and exotic places as Sicily, Spain, Syria, Palestine, Castile, Poland, and Prussia, as well as places like England, Scotland, Wales, and Ireland that, to us, seem much less exotic and alien, but which to their Norman conquerors must have seemed like the borderland between culture and utter chaos. It is during this period almost simultaneously that both genres—vernacular history and romance—first emerged (or re-emerged). Both genres manage the anxieties of both the conqueror and the conquered, the powerful and the destitute, about the chaos that lies beyond what is known during a period of rapid expansion, during a period in which boundaries—geographical, political, and social, both at home and abroad—are forming and reforming.

This concern with boundaries suggests that the kind of continuous history Žižek associates with official historiography requires not only a particular ordering of time (the succession of one king after another) but of space as well. In *The Sacred and the Profane*, Mircea Eliade describes anthropologically the symbolic construction of territorial boundaries in what he refers to as "traditional"—or preindustrial—societies, such as that of twelfth-century Europe. He argues that "traditional" societies create rigid boundaries between what he calls sacred territory—territory consecrated, inhabited, and known—and that territory that lies beyond, in which lurk danger, demons, turmoil (20–65). Sacred territory has been claimed from the chaos, from the monsters who ruled before. It has been cleansed and marked by reminders of the victory over disorder and the possibility that disorder may once again reign without continued vigilance.

Vernacular histories, like Wace's *Roman de Brut*, that represent the antique history of England, illustrate just this process of marking geographical spaces with the signs of the political body. Wace, for instance (like Geoffrey of Monmouth before him), describes Brutus landing at Totnes on the Cornish coast and discovering the land inhabited by giants. The giants are horrific; they are described as demons and fiends. Their leader, Gogmagog, is the worst of all. Wace stresses his huge size; he is leader of the giants because of his "force" and "grandur" (1071). To establish their claim to this new land, Brutus and his men must immediately banish these creatures to the geographical margins of the land, to the mountains. Banishment to the periphery, however, is not enough to secure the new boundaries. The giants return and violate the Trojan's religious observations, their sacred space. The Trojans kill nineteen of the giants and force the leader, Gogmagog, to wrestle Corineus in front of Brutus. Corineus dispatches the last threat to the Trojan conquest of the island by throwing him over a cliff, thus securing Brutus's claim to the land.

Eliade's model, however useful, neglects the political, economic, and ideological implications of the differentiations he identifies between sacred space (secured and ordered space) and what lies beyond. He neglects to recognize, for instance, how such differentiations provide the ideological justification for imperialistic ventures, in traditional societies and even in largely secular, postindustrial cultures. If all margins are a threat to the integrity of the social body, as Eliade's argument suggests, how does the social body manage anxieties about what lies beyond its borders? The physical body, as Mary Douglas has argued, can be a model for any bounded system and we must be prepared to see in the body a symbol of society, "to see the powers and dangers credited to social structure reproduced in small on the human body" (115).

The migrations of Bartlett's "aristocratic diaspora"—of which Norman expansionism was a part—were primarily the result of pressures created by the medieval dependence on land as a source of economic wealth. Land by its very nature is a finite resource, so that landless aristocrats, disinherited because they were younger sons in a system of primogeniture that favored eldest sons (or because they were not legitimate sons), needed to go elsewhere to make their fortunes. Control of the land as an economic resource, however, also depended on control of women—and their bodies—as economic resources. Strategic intermarriage with conquered people forged necessary political alliances and ensured orderly succession and inheritance of property through the production of legitimate heirs. By the late twelfth century, the collective social practices of the Norman aristocracy that sustained conquest and intermarriage spawned a host of new genres—including romance and vernacular history—that preserved and reproduced this metonymic link between land and women (see chapter 2 above).

Women's bodies, then, occupy, at least symbolically, a strategic, if passive, position within this process of marking boundaries during a period of instability. But if marriage could be used in conjunction with conquest to expand wealth and political influence, then, failing that, rape and abduction might accomplish the same thing (Duby, *Knight*, 38–40, 237–38). The rape of women—the violation of the intact physical body—can figure symbolically the violation of political boundaries by an "other" that is represented as grotesque and monstrous. Following Žižek's analysis of ideology, we can understand rape as a symptom, "a particular, 'pathological' feature, signifying formation, a binding of enjoyment, an inert stain resisting communication and interpretation, a stain which cannot be included in the circuit of discourse, of social bond network, but is at the same time a positive condition of it, . . . a terrifying bodily mark which is merely a mute attestation bearing witness to a disgusting enjoyment" (75–76). In other words, we might explore in Wace rape's imaginative construction as a symptom or trope in the writing of history that functions as a "quilting point" binding together the floating elements that make up ideological space, thereby creating and sustaining a particular ideological formation (87). What anxieties about boundaries—political as well as bodily—about exogamy and purity are being enacted in Wace's narrative? What is the generic function of rape narratives in historical writing?

The view of women as resources in dynastic expansion no doubt explains the extent to which abduction and rape tend to collapse into each other in medieval law. The term "rape" derives in antiquity from the word *raptus,* literally to carry off by force. Gratian defined rape as involving the abduction of a woman in addition to unlawful intercourse with her (Brundage, "Rape and Seduction," 141–42). The offense of rape was as much about stealing a woman away from those under whose authority she lived as it was about sexual intercourse. These legal distinctions find their way, for instance, into Wace's description of the Mont Saint Michel giant's rape of Eleine. When Eleine's nurse describes the events, she distinguishes between the actual abduction and forced sexual coitus. For the former, she uses the term *ravie:*

> Lasse, pur quei l'ai tant nurrie
> Quant uns diables l'ad *ravie,*
> Uns gaianz mei e li *ravi*
> E mei e li aporta ci. (11403–6; emphasis ours)

> [Alas, why did I nurse her so much
> If some devil ravished her away;
> A giant ravished me and her
> And me and her he brought here.][18]

For the latter, she uses the verbs *purgesir* and *desforcier:*

> La pucele volt *purgesir*
> Mais tendre fu, nel pout suffrir
> . . . .
> Par force m'ad *purgeüe.*
> Sa force m'estuet otreier,
> Ne li puis mie *defforcier* (11407–08, 11428–30; emphasis ours)

> [[The giant] wanted to couple with the maiden
> But she was tender, she could not endure him.
> By force he detained me here
> And by force he coupled with me.
> I had to yield to his strength,
> I could never thwart him.]

Eleine dies before the giant can deflower her, so that forced sexual intercourse is displaced onto the ancient and lower-class nurse. But the giant's crime—and the horror for which he must be violently dispatched—is his abduction of Arthur's kinswoman, Eleine. The violation of the nurse is at best a secondary incentive for Arthur's revenge.

If we understand the story of Arthur, as it is related in Wace's *Roman de Brut*, to be an ideological legitimation of the imperialistic ambitions of the Anglo-Norman monarchs, then we should be struck by the centrality of rape to the legend, by its obsessive and symptomatic repetitiveness. Arthur's history is structured by rape. Uther Pendragon's rape of Igerna, which leads to Arthur's conception, begins the story. Mordred's rape of Guenevere ends Arthur's career and life.[19] The Mont Saint Michel giant's rape of Eleine and Arthur's vengeance for that act occupy a pivotal moment in Arthurian history. Having previously received an embassy from the Roman emperor demanding tribute, Arthur refuses to pay or to recognize the emperor's authority over him. He assembles an army and travels to Brittany, which will serve as a staging point for his conquest of the Continent. With this move, Arthur's dynastic ambitions become imperial ones. No longer content to be merely king of England, he lays claim to the imperial crown, establishing the legitimacy of his claim through a genealogical link with his predecessors Belinus, Constantine, and Maximian. While in Brittany Arthur hears of a giant, called Dinabunc by Wace, who has abducted his kinswoman Eleine, niece of King Hoel. The giant has taken her to the remote and inaccessible Mont Saint Michel. How, we might ask, does the narration of this incident function generically to transform Arthur from local to world historical hero? How does it serve as an ideological "quilting point" for the legitimation of imperial ambition?

The rape of Eleine functions as a spectacle of political hegemony, of Arthur's imperial and dynastic ambitions. Arthur defeats the giant/rapist not simply as an individual knight errant out for personal glory—a marker of the romance as a genre—but as an established king of England and potential emperor of Rome. His act of vengeance against the giant provides a fitting transition for Arthur from king to emperor.

On the surface, though, rape would seem to constitute a threat to official historiography. It would seem to constitute just the kind of disruptive moment that enables the dispossessed to write their own histories. Rape creates anxiety in a patrilineal caste by threatening the orderly transfer of power and property from generation to generation, which is why incidents like the Mont Saint Michel giant's abduction of Arthur's kinswoman must elicit a swift and violent response. But how does this episode differ from other instances of rape that go unpunished? We might ask instead what are the circumstances under which the sexual exchange of women between strangers (exogamy) is seen as an acceptable means of establishing political alliances and what are the conditions under which such exchanges are constituted as involuntary and hence as rape.

The Mont Saint Michel giant's rape of Eleine serves as a nodal point (*point de capiton*) that "quilts" together networks of ideological relations histories like Wace's were designed to reproduce, while itself producing a certain excess (Žižek calls this "surplus-enjoyment") that exceeds the rape's ideological and structural function. The event coalesces several anxieties about the maintenance of boundaries during times when they are being redrawn in potentially disturbing ways. The particular ideological field being quilted by the rape involves the relationship between the familiar and the foreign during a period of geographical expansion.

Wace represents the giant not as a homegrown threat, but, following Geoffrey of Monmouth, as an exotic outsider; he is said to be from Spain. The giant's origin strikes us as significant, as it has other scholars working on insular histories. Geraldine Heng attempts to relocate the giant in Geoffrey's *Historia* from Spain to Syria (or at least to argue for a doubled origin, focusing on Geoffrey's genitive plural *Hispaniarum*). She argues that the name *hispania* was often "applied vaguely to Moslem regions in Asia Minor and eastward," seeing in the giant a displacement of European anxieties about the oriental "other" ("Cannibalism," 117–18). While her argument strikes us as plausible, once again we would like to focus attention on the "internal" colonization of Europe itself, on the ways in which Europe contained within its own borders the hybridity postcolonial scholars find in conflicts between East and West during the Middle Ages.[20] The second half of the eleventh century witnessed extraordinary upheaval in Muslim Spain, ripples of which almost certainly were felt as far north as England. In the last decades of the eleventh century, the Muslim rulers of al-Andalus came under considerable criticism from Islamic fundamentalists, known as the Almoravids, for embracing increasingly secular lifestyles and forging alliances with Christian Europe. The Muslim strategy of appeasement in Spain, along with its concomitant cultural assimilation, was not enough, however, to satisfy the increasing pressures of the Christian world's expansionism. Christian rulers in Spain were forced to acquire more and more resources to meet the escalating demands of their vassals, which included not just gold, but also slaves, horses, and land. The increasingly aggressive posture of the Christian lords toward Islamic Spain drove the taifa rulers into the arms of the fundamentalist Almoravid factions. Finally, like Hengest and Horsa of Britain's early history, the Almoravids ultimately displaced the very leaders they came to protect from an immediate external threat.[21]

The ascendency of the Almoravids in Islamic Spain dramatically altered the relationship between the Islamic and Christian worlds. Compared with their highly cultivated predecessors, the taifa rulers of al-Andalus, the Almoravids must have seemed grotesque to European Christians. Fletcher describes them as "outsiders... unsophisticated tribesmen, materially and culturally impoverished." Their leader, Yusef, "dressed in skins, reeked of camels, and spoke Arabic only with difficulty. It is impossible to imagine him at the elegant soirées of the Abbadid court of Seville" (Fletcher, *Moorish Spain*, 108). During the early twelfth century, the relationship between Christians and the Almoravids was marked by escalating belligerence. Christian rulers abandoned all pretense of benign exploitation in favor of a policy of outright conquest. Within a generation, Almoravid rule was being torn apart by Christian incursions from the north, internal strife, and the threat of even more radically fundamentalist Muslims—the Almohads—from the south. Reports about conflicts between Christian chivalry and what to Europeans must have seemed like an alien, even demonic, mass, however exaggerated by propaganda, would likely have reached even England, where they may have found their way into Geoffrey's characterization of the Mont Saint Michel giant.

The giant figures foreignness represented as monstrosity. His defeat carries world historical import in the context of the larger conflict between Arthur and the emperor Lucius, which is curiously portrayed as a conflict between Christian Europe and the rest of the non-European, and largely Muslim, world. While from our geographical and historical perspective, Arthur might seem, at best, king of a marginal outpost of the Roman Empire who is invading a wealthier and more powerful neighbor, Wace—once again following Geoffrey—reconfigures the sides. Arthur's army is composed of knights from England, Scotland, and Ireland, but also Gutland, Iceland, Norway, Denmark, Orkney, Man, Normandy, Anjou, Poitou, Flanders, Boulogne, Lorraine, and Lovaine. Together, these principalities, coupled with Arthur's claim to the lineage of former emperors Belinus, Constantine, and Maximian, define much of what we usually think of as the Western European hegemony. The emperor's army, on the other hand, seems composed almost exclusively of foreigners from alien, exotic, and primarily Middle Eastern and Mediterranean lands. They include the king of Greece and the duke of Boeotia, as well as the kings of Turkey, Egypt, Crete, Syria, Phrygia, Babylon, Media, Libia, Bitunia, Ituria, Africa, and

Ethiopia. Like the giant of Mont Saint Michel, these potential invaders from the south represent the threat of cultural, political, and sexual violence. Destroying them ensures not only domestic tranquility but the expansion of the European hegemony.

Curiously absent from the ranks of both sides are the Spanish, who are represented only by the giant, though, as we suggest above, Spain was at the heart of Christian–Muslim conflict for much of the eleventh and twelfth centuries. In the form of the giant, the actual threat is dehumanized—literally made monstrous—in the interests of creating a credible opponent, a giant, with whom Arthur can exchange violence and, by doing so, win the right to lay claim to Empire.

Justification for political, economic, and ideological expansionism is frequently found in the demonization of those "others" who populate contested territories, and this demonization almost always includes a sexual component (Moore, 100–101). The colonial "other" is invariably seen as sexually menacing. As Moore writes, "Pollution fear . . . is fear that the privileged feel of those at whose expense their privilege is enjoyed. Marked sensitivity to the possibilities of sexual pollution may therefore suggest that the boundaries which the prohibitions in question protect are threatened, or thought to be. Conversely (what may in practice amount to the same thing) if new social boundaries are being established it will be appropriate to consider whether heightened vigilance over sexual matters may be one means of securing them" (101). As boundaries are extended, those at the margins must either be assimilated, pushed to more distant margins, or destroyed. These sometimes contradictory impulses—assimilation, marginalization, and destruction—allow for contradictory mythologies of the other as sexually attractive (perhaps even endowed with extraordinary sexual prowess), sexually dangerous, and sexually hideous. These mythologies allow for such various kinds of domination as rape, dispersion, and murder.

Wace's treatment of the Mont Saint Michel rape demonstrates Mary Douglas's argument that violations of physical bodies can be metonymies for violations of the political body by representing the giant as aggressively disruptive of the social order; he threatens not only the intactness of Eleine's female body, but that of the social body as well. The giant not only abducts and rapes a high-born virgin, he also lays waste the countryside:

Mult veïssiez les païsanz
Maisuns vuider, porter enfans,

> Femes mener, bestes chacier,
> Es munz munter, es bois mucier.
> Par bois e par deserz fueient
> E encor la murir cremeient.
> Tute esteit la terre guerpie,
> Tut s'en est la gent fuïe. (11309–16)

[You could see peasants all leaving their houses, carrying children, leading women, hustling animals and climbing mountains or hiding in the woods. They fled into forests and wilderness, still fearing to die even there. The whole land was abandoned, all its people fled.] (285)

Wace—who, throughout most of his career profited from the largesse of Norman imperialism—suggests that Arthur's destruction of the giant comes as a boon to the peasantry, which has been especially harassed by the creature. His narrative thus indicates that the aristocracy must keep the foreign "other" in check not only to maintain its own privilege, but for the sake of the peasantry as well.

Simultaneous to expansionism—and coincidental to the demonization of foreigners—lurks an anxiety that those at the margins not only may succeed in reclaiming their previously held properties, including the women that have been taken from them by invading forces, but also might embark upon imperialistic ventures of their own. Just as imperialistic forces make claim to the women and land they capture, causing their forced assimilation, these same forces anxiously eye the situation of their own property—their own women—lest those on the margins attempt an incursion. Their anxiety hardens defenses against incursions while at the same time fueling further imperialistic enthusiasms—there can be no rest until "difference" is obliterated. The genre of historical narrative necessarily reflects these anxieties and their antidotes, justifying Arthur's expansion of his borders, provoking further acts of imperialism, and legitimating his ambitions of world conquest. In Wace Žižek's continuous history serves the needs of Empire and appeals to patrons enjoying the fruits of Empire. Whatever discontinuities might emerge in the narrative, whatever arresting moments offer glimpses of alternative histories are quickly contained by the simple expedient of turning the crime back on those who are to be conquered: the Britons tell lies about Arthur; the Mont Saint Michel giant can be dispatched because he is a rapist. In the next chapter, we will explore more fully the possibilities for alternative histories by examining the changed circumstances under which Laȝamon's thirteenth-century *Brut* emerged.

4

Discontinuous Time

History in the Eyes of Its Losers

To our knowledge, Wace has never been accused of being a nationalist poet; perhaps because of his position as a French historian writing about English history, his interests seem more cosmopolitan than his successor and translator, Laȝamon. It has, however, been the fashion among literary scholars to suggest that Laȝamon's thirteenth-century *Brut* represents that poet's self-fashioning as a patriotic Englishman, "an attempt to kindle a spirit of solidarity between the Welsh and the English, the legitimate inhabitants of Britain, against the [Norman] invaders" by combining Celtic material with Anglo-Saxon forms (Le Saux, 227).[1] To what extent ought we to read into Laȝamon's *Brut* the kind of open rejection of Norman political and cultural dominance that Thierry describes in the passage we quoted at the opening of the previous chapter? The *Brut* does not conceive of a "project of deliverance conceived with common accord by a great mass of men." It does not resound with "the old English cry, No Normans!" To the extent that Laȝamon was required to please his patrons, who were as likely to think of themselves as Norman as English, his *Brut* bears the marks of a performance in the public transcript, of official historiography. At least on the surface it seems to present the same kind of continuous progressive history we found in Geoffrey and Wace, the same celebration of dynastic continuity.

Indeed the layouts of two extant *Brut* manuscripts illustrate visually the chronotope of continuous history. As Elizabeth Bryan has noted, Cotton Otho C. xiii's use of historiated initials calls attention to the succession of English kings from Brutus through Arthur to Cadwallader and, in the Arthurian section, the amassing of territory through imperialistic adventuring (64). Cotton Caligula A. ix indicates the names of successive rulers in the margins in red ink at the points of their first appearance (Stein, 107). The manuscripts themselves delineate history's unfolding in continuous space and time. As Rosamund Allen writes, Laȝamon's "main contribution to the story of Britain is to present a picture of 'merry Britain' where law and order create a world in which populations thrive and society achieves stability and security" (Lawman, trans. Allen, xxiii), hardly the description of a revolutionary out to overthrow the status quo.

However, the hidden transcript of Laȝamon's distaste for the Normans erupts from time to time in references to the French conquerors "þa mid fehte heo bi-wonnen" (1030) [who won [England] through fighting], and of the Normans "mid heore nið-craften" (3547), which Allen translates as "with their nasty malice" (92).[2] Such outbursts suggest that it might be possible to read in the margins of Laȝamon's *Brut* the kind of discontinuous historical narrative Žižek attributes to history's losers, in particular "its capacity to *arrest*, to *immobilize* historical movement and to *isolate* the detail from its historical totality" (139).

Laȝamon did not write for the same audiences and under exactly the same circumstances in the thirteenth century as Wace did in the twelfth. Changes occurred in the intervening years between the two translations that make it possible for Laȝamon to write a history of the kings of England in the English language. The change that looms the largest during this period is the loss of Angevin lands in France during the reign of King John (1199–1216). By the early thirteenth century, the kings of England no longer rule a vast empire. The Anglo-Norman aristocracy was forced, as one historian notes, "to concentrate on English interests. They would continue to think feudal thoughts and work in feudal ways, but their problems were basically English, and English ways and traditions would sooner or later influence the manner in which those problems were solved" (Sayles, 397). The loss of Continental lands did not prevent a nostalgia for past glories that fueled the imperialistic ambitions of subsequent monarchs, as we shall see, down to the fifteenth century, but it did physically limit the scope of their activities. At the same time, the centers of patronage were beginning to move from the royal courts to the barons of the realm, and to the margins of the kingdom where contact with the cosmopolitan royal court was sporadic. These developments undoubtedly helped to create an audience interested in reading about the history of English kings in the English language.

The Romance of the Nation

Before we can say what the chronotope of discontinuous history might look like we must distinguish it from the kind of romantic historicism that seeks in Laȝamon some glimpse of the English people (the true inheritors of a pure Anglo-Saxon culture) rising up against their foreign overlords. As Thierry notes, this sort of open rebellion—if it ever existed—was pretty much finished seventy-two years after the Battle of Hastings. But critics persist in reproducing a romantic view of history that sees Laȝamon as a part of a continuous tradition of English poetry that springs from and feeds an English national identity that thumbs its nose at alien Continental influences. Henry Cecil Wyld, for instance, in 1930 claimed that Laȝamon's "poetry has its roots, not merely in the old literary tradition, but also . . . in the *essential genius of the race*. The intensity of feeling, the wealth of imagery, the tender humanity, the love of nature, the chivalric and romantic spirit, which distinguish the poetry of Laȝamon would give him a high place among the English poets of any age" (2; emphasis ours). While Françoise Le Saux, writing in 1989, is more careful than earlier critics in warning her readers that to call Laȝamon's so-called Englishness "'patriotism' or 'nationalism' is dangerous, for these words have connotations which do not tally with the ideological background of the twelfth or thirteenth century," she still cannot help but attribute to the poem a "national feeling of a sort" (227).

Characterizations throughout much of the last century of Laȝamon's *Brut* as an expression of English nationalism result from the romance of seeing the *Brut* as "the eccentric work of an obscure country priest, isolated in the west midlands, and celebrating, in a rather old-fashioned way, the glories of this island's past" (Salter, 66). Such critics read the *Brut* as a poem written in reaction to the kinds of literary forms promoted by a dominant, but essentially alien, Norman culture. They point to such elements of composition as vocabulary, versification (especially Laȝamon's use of the alliterative long line), the presence of epic formulas such as those found in Old English verse, and mythological references to Germanic deities as evidence of Laȝamon's allegiance to a specifically "English" culture untainted by Continental influences (Le Saux, 189–205). These nationalist readings of Laȝamon's *Brut* are of a piece with a historical view, present in Thierry, that medieval English nationalism issued from a class divide between a Norman aristocracy and an English populace. As Thorlac Turville-Petre expresses it, the lords were of Norman origin, while the English "nation" consisted of "the *comun*, the *lewed*, or the *lowe-men*" (17). He cites Robert of Gloucester's *Chronicle* as evidence of this split:

Of þe Normans beþ heyemen þat beþ of Englonde,
And þe lowemen of Saxons, as ich vnderstonde. (Turville-Petre, 18)

Yet this characterization of the thirteenth century as fundamentally divided between two categorically distinct ethnic and class groups ignores the dialogically agitated environment of the period in which family and patronal loyalties could easily cut across and complicate ethnic and class identifications.[3] This interpenetration of cultural languages reveals itself aesthetically in Laȝamon's work. Salter and others have attempted to show that "what Laȝamon achieves is as much an extension of the range of English verse-writing, under the influence of twelfth-century materials and forms, both French and Latin," as a nostalgic retreat into an archaic but native Anglo-Saxon versification (Salter, 49). The internal rhyme of his long line owes as much to the French octosyllabic couplet of his source or the versification of Anglo-Norman homilies as to the Anglo-Saxon alliterative line (49, 57–59). His characteristic use of the extended simile more likely derives from the Latin heroic poetry of Henry II's court than from the Anglo-Saxon kenning (62). Both the form and content of Laȝamon's "glorious history" is marked by an environment of heteroglossia in which several cultures and several languages compete for hegemony.

Attempts to depict Laȝamon as a representative of thirteenth-century identity politics belong to the kind of continuous and progressive history that Žižek attributes to ruling class or "official" historiography: twentieth-century historians and literary critics construct the past retrospectively to culminate logically in the sort of nationalist enterprise that dominates the fields of English history and literature today. One of the discontinuities we must explore in the medieval history of Arthur, then, is the possibility that such "national feeling" could not be conceived within either the dominant aristocratic culture or the marginalized ethnic groups and classes of thirteenth-century England. Contrary to contemporary Western theories of nationalism, which place the emergence of the nation and nationalism in the modern (post-Enlightenment) world,[4] it has become fashionable among medievalists interested in postcolonial criticism to argue that "the similarities between medieval and modern expressions of national identity . . . are fundamental" (Turville-Petre, v). Indeed Geraldine Heng speaks of a "consensus" among medievalists who believe that "discourses of the nation are visible and can be read with ease in medieval England" ("Romance of England," 151); they disagree only on whether these discourses of the English nation begin in the ninth or thirteenth century.[5] Some even locate "the rise of the nation-*state* and statism during the European Middle Ages itself" ("Romance of England," 150; emphasis in original). The impulses for these arguments are understandable. Medievalists justly criticize contemporary theorists of nationalism, especially Anderson in *Imagined Communities*, for their ignorance of and indifference to the complexities and heterogeneity of medieval cultures and of those cultures' salience for understanding contemporary political formations. They rightly accuse these theorists of grounding the emergence of the nation on a decisive break with a medieval past characterized as a homogeneous "field of undifferentiated otherness" against which modernity can emerge (Cohen, "Introduction," 4; see also Davis, "National Writing," 612–13, and Heng, "Romance of England," 150–51).

Despite our fundamental agreement with these criticisms, however, we are not quite ready to join the consensus on the emergence of national sentiment in the Middle Ages. We want to resist the impulse to naturalize the discourse of the nation as, for instance, Turville-Petre does when he begins with the assumption that nationalism (and the idea of the nation that nationalism invents) already existed in England by the late thirteenth century. He argues that English writers defined the nation in terms of its territory, people, and language (vi), though he takes it for granted that the sum of these disparate entities is necessarily the nation; he never actually demonstrates that, for the writers he cites, the relationships among territory, people, and language add up to the political entity we now call the nation. He assumes its prior existence. Those medieval scholars who critique contemporary theorists of nationalism for defining modernity against the alterity of the Middle Ages end up reinscribing the very same break under different terms. Both Heng ("Romance of England," 150) and Davis ("National Writing," 613), for instance, argue that medieval "nations" are qualitatively different from modern ones. But at what point do they become so different that it ceases to be meaningful to call them nations at all? Susan Reynolds is more circumspect. She avoids the terms "nation" and "nationalism" in her study of medieval communities, finding them "misleading" (*Kingdoms and Communities,* 253). Instead she refers to the "community of the realm," which enables her to consider how these communities may have been imagined differently from the nation-state.

Resisting this emerging consensus, we want to insist that the nation is a cultural artifact of a particular kind and that, as a cultural artifact, it has a history that must be investigated, not assumed. Part of the difficulty in separating medieval conceptions of political community from modern ideas about the nation is the way in which the terminology, documents, symbols, and narratives of medieval political communities were assimilated into modern discourses of the nation. For this reason, we find Jeffrey

Cohen's appropriation of the Lacanian notion of *extimité* an extremely useful starting point for a discussion of medieval imagined communities. The Middle Ages, he argues, "as a formal effect of their very middleness could... be located as extimate to the modern: intimate and alien simultaneously: an 'inexcluded' middle at the pulsing heart of modernity" ("Introduction," 5). The language of medieval political communities, we would argue, is both tantalizingly familiar and bafflingly strange.

Approaching the Middle Ages as extimate—intimate and alien—to modernity, we want to return to Benedict Anderson's definition of the nation as a starting point for an exploration of alternate forms of political community. Anderson defines the nation as "an imagined political community," one that is imagined as "both inherently limited and sovereign" (*Imagined Communities*, 6). Ernest Renan, in his 1882 lecture "What Is a Nation?" anticipates Anderson's characterization of the nation. Rejecting dynasty, race, language, religion, and territory as the bases of nationhood, he argues that the nation is "a soul, a spiritual principle," a "daily plebiscite" (19). For Renan, nations are made by human will (Gellner, 8). The nation, then, is "*imagined* because the members of even the smallest nation will never know most of their fellow-members, meet them, or even hear of them, yet in the minds of each lives the image of their communion" (Anderson, *Imagined Communities*, 6). Of course, the same is true of many other kinds of communities, even medieval ones; what distinguishes the nation from other imagined communities is the *style* in which it is imagined. The nation, Anderson argues, is imagined as limited; it has finite boundaries beyond which lie other nations, conceived of as more or less equivalent and even interchangeable. The nation is imagined as one in a series of nations; no nation, even the most imperialistic, imagines itself as "coterminous with mankind" (7).[6] Furthermore, the nation is imagined as sovereign. It must subscribe to the notion that "alien rule is illegitimate rule" (Smith, xxi): "nations dream of being free ... the gage and emblem of this freedom is the sovereign state" (Anderson, *Imagined Communities*, 7). Finally, the nation is imagined as a community of a particular sort: "regardless of actual inequality and exploitation that may prevail in each, the nation is always conceived as a deep, horizontal comradeship" (7). According to Smith, it was the coming together of these three notions—the abstract idea of popular sovereignty, an ideology of at least theoretical equality, and the popular notion of a particular, ethnically defined people—in the French Revolution that "set nationalism on its path of self-propelling growth and expansion, a process vastly amplified and now brought to the remote European hinterlands by technologies, communications, and mass education" (Smith, *Ethnic Origins*, xxii).

Given this definition of the nation, it seems to us premature to assume that medieval England can be understood as a nation without at least exploring other kinds of communities—imagined or face-to-face—that might have bound people together. We believe this to be the project of postcolonialism as it is articulated by Homi Bhabha. To imagine medieval England as a homogeneous political and cultural unity, to privilege "the natural(ized), unifying discourses of 'nation,' 'peoples,' or authentic 'folk' tradition" masks "the spatial histories of displacement, relocation"—of subjugation, domination, colonization, and diaspora—postcolonialism seeks to expose (Bhabha, "Postcolonial Criticism," 438). While it is possible, as Smith suggests, to admit the "antiquity of collective cultural ties and sentiments," this does not mean we must assimilate them retrospectively to nation-states or nationalism. It does not require that we understand medieval collective units as "simply small-scale, primitive forms of modern nations and nationalisms." Rather we must investigate variations in "scope, intensity, salience, and political importance" of these collective cultural ties (*Ethnic Origins*, 13). The question we need to ask is whether a community united by the possession of territory, people, and a potentially common language (although significantly, in the thirteenth century, neither the English people nor territory shared a common language) can imagine itself in ways that are not limited or sovereign, or in which people are not bound horizontally to one another as they are in the modern nation-state.

One way to test this question is to look at the kinds of vocabulary medieval documents use to describe the political communities that are their subjects. Because it is roughly contemporary with Laȝamon's *Brut*, the language of the Magna Carta (1215) might reveal something of the ways in which the thirteenth-century inhabitants of England imagined corporate bodies of various sorts. The text of the document most frequently uses the term *regni* (realm) to designate the territory ruled by King John; *corone* (crown) and *terre* (land) also appear. Richard Mortimer argues that the Magna Carta "presupposed the existence of the realm as a corporate body" (as it does other corporate bodies as the "English church" and the "city of London"). However, he goes on to say that, while the Magna Carta speaks of "the commune of the whole land" (*commune totius terre*), "the idea behind these words is perhaps more likely to have been the sworn confederacy such as the 'communes' of city government, often found on the continent and in the 1190s in London, than a developed idea of the 'community of the realm.'" (104).⁷

According to the Middle English Dictionary (MED) and the Oxford English Dictionary (OED), the word *nation* is not attested in Middle English before the fourteenth century. And even then its semantic range is considerably wider than it is today. The word could refer to virtually any kind of classification of humans or animals; its delineation of specific political polities or ethnic groups was undercut by its generality in other usage. For instance, in the following passage from Trevisa the word refers to a particular way of classifying humans: "Children in scole, aȝenst þe vsage and manere of alle oþere naciouns, beeþ compelled for to leue hire owene langage" (MED, 814–15). In these lines from Gower the word refers to all mankind: "Out of mannes nacioun / Fro kynde thei be so miswent" (OED, s.v. nation). The word appears in Latin as *natio*, from which it was derived in English, but with meanings that range from "birth, origin, breed, stock, species" to "race of people, nation, people" (Lewis, *Latin Dictionary*, s.b. *natio*, 527). Indeed, the Latin ranges of such words are difficult to pinpoint with any precision, and must rely heavily on contextual clues. Other vocabulary, however, was available for specifying various sorts of political and ethnic communities. William of Malmesbury says that he wrote *The Chronicle of the English Kings* "propter patriae caritatem," which Giles translates "for the love of my country" (ed. Stubbs, 1:2; trans. Giles, 4). Giles's nineteenth-century translation of the *Gesta* literally rings with terms associated with nationalism; words like *country* and *nation* translate frequently used Latin terms like *patria*, *populis* [people], *terra* [land], and *gens*. It is difficult to determine, however, given the inevitable imprecision of any translation, the extent to which Giles's choice of vocabulary is colored proleptically by the ways in which these Latin terms were adapted to describe sovereign nation-states during the heyday of European nationalism (a time when Latin was still in use at least among the learned).⁸ *Patria* is glossed in C. T. Lewis's *Latin Dictionary* by "fatherland," "native land," and "country," but also by "native place" and "dwelling place." It is cognate with words indicating "father," "ancestors," and "household gods"; it is possible that the semantic range of the word was wider in the Middle Ages than in later periods. Armstrong, in fact, argues that the city, not the state, was the original *patria*; that "citizenship ... began with the experience of intimate participation in a small political entity," small enough even to be limited to networks of personal acquaintance and so not necessarily an imagined community at all (93, 104), and in which citizenship was limited not only by ethnicity or territory but by social class as well. *Gens* is glossed by a wide range of words that suggest very different kinds of social organizations and classifications, including "race," "clan," "house," "tribe," "species," "people," "region," and "country." None of the Latin terms William uses to designate communities requires a sense of nation as Anderson defines it. Wace, like William, also uses a vocabulary that has evolved into the very language we use to describe nation-states. He most frequently uses the French words *cuntree* [country], *terre* [land], and *regne* [realm] to describe political communities in the *Roman de Brut*, but it is unclear whether the semantic range of these words coincides with that of modern French.

Laȝamon's vocabulary for imagined communities is the most diverse and, for this reason, the most interesting. His self-consciously archaic use of an Anglo-Saxon idiom that was probably obsolete in his own time is the primary reason he is so frequently described as a "nationalist" writer; yet his archaic vocabulary ensures that the words he uses to designate imagined communities are those least likely to be used of the modern nation. He does use some familiar terms like *londe*, suggesting that the sorts of collectivities he imagines occupy territories; they are based on land. For instance, Germany is described as "aðelest alre londe" (6911) [most glorious of all lands]. Other terms like *ænd* (6912) and *ærde* (11213) also refer to political entities that occupy a physical territory or land; according to the MED, these words indicate a district, territory, dwelling, or land. Words like *kine-lond* (11109) [royal land] and *riche* (11090) [kingdom], however, suggest that such territory is imaged to cohere because it is ruled by a king as a personal possession. Such a reading is further suggested by Laȝamon's opening declaration that he has decided to tell the story of those who "Englene londe; ærest ahten" (9) [those earliest owners of England]. At the end of the poem, Laȝamon returns to this point noting that "Alemainisce men; Ænglen scullen aȝen. / and neuermære Bruttisce men" (16018–19) [men of Almaigne will be owners of England, / and nevermore may British men].[9] It is possible, then, to imagine a kingdom that is not a nation, but real estate held or possessed by a landholder whose inhabitants are bound together by a common fealty to a king.[10] Other lexical items define the imagined community by its people and their relations to one another. Examples include *iledene*, which the MED glosses as compatriot or fellow countryman, *leode(n)* and *þeode* (from the Latin *gens*), which refer to people, and *uolke* or folk. The MED glosses *leode* and *þeode* as "people, race, nation," but it is just as likely that, like "duȝeþe" (11249), these words refer to the body of retainers of a king or nobleman and so designate a community that is bound together not through imagined relations, but rather through the face-to-face ties of patronage networks.

We might further investigate the possibilities for imagined and real corporate identities in Laȝamon's vocabulary by looking more closely at the *Brut*'s depiction of Arthur's conquest of other political communities. An exploration of Arthur's imperial ambitions may suggest more specifically the ways in which thirteenth-century writers imagined political communities as neither limited nor sovereign. Arthur's first task after his coronation is to repel the Saxon invaders (in this, Laȝamon follows his source text closely). Once he has succeeded (at least temporarily), however, he is not content to rule his own realm in peace. Rather, because "his folc gode; aswunden ne læie þere" (11105) [his good people should not lie in idleness], he turns his attention to his neighbors. He campaigns first in Scotland because of the aid the Scots had given the Saxons. When he defeats them, they swear oaths to him and "þas kinges men bi-comen" (10953) [they become the king's men]. From there he moves on to Ireland to "wenden al þat kine-lond; to his æhȝere hond" (11109) [to transfer all that kingdom into his own hand]. After a battle in which Arthur's army triumphs, the Irish king Gillomaur swears an oath; he too promises to "become Arthur's man" (11166). Arthur's ambitions then take him successively to Iceland, Orkney, Jutland, Wendland, Norway, and Denmark, and in each place the same scene is replayed. With or without battle, the rulers of each of these territories swear the same oath: "ich wulle þi mon bicumen" (11224):

> Þu scal beon min hæhȝe king; and ich wul beon þin under-ling.
> Ich þe wullen heren; swa mon scal don his hærren. (11222–23)
>
> [You are to be my high king, and I shall be your underling;
> I shall owe you such obedience as one ought his overlord.]

Each understands his relationship to Arthur as a feudal relation of vassalage, a relation of patron to client. Arthur neither assimilates these conquered lands into a British "nation" nor imagines them as independent polities whose sovereignty underwrites England's.

The essentially feudal nature of Arthur's conquests becomes clear as Arthur is about to attack France. He assembles his army by calling upon the military service his feudal clients from all the conquered territories owe him:

Þa ȝet cleopede Arður; aðelest kingen.
Faren ich wulle to France; mid muchele mire ferde.
Ich wulle habben of Noreweie; niȝe þusend cnihtes.
& of Denemarke ich wulle leden; niȝe þusend of þan leoden.
and of Orkaneie; enleuen hundred.
and of Mureinen; þreo þuseond monnen.
and of Galeweien; fif þusend of þan leoden.
and of Irlonde; elleuen þusend.
and of Brutaine; mine cnihtes balde.
scullen þræsten be-foren me; þritti þusende.
and of Gutlonde; ich wulle leden; ten þeuseond of þan leoden.
and of Frislonde; fif þusend monnen.
and of Brutaine; Howel þene balde.
and mid swulche uolke; France ich wulle i-sechen. (11655–68)

[Then Arthur cried again, that most admired of kings:
"Now I wish to go to France with my enormous force:
I desire to have from Norway nine thousand knights,
And out of Denmark I shall conduct nine thousand of the countrymen.
And from the Orkneys eleven hundred,
And out of Moray three thousand men,
And out of Galloway five thousand of the people,
And out of Ireland eleven thousand.
And out of Britain from my own bold knights
There shall throng past me thirty thousand,
And from Jutland I shall lead ten thousand of the people,
And out of Friesland five thousand men,
And from Brittainy Howel the brave,
And with such folk I shall invade France."]

Laȝamon's account of Arthur's conquests suggests that the imagined community Arthur forges as king corresponds less with a twentieth-century notion of the nation than with an older imagining in which "states were defined by centers, borders were porous and indistinct, and sovereignties faded imperceptibly into one another" (Anderson, *Imagined Communities*, 19). Borders are not clearly delimited in Laȝamon's narrative, nor were they in thirteenth-century England. Magna Carta's separate treatment of the Welsh and Scottish suggests something of the porousness, the complexity of political identities and territories during this period. These groups are at one and the same time represented as part of the community of the realm and separate from it, requiring separate clauses to enumerate their rights. They are clearly not "English," yet they are part of the collectivity that Magna Carta addresses: "If we have disseised or deprived Welshmen of lands, liberties or other things without lawful judgement of their peers in England or in Wales, they are to be returned to them at once; and if a dispute arises over this it shall be settled in the march by judgement of their peers; for tenements in England according to the law of England, for tenements in Wales according to the law of Wales, for tenements in the March according to the law of the March. The Welsh are to do the same to us and ours" (Holt, *Magna Carta*, 333). At the end of the century, Edward I's strategy for controlling the Scottish aristocracy and his own rebellious northern barons was to give away English land to Scottish lords and Scottish lands to English lords. His aim was to blur the borders between the two territories, not make them more distinct; he saw no advantage in encouraging identification with any kind of imagined or corporate communities; rather his goal was to foster the interpersonal relationships of clientage that bound both the English and Scottish lords personally to him.

The collectivities Laȝamon describes in Arthur's conquests fail to meet any of Anderson's criteria for a nation. As the passage cited above suggests, relationships among the constituent members of Arthur's polity are vertical not horizontal. Hierarchy predominates; it defines individuals' identities and their relations to others. Arthur would never declare (even as propaganda), as Shakespeare's Henry V does, that "he who sheds his blood this day with me / Shall be my brother. Be he ne'er so vile, / This day shall gentle his condition" (IV.iii, 65–67).[11] Furthermore, there is no sense that Arthur's territory is limited. At the height of his power, Laȝamon says, "al þat Arðure isæh; al hit him to bæh" (11334) [Everything that Arthur gazed at paid homage to him]. Laȝamon, like his predecessors, gives the impression that Arthur will go on conquering others until his resources are exhausted or until someone stronger comes along. In fact, it is only insurrection at the center of his empire that forces him to abandon his attempts to swallow up the margins through conquest. Finally there is in Laȝamon no concept of sovereignty, of the freedom of the state from foreign influence and control. There is no recognition in Laȝamon of the existence of other states, equal to Arthur's, entitled to recognition as sovereign states—political entities can be only greater or lesser. As Arthur's encounter with the Roman senators suggests, there can be no equality between territories any more than between individuals. One is either a patron or a client territory; one either pays homage or receives it.[12]

It might be possible to see the kind of imagined community Laʒamon represents as the collective Smith calls an *ethnie*, or ethnic community. "It is [a] sense of history and the perception of cultural uniqueness which differentiates populations from each other and which endows a given population with a definite identity, both in their own eyes and in those of outsiders" (*Ethnic Origins,* 22). The kinds of imagined communities Laʒamon describes do possess many of the features Smith attributes to the *ethnie*. It is characterized by a collective name (the "British" or "English"),[13] a common myth of descent (from Brutus), a shared history, culture, and territory, and a sense of solidarity (Smith, *Ethnic Origins,* 22–30). However, even this designation has its problems. While it does seem reasonable to suggest that ethnic identity was possible in medieval England, the proliferation of international marriages and patronage networks virtually guaranteed that the ruling class of medieval England maintained close ties with the Continent—even after John's loss of the French lands—and that its political outlook and makeup would be multicultural rather than ethnically homogeneous. Intermarriage in particular tended to prevent ethnic identification from becoming synonymous with the state. Henry I's daughter and only heir, Matilda, returned to England to reclaim her territorial possessions only after being married, at a young age, first to a German emperor and then to the count of Anjou. Henry II was raised on the Continent and married a French wife; he spent most of his reign living on the Continent. No English king in the three centuries between Henry I and Edward IV took an English queen and, as John Carmi Parsons has argued, thirteenth-century queens like Eleanor of Provence (queen of Henry III) and Eleanor of Castile (queen of Edward I) brought with them to England their own cultural and ethnic identities, as well as their own patronage networks (Parsons, 176–88).

Discontinuous Identity and Patronage Networks

The extent to which Laʒamon's vocabulary of political community highlights the face-to-face relationships of patronage networks is suggestive. While histories of King Arthur or documents like the Magna Carta would in later centuries become icons of British nationalism, we cannot simply assume that this was how their original audiences understood these texts without examining not only the ways in which they *imagine* the "community of the realm" (to use Reynolds's term) but also the ways in which they *fashion* that community through specific material practices. The Magna Carta does at some points appear to represent a large-scale corporate and impersonal body, both abstractly, as, for instance, in the famous clause 39—"No free man shall be taken or imprisoned or disseised or outlawed or exiled or in any way ruined, nor will we go or send against him, except by lawful judgement of his peers or by the law of the land"—and materially, as in the call to establish a single standard for weights and measures throughout the kingdom (Holt, *Magna Carta*, 327). Historians have long held that the Magna Carta represents the extent to which Henry II and his sons had successfully established a political and administrative machinery capable of extending royal government throughout the realm (Holt, *Magna Carta*, 19–38).

However, the greatest part of the Magna Carta is taken up with articulating ever finer points of feudal law, of defining the quite specific face-to-face relationships on which patronage networks are built; many of its clauses attempt to limit the king's power to the exercise of his feudal prerogatives. This should not entirely surprise us since whatever procedures for governing the Angevin kings put in place—whether for settling legal disputes, collecting taxes, or regulating weights and measures throughout the kingdom—they could only be implemented through the patronage networks that everywhere dominated social relationships and through which imagined communities became a reality (Holt, *Medieval Government*, 39–40). Magna Carta is quite specific in its reformation of the king's patronage networks, not only attempting to eliminate perceived abuses of feudal law, but even to force the king to cut himself off from particular clients: "We will dismiss completely from their offices the relations of Gerard d'Athée that henceforth they shall have no office in England, Engelard de Cigogné, Peter and Guy and Andrew de Chanceaux, Guy de Cigogné, Geoffrey de Martingny with his brothers, Philip Marc with his brothers and his nephew, Geoffrey, and all their followers" (clause 50). The imagined community of the realm expressed itself functionally only through the vast system of patronage networks that spread out in ever widening circles from the king's court, reaching to the most far-flung corners of the kingdom.

In the thirteenth century, then, individuals might imagine loyalty to their family, their kin group, or they could conceive of loyalty to their patrons or clients. They might even conceive of themselves as members of a distinctive ethnic group. But individuals in the thirteenth century were ill-equipped to conceptualize anything as abstract as nationalistic fervor. In exploring the ways in which thirteenth-century writers imagined political communities, we begin to uncover some of the historical discontinuities Žižek attributes to history's losers. In contrast to Wace's presentation of the orderly succession of British kings, one following the other, Laȝamon, early on in his *Brut*, conceives of the ancient history of England as one of unstable and discontinuous identities. For Laȝamon, throughout the island's history, one wave of "uncuðe leoden" follows another; the vanquished are neither obliterated nor assimilated.

> Swa is al þis lond iuaren. for uncuðe leoden;
> þeo þis londe hæbbeð bi-wunnen. and eft beoð i-driuen hennene.
> And eft it bi-ȝetten oðeræ; þe uncuðe weoren.
> & falden þene ælden nomen; æfter heore wille. (3549–52)

> [So has all this land fared, with aliens landing
> Who have conquered this land and in their turn been driven away,
> And others again would gain it, who were foreign people,
> And would refashion the old names according to their whim.]

Nor do they form entirely separate *ethnies*. Their laws, customs, and languages intermingle, sometimes peacefully and productively, as when the English king Alfred translates the British laws handed down by Queen Marcie into English (3145–53), sometimes more confrontationally, as when, at the end of the *Brut*, the British have retreated in the face of English invasions to the "Walisce lond" [Welsh land] where they could keep their own laws and customs (16088), awaiting the moment that Merlin has prophesied (16020) when British supremacy will one day reassert itself, while the English kings "walden þas londes" (16091) [hold sway in this land].

Ethnic identity in Laȝamon is always, then, complicated by the intricacies of patronage networks because identity in thirteenth-century England remained first and foremost private, defined by social, political, and economic exchanges between lord and vassal, patron and client. Both colonizer and colonized participated in the complicated networks of personal patronage we described in chapter 2. These hindered the creation of the impersonal and corporate relationships we associate with the nation or even the *ethnie*. For this reason, we must investigate Laȝamon's understanding of the role of patronage networks in the formation of political communities.

Laȝamon's representation of Vortigern's dealings with the Picts illustrates the ways in which the patronage system disrupted the formation of specifically ethnic communities. It also shows the instability of the system, the irreconcilable contradictions within the ideology of patronage. Laȝamon amplifies Wace's account of this episode considerably. In Wace, narrative emphasis is placed on the Picts' drunkenness. When they arrive at court ostensibly to protect Constantine from foreign invaders, "Vortigern mult les enura, / Bien les pout, bien les abevra; / A grant joie les faiseit vivre, / Assez suvent esteient ivre" (ed. Winters, 6603–6) [Vortigern did them much honour: he gave them good food and drink and a merry life, so that very often they were drunk (trans. Weiss, 167)]. In this drunken stupor they are manipulated by Vortigern into killing the king and setting Vortigern up as a new king. Vortigern treats them not as clients, but as mercenaries. It is even possible that Wace's account may express some of the anxieties about mercenaries prevalent during Henry II's reign (see chapter 3).

In Laȝamon's *Brut*, however, while Vortigern still manipulates the Picts into doing his dirty work, he does so using not drink but the ideology of patronage. From the first, he cultivates the Picts as his own clients, beloved members of his household, at the expense of his British clients:

> Þas cnihtes weoren an hirede. hæhliche iwurðed;
> . . . .
> A he seide þat Bruttes; neoren noht to nuttes.
> ah he seide þat þa Peohtes; weoren gode cnihtes.
> A weoren Bruttes godes bidaled;
> & þa Peohtes walden. al þat heo wolden;
> heo hafden drænc heo hafden mete. heo hafden muchel blisse æke;
> Vortiger heom salde. al þat heo wolden;
> & heom wes al swa leof. swa heore aȝene lif;
> . . . .
> Vortiger ȝef þissen gumen; swiðe muchele gærsume.
> (6699, 6702–8, 6712)

> [Those knights in the retinue were highly respected;
> . . . .

He kept on saying the British were no more than rubbish,
But he said that the Picts were very good knights.
Constantly the British were deprived of their goods,
While the Picts commanded everything they wanted:
They had drink, they had food, and they had great fun as well;
Vortigern gave to them everything they wanted,
And he was as dear to them as their own life,
. . . .
Vortigern gave these characters a great deal of treasure.]

La3amon stresses the interpersonal elements of patronage in this passage by describing the Picts as a "hirede," a term that the MED defines formally as a household or a court or even an army, but one that emphasizes the interpersonal rather than contractual relationships among men. Vortigern gives lavishly to his Pictish clients and as a result they love and serve him (he is as "dear" to them as their own lives). When he is certain of their loyalty, he threatens to withdraw his patronage, claiming such poverty he can no longer support his clients:

ne mæi I noht for muchele scome. habben here þesne wone;
ah forð ich mot liðen. to uncuðe leoden;
& 3if auere cumeð þe dæi; þat ich æhten bi-3iten mæi.
and ich ma3en swa wel iþeon; þat 3e cumen a londe þer ich beon.
ich eow wulle wel biwiten; mid muchelere wurðschipe. (6733–37)

[I cannot, for fear of great disgrace, retain here this dwelling-place,
But I've got to go, off to foreign places,
And if the day ever comes when I can gain some goods,
If I can succeed in this so well that you come to the land where I
    have gone,
Then I shall protect you well with the greatest honour.]

Like those involved in the aristocratic diaspora of the twelfth century, Vortigern claims he is driven by poverty to seek his fortune in "uncuðe leoden." He alludes to the ideology of love and protection that is the ostensible basis of their relationship, claiming that only his lack of resources prevents him from continuing as their patron. The Picts react as disappointed clients, keenly aware of their loss:

Whæt ma3e we nu to rade. Whæ scal us nu ræden;
Wha scal us feden Wha scal us scruden;

Wha scal an hirede beon ure lauerd;
Nu Vortiger is iuaren. alle we mote fusen. (6751–54)

[What shall we do now for advice? Who will advise us?
Who is going to feed us? Who is going to clothe us?
Who at the court is going to be our lord?
Now Vortigern has gone away we must all scurry off.]

Although they are still drunk when they murder Constantine, Laȝamon portrays the Picts as acting out of rational calculation as well. They feel a keen sense of their loss of a patron. They "grieve" and "mourn" ("kare" 6747, and "menden" 6749) because Vortigern is so dear to them ("leof" 6749). And, like good clients, they act to ensure the continuing patronage of their lord by murdering his rival. Vortigern becomes king by manipulating his patronage network, disrupting the genealogical continuity that would have placed Aurelius Ambrosius on the throne.

Likewise, as a poet, Laȝamon could only have conceived of his authorship within this regime of aristocratic patronage, whatever its flaws. Indeed, Laȝamon's *Brut* serves as an example of literature written at the margins of the Anglo-Norman patronage system, literature that demonstrates not the horizontal relationships of the nation, but the vertical and highly mediated nature of patron–client networks that required hierarchy and stratifications of power. Laȝamon's understanding of patronage is from the beginning mediated by the experience of his Norman predecessor, Wace, who, as we have seen, was positioned more centrally within the dominant Norman aristocratic culture. In the first lines of the *Brut*, Laȝamon acknowledges the *Roman de Brut*'s authority. He tells us that Wace presented his book to "þare æðelen; Ælienor / þe wes Henries quene; þes heȝes kinges" (22–23) [to the noble Eleanor, / She was the queen of Henry, the king of such high fame]. Irrespective of the truth of Laȝamon's claim, where did he come upon this information about Eleanor's patronage of Wace? Obviously he could not have been there; he most likely would not even have been born when Wace made this presentation. Yet Laȝamon is the only source for our belief that Wace produced the *Roman de Brut* specifically for Henry and Eleanor. If Laȝamon was a minor Anglo-Saxon poet writing at the margins of the kingdom on the Welsh border, how did he know what was happening at the royal court? Critics have always assumed his knowledge was textual, that he read about it somewhere. Yet there is no dedication, nor any other statement, in any of the manuscripts of the *Roman de Brut* that might indicate who Wace's patrons were. It is possible that during his travels, while he was researching his book, Laȝamon might have come across a copy of the *Roman de Rou* in which Wace names Eleanor and Henry in a general way as his patrons (see above, chapter 3), although that text does not specify that they patronized any particular work. The more likely answer is that someone told him about it. It seems much more probable that the source of Laȝamon's knowledge lies in his own participation in patronage networks, which are formed through chains of interpersonal relationships. Indeed, the mysterious source of Laȝamon's information points to the disseminated nature of patronage networks, which radiate out from a center in ever widening concentric circles. While Laȝamon's patron, the "gode cniþhte" of the Otho manuscript, probably did not have firsthand knowledge of the royal court, he most likely knew someone, a patron higher up in the aristocratic pecking order, who did.

Laȝamon's remark about Wace's gift seems calculated to set up some kind of equivalency between his situation and his predecessor's. His ingenuousness masks the transaction occurring when a "Frenchis clerc...þe wel couþe writen" (20–21) [skillful French clerk] gives a metrical history of Britain's antique past to a queen. It also obscures the nature of the gift and what it represents to both the giver and the recipient because the elaborate rituals, codes, and rules that govern patronage networks required the "euphemerization" of the economic and social power that participants sought (Finke, *Feminist Theory*, 42; Scott, *Weapons of the Weak*, 307). Wace surely expected to benefit materially from the transaction Laȝamon describes, as no doubt Laȝamon hoped to benefit from his, though perhaps more modestly. Wace's commission in 1160 to begin his chronicle of the dukes of Normandy, the *Roman de Rou*, suggests that his gift to the king and queen of the *Roman de Brut* had the desired effect. In the *Chronique ascendante*, Wace writes of his patrons' generosity: "de dons et de pramesses chascun d'euls m'asouage" [each of them soothes me with gifts and promises] (Blacker, 37), suggesting that, even if their gifts were never enough ("mez besoing vient souvent qui tost sigle et tost nage" [but need comes soon, sailing swiftly on]) (Blacker, 37), he was a successful client to a very powerful set of patrons, a fitting model for an ambitious poet. By reminding his patron of the relationship between Wace and the queen, Laȝamon subtly reminds his patron of his own obligation. As Marcel Mauss writes, "The gift not yet repaid debases the man who accepts it" (41).

What the patron, Eleanor, stood to gain from Wace's gift is less clear-cut for the modern reader. In societies dominated by patronage networks, as we suggested in chapter 2, gift and countergift are mediated by the symbolic capital the gift creates, in this case the prestige and status that would accrue to the possessor of such a distinguished lineage. Ultimately, this prestige would be turned back into forms of social control and wealth—in this case the legitimation and extension of the monarchy.[14] Eleanor of Aquitaine was particularly adept at accumulating symbolic capital. Her manipulation of patronage networks not only made her the greatest literary patron of the twelfth century, almost single-handedly responsible for the diffusion of both courtly love and Arthurian literature throughout Europe (McCash, 15–16), it also enabled her to wield considerable political authority, more than was usual for a woman. Indeed, she became so powerful as a player in the political conflicts between Henry and his sons that Henry could curb her only by imprisoning her for some sixteen years. Laȝamon's choice to invoke a figure like Eleanor, however distantly, stresses the potential benefits to patrons of the symbolic capital he is offering.

Laȝamon's anxieties about the historian's claims to record "what really happened" illustrate the role of patronage networks in the dialogically agitated environment of thirteenth-century England.[15] In a passage that translates Wace's account of the founding of the Round Table, he claims, like Wace, that history is subject to the prejudices of its tellers; the Britons "sugeð feole cunne lesinge; bi Arðure þan kinge" (11455) [speak many falsehoods about King Arthur]. Following Wace closely, Laȝamon continues "Ne al soh ne al les; þat leod-scopes singeð" (11465) [It's not all true, it's not all false which poets are proclaiming] about Arthur:

ah þis is þat soðð; bi Arðure þan kinge.
Nes næuer ar swulc king; swa duhti þurh alle þing.
for þat soðe stod a þan writen; hu hit is iwurðen.
ord from þan ænden; of Arðure þan kinge.
no mare no lasse; buten alse his laȝen weoren.
Ah Bruttes hine luueden swiðe; & ofte him on liȝeð.
and suggeð feole þinges; bi Arðure þan kinge.
þat næuere nes i-wurðen; a þissere weorlde-richen. (11466–73)

[But this is true fact about Arthur the king:
There has never been a king so valiant in everything;
It's found as fact in the annals just as it actually was,

From the start to the end, concerning Arthur the king,
No more and no less, just as his deeds were recorded,
But the Britons loved him greatly and often lie about him
and recount many things about Arthur the king
Which never really happened in the whole of this world.]

This passage, however, expands Wace's remarks about the reliability of history (see above, chapter 3) in a very different direction. Laʒamon's vacillations—between the truth of history and the lies of poetry, between writing he maintains ultimately contains the truth, but which he seems to understand really encompasses only many biased accounts—suggest that the historian's knowledge of the past is always inextricably bound up with his or her investments in and concerns about the present, and with the ideological conflicts and dialogic interactions that divide the present from the past.

For Laʒamon, these investments and concerns are inextricably bound up with the proliferation of patronage in thirteenth-century England in which the truth, "soðð," can be understood only within the context of "trouþe" or loyalty to one's patron. This passage, like Wace's, plays off "soðð" against its antonym "les," but also against its absent English synonym "trouþe," a play on words that would not be possible in Wace's Anglo-Norman dialect. If the Britons lie about Arthur, it is because that is usual when one loves another.

> Swa deð auer-alc mon; þe oðer luuien con.
> ʒif he is him to leof; þenne wule he liʒen.
> and suggen on him wurð-scipe; mare þenne he beon wurðe.
> ne beo he no swa luðer mon; þat his freond him wel ne on.
> Æft ʒif on uolke feond-scipe arereð.
> an æuer-æi time; bitweone twon monnen.
> me con bi þan læðe; lasinge suggen.
> þeh he weore þe bezste mon; þe æuere æt at borde.
> þe mon þe him weore lað; him cuðe last finden. (11456–64)

> [But so does every man who has great love for another
> If he loves that man too much then he is bound to lie,
> And in his fine praise he'll say more than he deserves;
> However bad a man is, his friend will back him up still;
> On the other hand if [enmity] should arise in the community,
> On any occasion between two individuals,

Lies will be invented about the one who isn't liked:
Even if he were the best man who ever ate bread at table
the man who found him hateful would invent some vices for him.]

On the margins of the patronage networks that everywhere marked feudal relations, Laȝamon can be suspicious of its contradictions and biases at the same time he must embrace it since there is no place outside that system. For him, truth cannot easily be extricated from the lies required by love (by which Laȝamon means the vertical and hierarchical relations between patron and client) and hate (by which he means the horizontal relations among competing patrons or among competing clients).

Mythomoteur or Discontinuous History?

Laȝamon, writing for a minor aristocrat near the Welsh border, glances anxiously at the figure of Wace, who had access to the person and power of a reigning monarch and who was responsible for providing the Plantagenet kings with what Anthony Smith has called a *mythomoteur*—"a constitutive myth of the ethnic polity" (Smith, *Ethnic Origins*, 15)—in their native language. Such myths of origins and descent, Smith argues, provide the *ethnie* with a "means of collective location in the world and the charter of the community which explains its origins, growth and destiny" (24). Susan Reynolds argues that one of the characteristics that sets the medieval "community of the realm" apart from the modern nation is its reliance on myths of origins that tell "how a band of migrants under their king had come and conquered the land," assuming that all the "currently settled inhabitants of an area who lived under one law were descended from the conquerors" (*Kingdoms and Communities*, 259). Wace's translation of Geoffrey appears to provide all the necessary ingredients of the *mythomoteur*. It locates the community's origins in time and in space, identifies ancestors, and contains myths of migration, liberation, a golden age, decline, and rebirth, of a "once and future king" (Smith, *Ethnic Origins*, 192). Smith even cites the Arthurian legends as an example of the *mythomoteur* of the English nation when it finally emerges (205). But simply to label the matter of Britain a *mythomoteur* fails to account for the fact that, at least in the twelfth century, these stories did not necessarily serve to unify a single *ethnie*; rather, as we suggested earlier, they are an attempt to smooth over the conflicts and friction created by the uneasy cohabitation of three distinct cultures or *ethnies*. Why else should the Normans choose a specifically Celtic *mythomoteur* to legitimate their rule except to link themselves with the antiquity of the land by connecting themselves, as Laȝamon observes, with those who first possessed the land? This question suggests that Laȝamon's position as Saxon priest compiling a Celtic narrative for Norman patrons using a Norman source—his role as mediator among three uneasily cohabitating cultures—might offer some insight into what Žižek means by claiming discontinuous history as the history of the dispossessed.

From a very early date (at least the fifth century) there existed in England a class of professional interpreters, called *latimarii*, who acted as "intermediaries and translators between one race and another" (Salter, 9). After the conquest, this group of professional mediators became strategically even more important in managing the cultural Babel created by frequent intermarriages among speakers of French, Breton, English, Welsh, Scandinavian, Scottish, Cornish, and Irish (not to mention the ubiquitous presence of Latin-speaking clerics) in the Anglo-Norman courts and their anxious coexistence within hierarchically integrated households bound tightly together by patronal ties. These professional mediators tended to be both English and Celtic, and, as Elizabeth Salter suggests, their influence on the development of cultural forms during the postconquest period must have been profound: "The ease with which materials concerning Arthur and other Celtic heroes passed into the 'neo-Celtic' literature of the French and Anglo-French writers of the twelfth century may find its most likely explanation in the royal and baronial *latimers*, with whom important poets like Wace, Thomas the author of Tristan, Marie de France and Chrétien de Troyes would have come into personal contact" (9). It is quite possible that Laȝamon was himself one of these *latimarii* or something like it. He certainly imagines himself in exactly this role of cultural mediator throughout the *Brut*, where he endeavors to capitalize on his own marginalization within the dominant structures of Norman patronage by allying himself with the counterhegemonic antistructures afforded by a Celtic culture barely containable within the Norman hegemony. In these moments when it refuses the tidy narratives of official Norman historiography, Laȝamon's narrative enables, within the homogeneous, rectilinear, continuous time of the historical narrative he has inherited from his Norman predecessor, glimpses of what failed in history, of what had to be repressed so that the continuity of "what really happened" could be established.

For this reason we would argue that Laȝamon's work is not a partisan response to Norman oppression; such an oppositional stance would belie his role as a cultural mediator. Laȝamon shows throughout the *Brut* that he can reproduce the kinds of progressive narratives that provide ideological justification for imperialistic ventures in traditional societies, that he can imitate the discursive style of his predecessor and even improve on his model. For instance, when he recounts the story of Brutus's defeat of the giants, he ends the episode with a scene in which Brutus surveys his recently acquired territory:

> Brutus hine bi-þohte; & þis folc bi-heold.
> bi-heolde he þa muntes; faire & muchele.
> bi-heolde he þe medewen; þat weoren swiðe mære.
> bi-heold he þa wateres; & þa wilde deor.
> bi-heold he þa fisches; bi-heold he þa fuȝeles.
> bi-heold he þa leswa; & þene leofliche wode.
> bi-heold he þene wode hu he bleou; bi-heold he þat corn hu hit greu.
> al he iseih on leoden; þat him leof was on heorten. (1002–9)

> [Brutus began reflecting, beholding all those people,
> He beheld the mountains, beautiful and mighty,
> He beheld the meadows which were most magnificent,
> He beheld the waters and the wild creatures,
> He beheld the fishes and all the birds and fowl,
> He beheld the grasslands and the lovely groves,
> He beheld the woodland flowering and beheld the cornfields growing;
> All this he saw in the country and his heart was light and happy.]

What is significant in this survey is not its content, but its form. The echo of the biblical creation story—and the story of God's victory over the giants (Genesis 6:4)—imparts ideological authority to Brutus's conquest of Britain; it legitimates it. Brutus sees, what he sees is good, and he founds the city of Troynovant, dispossessing its previous owners. Because the dispossessed giants are never considered fully human, Brutus's actions can be recast not as conquest, but as creation.

By its very nature, the kind of discontinuous history Žižek attributes to the dispossessed is fragmentary and incoherent, barely recognizable as history. Therefore, rather than looking for history written from a consistently oppositional viewpoint, we must look for those moments of discontinuity and disjunction through which we can glimpse what has failed in history, the stories of the dispossessed that had to be denied to produce an official account of the past. Laȝamon attempts to renegotiate the status of the marginalized through his various re-visions of Wace's Merlin. As in Geoffrey, the Merlin created by both Wace and Laȝamon embodies the knowledge required to govern, intellectual property that must be protected if the possessor is to benefit from that knowledge. Merlin's magic and powers of prophecy give him a virtual monopoly on information: how to keep Vortigern's tower from falling down, how to move Stonehenge across the sea, what will happen to the British kings in the future. His magic, as we suggested earlier (chapter 2), offers effective protection for his intellectual property and enables him to eliminate his competitors; in Laȝamon, he even has them executed. Wace portrays Merlin as a "new man," who suffers humiliation because he cannot trace his paternal lineage, yet who gains enormous power as the client of a succession of three illustrious British kings. For Wace, physical presence is imperative for the successful cultivation of a patronage relationship; Merlin's relationships with England's kings depend on his accessibility. In Laȝamon, Merlin directs the ascent of several British kings but he is rarely found among their retainers. Laȝamon complicates Wace's simple feudal relationships by placing several intermediaries between the magician and his royal patrons. His revisions of Uther's seduction of Igerna are among the most interesting in his characterization of Merlin. In Wace, when Uther is laying siege to the castle of his vassal, Gorlois, the duke of Cornwall, so he can procure his wife, Igerna, with whom he has fallen in love, Merlin comes to Uther's aid immediately upon being summoned; he is a member of the host carrying out the siege. In a curious revision of this scene, Laȝamon places a number of intermediaries and financial dealings between the king and the magician. Uther has to delegate his vassal (and client) Ulfin to locate Merlin (and indeed, as in Wace, the idea to procure Merlin's aid comes from Ulfin) in exchange for a reward of "þritti solh of londe" (9371) [thirty tracts of land]. But Ulfin alone cannot get access to Merlin. He is required to seek out someone more marginal than himself, a hermit who is dispatched with the promised reward of "seouen sulȝene lond" (9376) [seven ploughs of land], to locate Merlin, whom he finds in "in þene west ænde. / to ane wilderne" (9378–79) [the western wilderness]. The scene demonstrates the ways in which disseminated networks of interpersonal relationships (I know someone who knows someone who can get what you want) accomplish many of the same goals that, in a modern polity, we would expect to be handled by a bureaucracy.

Merlin's geographical inaccessibility, his place outside of Uther's patronage network—and its demand for mediation—Laʒamon suggests, ironically enhances the magician's power within the patronage network because it enables him to redefine its terms to his own advantage. Merlin seems to have a detailed knowledge of the financial transactions required to locate him.

> Þa sæde Merlin; muchel wisdom wes mid him.
> Sæie þu mi leofe freond; wi naldest þu me suggen.
> þurh nanes cunnes þinge; þat þu wældest to þan kinge.
> Ah ful ʒare ich hit wuste; anan swa ich þe miste.
> þat þu icumen weore; to Vðere kinge.
> and what þe king þe wið spæc; and of his lond þe bæd.
> þat þu me sculdest bringe; to Vðer kinge.
> And Vlfin þe sohte; & to þan kinge brohte.
> & Vðer Pendragun. Forð-rihtes anan.
> sette him an honde; þritti solh of londe.
> & he sætte þe an honde; seoue sulhʒene lond. (9387–97)

[Then Merlin remarked (he was really perceptive):
"Now tell me, my dear friend, why you didn't want to tell me
Not for any kind of thing, that you were going to the king!
But anyway I knew at once the moment that I missed you
That you had come to Uther the king,
And what the king was saying to you, and offering you his lands
On condition you should bring me to Uther the king,
And Ulfin, who had sought you, to the king had brought you.
And Uther Pendragon, straightway at once,
Placed into his hands thirty ploughs' worth of lands,
And into your hands seven ploughs' worth of lands."]

Yet he refuses to accept any material reward for his services, arguing that such reward would constitute a lessening of his power.

> for nulle ich aʒæn na lond; neouðer seoluer na gold.
> for ich am on rade. rihchest alre monnen.
> & ʒif ich wilne æhte; þenne wursede ich on crafte. (9444–46)

["But I don't want to own land, nor silver, nor gold,
Seeing that for giving good advice I'm quite the wealthiest man!
And if I wanted to own property my skills would grow the
    weaker."]

Like the latter-day academic, Merlin understands that to accept payment for his services would lessen the symbolic capital that would accrue to him otherwise as a great magician. He understands that the symbolic capital he stands to gain is worth far more than even the "þritti solh of londe" promised Ulfin. More basically, he understands that within the network of patron–client relations, a gift entails obligation and marks the receiver as the subordinate. Within the counterhegemony established by Merlin's magic, his expenditure—the expenditure of his magical powers—enables him to redefine the clientelistic relationship, laying a debt on those who receive his aid, recasting himself as the patron and the king he ostensibly serves as his client. And within the feudal system it is a very powerful patron indeed who is not himself also a client, the vassal of a still more powerful patron. Merlin's creation of this antistructure within the poem places him on an equal footing with the kings of England despite his humble beginnings.

What Laȝamon seems to recognize in structuring his scene in this curiously laborious manner is that within the chain of patronage that links the dominant group, those who are marginal—like the hermit who dwells in the wilderness outside of civilization—are most appropriately placed to make connections with those outside the system who are seen as possessing a more powerful magic. The hermit's situation, then, most closely parallels Laȝamon's as mediator—*latimarii*. As a Saxon priest writing for a minor Norman aristocrat, the poet sees himself as most appropriately placed to offer the ruling Normans access to the legitimating power of Celtic prehistory.

In the *Brut*, Merlin negotiates his relationships with kings in terms of symbolic capital, of power and influence, rather than material reward. Laȝamon uses Merlin to demonstrate the power of counterhegemonic spheres of influence and the authority that might be gained by the knowledgeable outsider. But Laȝamon does not conceive of Merlin as his own alter ego. He possesses neither Merlin's abilities nor his access to the centers of power. His role might more accurately be described as mediating between the centers of power and alternative hegemonies. Merlin acquires symbolic capital by performing astonishing feats of prestidigitation for royalty. Laʒamon can only offer the mediation skills of the disenfranchised and disempowered, history's losers.

That the Celts constituted an effective counterhegemonic sphere of resistance may be suggested by the history of the Angevin kings' dealings with them. At the height of his power, Henry II signed treaties establishing feudal relationships with Scotland, Ireland, and Wales (Warren, *Henry II*, 150–206). Nevertheless, as W. L. Warren notes in his history of Henry II, while these treaties recognized the king of England, they also left intact the status and authority of the native rulers and deferred any fantasies of restoring a "lost insular wholeness," Geoffrey of Monmouth's *totius insulae* (Ingham, *Sovereign Fantasies*, 3). Magna Carta, as we have seen above, treats Wales and Scotland as distinct jurisdictions. James Given also argues that English hegemony over Wales was, until Edward I's conquest in the 1280s, largely indirect, accomplished by binding various Welsh princes as vassals to the English throne (43). This characterization of English–Welsh relations is given credence by the accounts of Laʒamon's contemporary, Giraldus Cambrensis, in *Itinerarium Cambriæ*. The sheer inaccessibility of Wales, its hostile mountainous terrain, made military conquest virtually impossible and enabled local princes effectively to resist Norman influence for centuries. The only strategic recourse the Norman kings had was to strengthen their vassals along the borders, a tactic that ran counter to their attempts to fragment the power of the baronage to increase centralized rule.

Attempts to hold on to the Celtic fringes of the island, then, was just one factor that worked against the formation of any kind of unified national identity held together by allegiance to a central government. In the political situation faced by the English kings of the early thirteenth century, identity remains as disseminated and discontinuous as the political bonds that link people, territory, and languages. In the closing lines of the *Brut*, Laʒamon comments on the power of discontinuous identities to disrupt official history by calling to mind history's failures, reminding us that, in the final analysis, all history is the history of failure and loss.[16]

Nu nabbe we of þan londe; buten þene west ende.
þa Bruttes hafden iwuned here; wel feole wintre.
Þa comen Englisce men; mid heore ufele craften.
heo weore wiʒel-fulle; and þis londe al biwunne. (15802–5)

[Now from that land we have nothing but the western edge
When the British had been inhabitants here for very many winters
Then the English men arrived with their evil artifices;
They were full of trickery and took over this land entirely.]

The British are pushed to the margins by the invading English, just as, Laʒamon's readers must have concluded, the Normans displaced the English. But, he reminds us, past failures can coalesce into new forms of resistance. As Žižek notes, "the oppressed class appropriates the past to itself in so far as it is 'open,' in so far as the 'yearning for redemption' is already at work in it—that is to say, it appropriates the past in so far as the past already contains—in the form of what failed, of what was extirpated—the dimensions of the future" (138). If the British have lost their territory, if they have retreated to "Walisce lond," they do maintain some collective sense of identity through their laws and customs: "and heore laʒen; & heore leodene þæuwen" (16084) [And they loved their own laws and customs of their nations], which set the stage for the kind of "redemption" Žižek describes. This seems to be the message of the dream vision experienced by Cadwallader, the last of the British kings:

> ah Alemainisce men; Ænglen scullen aʒen.
> And næuermære Bruttisce men; bruken hit ne moten.
> ær cume þe time; þe iqueðen wes while.
> þat Merlin þe witeʒe; bodede mid worde.
> Þenne sculle Bruttes sone; buʒen to Rome;
> and draʒen ut þine banes alle; of þene marme-stane.
> and mid blissen heom uerien; uorð mid heom-seoluen.
> in seoluere and in golde; in-to Brutlonde.
> Þenne sculle Bruttes anan; balde iwurðen.
> al þat heo bi-ginneð to done; iwurðeð after heore wille. (16018–27)

[the men of Almaigne will be owners of England,
And never more may British men be its possessors
Until the time arrives, which was announced long ago,
Which Merlin the prophet pronounced in his words.
Then the British shall soon turn towards Rome
And draw out all your bones from their marble tomb
And carry them rejoicing away with them again,

Enshrined in silver and gold, into Britain's land.
Then at once the British will become emboldened:
Everything they begin to do will happen as they wish.]

Merlin's prophecy holds out the promise that the lineage that once failed will someday be miraculously revived, that those who have failed will redeem themselves. At some unspecified point in the future, the British will reclaim their land by reappropriating the symbols of the past, represented by the "once and future king." This myth was perhaps threatening enough that Henry II felt the need to urge the monks of Glastonbury to locate the tomb of Arthur, an event that Giraldus Cambrensis describes in his *Speculum Ecclesiae* (1216). The discovery of a body "reduced to dust" laid to rest the "stupidity" of the British people who believe he is still alive: "The fairy-tales have been snuffed out, and the true and indubitable facts made known, so that what really happened must be made crystal clear to all and separated from the myths which have accumulated on the subject" (ed. White, 521). The British disappear from history—and yet never quite.

> and ʒet wunieð þære; swa heo doð auere-mære.
> & Ænglisce kinges; walden þas londes.
> & Bruttes hit loseden; þis lond and þas leoden
> þat næuere seoððen mære; kinges neoren here. (16090–93)

[And so they still live there, and they will do for ever more.
And the English kings hold sway in this land,
And the British having lost this land and those who live here,
Since then have never more been the kings here.]

Despite their glorious history, those at the margins of Empire—history's losers—are bound together imaginatively not by the sovereign ties of the nation, but by shared experiences of loss, failure, and dispossession, their myth of origin appropriated by their conquerors along with their land. In the next chapter we locate the destabilizing forces of history—its discontinuities—in the failure of origin myths to secure origins.

5

Mapping Ambition

Imperialism, Nationalism, and the Logic of Seriality in the *Chronicle* of John Hardyng

The following inscription appears as an annotation in a fifteenth-century copy of Walter Hilton's *Scale of Perfection* owned by a nun, Anne Colvylle, of Syon Abbey.

> This book was maad of the Goodis of Robert Holond for comyn Profite. That that Persone that hath this book committid to him of the Persoone that hath Power to commite it, have the use thereof the terme of his liif, prayinge for the soule of the same Robert, And that he that hath the forseid use of the Commissioun whanne he occupieth it not, leeve it for a Tyme to sum other Persoone. Also that Persoone to whom it was committid for the teerme of liife under the forseid condiciouns, deliver it to another Persoone the teerme of his Liif. And so it be delivered an committed from Persoone to Persoone, Man or Woman, as long as the Book endurith.[1]

In this inscription, a book made "of the Goodis of Robert Holond" is physically conveyed to a successor who is, at the same time, enjoined to pray for its original owner's soul. The book is imagined being handed from one individual to the next, not anonymously or indiscriminately to "a reader," but specifically from "the Persoone that hath Power to commite it" to "that Persoone to whom it was committid for the teerme of liife." Though Hilton's *Scale of Perfection* appears to have been a widely accessible text during the fifteenth century, this book is imagined as a unique event, its readers particular persons. There is no sense that it might have been read by more than one person *simultaneously*, only that it could be handed on *sequentially*, from "Persoone to Persoone, Man or Woman, as long as the

Book endurith." This way of thinking about book ownership and about serials will strike the modern reader in the age of mechanical—and even electronic—reproduction as peculiar. We begin with this bit of manuscript minutiae because it provides a glimpse into the ways in which the fifteenth-century mind imagined not only book ownership but also the more abstract concept of collective subjectivity as it is expressed in serials, a concept crucial for understanding both the late medieval monarchy and, as Benedict Anderson has argued, the beginnings of nationalism in early modern Europe (*Spectre of Comparison*, 29–40).

In *Imagined Communities* and his more recent *The Spectre of Comparison*, Anderson explores the cultural work done by technologies such as the map, the census, and the museum in constructing the idea of the nation. He argues that these technologies promote "a totalizing classifying grid which could be applied to anything under the state's real or contemplated control." Things that might be classified by such grids include "people, regions, religions, languages, products, monuments, literally anything." The effect of this grid according to Anderson, "was always to be able to say of anything that it was this and not that; it belongs here and not there. It was bounded, determinate and therefore—in principle—countable.... The 'weft' was what one could call serialization: the assumption that the world was made up of replicable plurals. This particular [an Englishman, a reader] always stood as a provisional representative of a series" (*Imagined Communities*, 184). Anderson describes such serials as either bounded or unbounded, that is, either finite and countable or potentially infinite and incalculable. Some modern examples of bounded serials include the family or the nation; examples of unbounded serials include such "open to the world" plurals as nationalists, workers, medievalists, or historians. The interplay of these types of serials maps the terrain of what Anderson characterizes as the "homogeneous, empty time" of nationalism.

The above manuscript inscription suggests a refinement of Anderson's account of serials to describe yet another dimension of serialization: serials can be imagined as either simultaneous or sequential. The series of readers (an unbounded series) of this particular copy of Hilton's *Scale of Perfection* equals the series of subsequent owners of the book. The strangeness of this kind of serial thinking becomes more apparent when we look at another inscription in the same book—a rejoinder in a much later hand:

> James Palmer owneth this Booke, yet without the least Intent to pray for the Soule of Robert Holland, being a Wicket and Simple Custome

of sottishly ignorant Papists. (MS Harley 993; cited in Bartlett, *Medieval Authors*, 166)

As James Palmer rejects the injunction to pray for Robert Holland's soul as a "Wicket . . . Custome," he also subtly redefines the nature of the series. He imagines Holland as a member of an impersonal group and an unbounded series of individuals who might be imagined to exist simultaneously. Though they might not know one another personally, all can be grouped under the heading of "sottishly ignorant Papists." Palmer can imagine a social space filled will comparable "Papists," none unique in importance, all representative of the same "sottish ignorance."

Anderson's concept of serialization, modified as we have suggested, may provide a means of understanding how individuals come to conceive of themselves as members of social groups or collectives, how they take their political identities from their identification with a group. Anderson argues that this act of political imagination—and its attendant temporalization and spatialization—is required to create the imagined political community we understand by the term "nation," a community that is both limited (a bounded serial) and sovereign (see chapter 4). The nation, he argues, depends upon particular cultural understandings of "deep horizontal comradeship" among its members, of time as "empty, homogeneous time" and of space as bounded and finite (*Imagined Communities*, 6–7). The cultural practices, institutions, and technologies he examines all helped to create the abstract concept of bounded serials—nations, citizens, fellow Americans—necessary for the political construct of the nation.

However, while nationalism, according to Anderson, requires a seriality in which horizontal and simultaneous (syntagmatic) identifications predominate, an institution like the medieval monarchy, we would argue, requires a sequential (or paradigmatic) notion of seriality in which one king follows another in succession. One might argue that so too do presidents, prime ministers, and premiers. Yet, these political figures—important and powerful though they may be—never embody the sovereignty of the political body, the nation, Anderson (and others) suggest is central to the modern conception of nationalism. In the modern nation, that sovereignty is always imagined as a corporate body—a bounded serial: the citizens or the people. In the medieval monarchy, however, sovereignty is always vested in the divinely anointed body of the monarch. These axes of seriality—bounded and unbounded, sequential and simultaneous—suggest a possible medieval grammar of seriality in which the interplay of paradigmatic and syntagmatic serials fashion complex social formations that include the monarchy, patronage, and, by the late fifteenth century, a nascent sense of nationalism. But these formations differ from their modern counterparts in that people are not imagined primarily as members of large impersonal collectives; rather they are linked, as we saw in the last chapter, in a sequence through quite specific face-to-face interactions of patronage.

Our test case for our claim about the relationship between serials and imagined communities will be John Hardyng's *Chronicle*, a fifteenth-century history of English kings from Brutus to Edward IV that purports to establish the sovereignty of the British monarch over Scotland. Hardyng has generally been dismissed as a terrible historian and a worse poet. Suspected of forging the documents included in his manuscripts that he claims established the British monarch's claims to the throne of Scotland (see Kennedy, 189), Hardyng has seemed to most scholars little more than a political hack and not a terribly successful one at that. Thomas Warton in the seventeenth century called him "the most impotent of our metrical chroniclers" (Kennedy, 186). What then is there to be learned from a serious consideration of such bad history? It is important to note that while Hardyng's ineptitude may be obvious with the benefit of hindsight, to his contemporaries he may not have looked so preposterous. His history provided a pedigree supporting the Yorkist claimants to the British throne and fuel for the intermittent conflicts between the English king and the Scottish aristocracy that broke out again in earnest about a decade after his death. In fact, in its obvious attempts to advance the political, ideological, and territorial ambitions of the patrons who supported its production, Hardyng's text is illustrative of at least one of the primary functions of medieval chronicles. Hardyng's *Chronicle* offers us a glimpse into the negotiations of power between the king and his subjects during the last half of the fifteenth century. In particular it demonstrates how imperialistic agendas can be advanced even in the absence of a concept of the nation.

Hardyng's *Chronicle* survives in two distinct versions, each dedicated to a different monarch. The first was compiled around 1457; it is extant in a single copy, London, British Library, MS Lansdowne 204, which appears to be a presentation copy made for Henry VI from whom Hardyng hoped to receive the patronage allegedly promised by Henry's father and predecessor, Henry V. In particular, he notes in his Proem, he hoped to get the manor of Gedyngton that had been promised "to me and to myne hayres in heritage."[2] As Felicity Riddy has shown, Hardyng's several attempts to secure rewards from the king were not nearly as direct as they seem from reading the dedication, but were intimately bound up with his participation in various local patronage networks, particularly those of the Northern Marcher lords Henry Percy and Robert Umfraville. His association with those barons who were responsible for guarding the Scottish border may explain his obsession with England's claims to Scotland. Riddy suggests that Hardyng may have felt the need to press his claims with the king after the death of Umfraville, when his patron's estates passed to the Tailbois family and Hardyng's financial position became more uncertain ("John Hardyng's *Chronicle*," 91–96). Hardyng's chief opponent at court was the cardinal of York who, perhaps because he was a rival of the Percys or because he knew a forger when he saw one, "rather wolde, er I had Gedyngton, / Ye shulde forgo your ryall soueraynte / Of Scotland" (fol. 4r). Hardyng finished the Lansdowne copy of his *Chronicle* in 1457 when he was seventy-nine years old and appears to have gained from the king an additional twenty pounds a year (Riddy, "John Hardyng's *Chronicle*," 97; Kennedy, 188–89).

Within three years of that date (1461), however, Hardyng, by now in his eighties, had begun a second, shorter version, this time dedicated to Richard, the duke of York, that updated the history to include the coronation of Richard's son as Edward IV, suggesting that Hardyng's quest for royal patronage was ongoing and that the sectional interests represented by his patronage networks at the periphery of the kingdom were stronger than the conflicts between the Lancastrian and Yorkist monarchs at the center. This version, though it exists in twelve complete manuscripts and four fragments, was apparently unfinished at his death. The existence of significantly more manuscripts of the later version, Riddy suggests, points to the different uses to which it was put by various factions. The presentation copy of the long version, like Robert Holland's copy of the *Scale of Perfection*, is imagined as a unique text passed sequentially from hand to hand, while the multiple copies of the short version allow for a wider circulation. In the changed political climate of the 1460s, Hardyng's new and revised *Chronicle*, perhaps commissioned by Thomas Burgh, who was granted the Tailbois estates when William Tailbois was attainted, participated in the ideological disputes over the legitimacy of Edward IV's claim to the throne (Riddy, "John Hardyng's *Chronicle*," 102–4).

The dedication of the unique 1457 version offers another example of the sequential notion of seriality, one that links consecutive serial book ownership to the economic exchanges that mark patron–client relationships. He writes:

> O Souerayne lord / be it to ȝoure plesance
> This book to take / of my symplicite
> This newly made / for rememorance
> Whiche no man hath in worlde bot oonly ȝe
> Whiche I compiled / vnto ȝour rialte . . .
> To know thestate / of your domynacion.³

Hardyng imagines this particular manuscript as a unique event, which indeed it was, a book that only the king can possess (at least until he passes it on to another). Its purpose, to record significant events of the past so they can be remembered, is not a collective "rememorance" for an entire nation, such as the modern historian might expect from a history, but a unique one, unique only to the king who has the book in his possession. Hardyng imagines a single reader for his text; he characterizes the book as a marker—an artifact—in a specific economic exchange of patronage. He gives the book to the King

> to been euermore / within your gouernance
> for soueraynte / and your inherytance
> Of Scotland hool / whiche shulde your Reule obaye,

linking his text to the king's successful exercise of "sovereignty" over a rebellious Scotland and expecting in return the manor of Gedyngton.

Virtually every aspect of this text's production calls attention to this sequential dimension of serials. The choice of the rhyme royal stanza, a nod to the pervasive influence of Chaucer in the fifteenth century,[4] adapts itself to the genre of the chronicle, which is structured primarily around sequence. The narrative follows the logic of "next" rather than that of "meanwhile"; events do not happen simultaneously, but sequentially. One year will follow the last, or in Hardyng's case, each king succeeds the last one. The dedication to Richard of York that prefaces the shorter 1461 version even suggests that this *mentalité* cannot imagine more than one king at a time. Kings, in this mind-set, cannot be a bounded or unbounded serial, but only an unbroken string of successive kings. In this prologue, Hardyng rehearses the lineage of the house of York:

> Now be ye knowe of your title to Englande
> By consequens to Wales and Scotlande
> ffor þay perteyne as ye may vnderstonde
> Of auncyent tyme to the crown of Englande
> By papall bull have þe right to Irelande

> Gastoigne, Paitowe, and Normandy
> Pountyfe, Bebuile, Saunge & Sauntoignye
>
> And all the lande beyonde the Charente
> of Dangeolesme, Dangolismoys & Luyrezyne
> Of Caoure, Caourenon, Poridor & Pirygunt contre
> Of Rodis, Rongeauis, Dagon, Dagenoise þe fine
> Charbe, Wigor & Gaure should to you enclyne. . . .
>
> Calys and Marke colne Hammys Dye & Wale
> Sandegate & Guysons with all þe whole contre
> Wt all the londes & townes betwen hem all . . .
> To Jerusalem I saye ye have grete right. (ed. Ellis, 21–22)

By the time he has rehearsed the titles York has amassed through marital alliances, births, deaths, and conquest to France, Ireland, Scotland, Italy, Spain, Portugal, and even Jerusalem, the house of York that succeeds to the English throne has become not one king among many, but literally king of all the known world. The reference to Jerusalem is decisive. As we will discuss later, in the medieval imagination, Jerusalem was the center of the known world (Akbari). And that title is imagined as continuing into the future. The book, Hardyng writes, is meant not only for the duke of York, but

> also for your heyres and for your successours
> In tyme comyng to have a cler knowledge
> How of þys realme the noble gouernours
> Haue kept it wt help of baronage . . .
> Sith Brute it wan. . . . (ed. Ellis, 23)

In this profoundly conservative text, lineage is all, a straight, preferably unbroken, line of succession that leads from Brutus down to the soon-to-be reigning monarch and beyond.

The text of the *Chronicle* itself rarely imagines kings existing simultaneously. Even in such obvious counterexamples as the "English Kings and Saxon" (ed. Ellis, 182)—"In Englande yet were kynges seuen" (ed. Ellis, 183)—these kings are always understood as lesser rulers owing homage to a single and true king; usually a Wessex king. Of Cuthred, for instance, Hardyng writes,

> Cuthred was kyng crouned of al Westsex,
> And protectour of all Englande that daye,

> His kynges vnder hym, þt then were full sixe,
> Did hym homage anone withoute[n] delaye. (185)

For Hardyng, kings do not rule over autonomous political entities. They reign over ancestral properties interconnected by relations of vassalage and patronage. In the Arthurian section, after Arthur's conquest of France, Lucius Hiberius, the emperor of Rome, demands a withdrawal. Lucius's concern is not that Arthur has violated the borders of a sovereign state, overthrowing and murdering its monarch. Rather, he speaks of "our lande of Fraunce" (139), challenging Arthur's right to annex that which belongs to Rome. As emperor of Rome, Lucius makes claim to all of Arthur's holdings as well and demands tribute, which he insists has long been withheld. Arthur does not dispute Rome's authority, does not argue that England is a sovereign nation that deserves freedom from external control. Rather, he argues that it is he who should be acknowledged "kyng of all the greate Brytain, / And emperour of Rome by title of right" (140). Arthur produces considerable, if not entirely unproblematic, genealogical evidence to support his position.

> For kyng Belyn, that was our auncetour,
> And Brenny also, the kyng of Albanye,
> All Roomain did wyn by [conquest there;]
> Of Roome thei had, and all greate Italie,
> [And sleugh themperour by their great maistrie,]
> And crouned were in [the sea] empiriall,
> Wher no prince was that tyme to them egall.
>
> But yet we haue a better title of right
> To thempire whiche nowe we will pretende;
> For Constantyne, sainct Elyn soonne of right,
> By right of bloodde, of Constaunce downe discende,
> Emperor was, that Roome did well defende
> Again Maxence, and his feloes tweyn,
> Which there made muche Christen people [to dien.]
>
> Maximian kyng of Greate Brytain,
> By whole decre, and will of the senate,
> Was emperor of Roome, and ruled Almaigne,
> Whose rightes we haue, and al their [whole] astate,
> And heire of bloodde borne and generate;

Wherfore we clayme the throne empirial,
From hens furth by lawe iudicial. (141)

More significant than the lineage of former emperors from the British Isles familiar from Geoffrey of Monmouth—Arthur's "auncetours" from Constantine to Maximian—is the juridical vocabulary of inheritance and property (the "lawe iudicial") that stresses sequential succession. His ancestors were crowned in the "sea^5 empiriall" (the imperial throne) and "no prince was that tyme to them egall." As elsewhere, Hardying resists understanding the monarchy as a simultaneous serial. Arthur claims ("pretends"[6]) the Roman Empire—Lucius's "astate"—by "right of bloodde," as well as by "title of right." He claims to be "heire of bloodde borne and generate." Arthur's legal claim to Rome is supported, as he suggests, by military might, and he ultimately defeats Lucius in battle. Hardyng's *Chronicle* is one of two medieval texts—the other is Malory's *Morte Darthur*—in which Arthur becomes crowned emperor of Rome, in essence king of all other, lesser kings. As Hardyng would have it, the king of England is king of the world.

Visual Seriality

In the luxury manuscripts that have them, even the visual programs contribute to sequence and linearity, the sense of unbroken succession. London, British Library, MS Harley 661, one of the sixteen manuscript copies of the 1461 Yorkist version, contains a visual genealogy that runs throughout the entire manuscript. Along the outside margin of every folio the artist has run a red line from the top of the page to the bottom. Interspersed along that line, at appropriate points in the text is a crowned roundel, each containing the name of one of the kings of England; those kings (like Arthur) who achieve the status of emperor are given a roundel with a more ornate crown. This genealogical table provides a visual marker for the text. If the narrative of a particular king runs more than a single page, the red line is unadorned, maintaining the sense of unbroken lineage (even though the lineage is, in fact, not unbroken), of descent from a single originary founder. When lateral filiation occurs (as in the case of the twenty sons and thirty daughters of King Ebranc or the complex genealogy that constituted Edward III's claim to the throne of France), it is indicated with blue connecting lines extending from the red line. Despite the occasional interruption, the visual focus is on linearity, one king following the next in an unbroken sequence that is often belied by the text.

Perhaps the most spectacular instances of sequential serialization in Hardyng's text, however, are its representations of Scotland itself. In at least two of the manuscripts, Hardyng has included an invasion map so that the king will know the best routes for his armies to use. Before we turn to these maps, a word or two about medieval maps themselves might be in order. Looking at maps produced before 1500 can be a disorienting experience; by itself the experience subverts our sense that concepts like the nation-state and the borders between them are natural and universal. Indeed, the experience even shakes ones faith in direction as a constant.[7] In the *mappæmundi* included in a late-fourteenth-century exemplar of Ranulf Higden's *Polychronicon* (London, British Library, MS Royal 14 C ix, fols. 1v–2; see Harvey, 34), the orientation is not north, but generally east, a common convention of many medieval world maps, or *mappaemundi*, which represent Asia at the top, Europe on the left, and Africa on the right. Jerusalem is, of course, at the center of the world, in Hrabanus Maurus's words "quasi umbelicus regionis et totius terre" [the naval of the region and of the whole world].[8] England is tucked obscurely away in the bottom left-hand corner. A glance at this map suggests that medieval maps were scarcely maps at all (at least as we understand them) but diagrams, best understood as an open framework into which all kinds of information might be placed in the relevant spatial sequence (Harvey, 7–8), not unlike a chronicle in which information would be placed according to chronological sequence and, indeed, not unlike a medieval painting in which temporal narrative is rendered spatially. To read them we must understand medieval maps as having both spatial and temporal dimensions, sequence as well as the seriality with which we invest modern maps.

This is clearly the way in which the invasion maps included in the Lansdowne and Harley manuscripts of Hardyng's *Chronicle* must be understood. To "read" these maps we must encounter them at "ground level," not aerially as we would a modern map. We are not meant to take the whole map and all its features in at once, serially, but rather to move sequentially from marker to marker, from town to town (generally designated by a castle or, in the case of Glasgow and Dumferline, churches). The Lansdowne map is oriented with west at the top and east at the bottom so that the course of Hardyng's imagined invasion of Scotland is from left to right, not bottom to top as we might "naturally" imagine. (The Harley map is oriented north–south so this appears to be a somewhat arbitrary

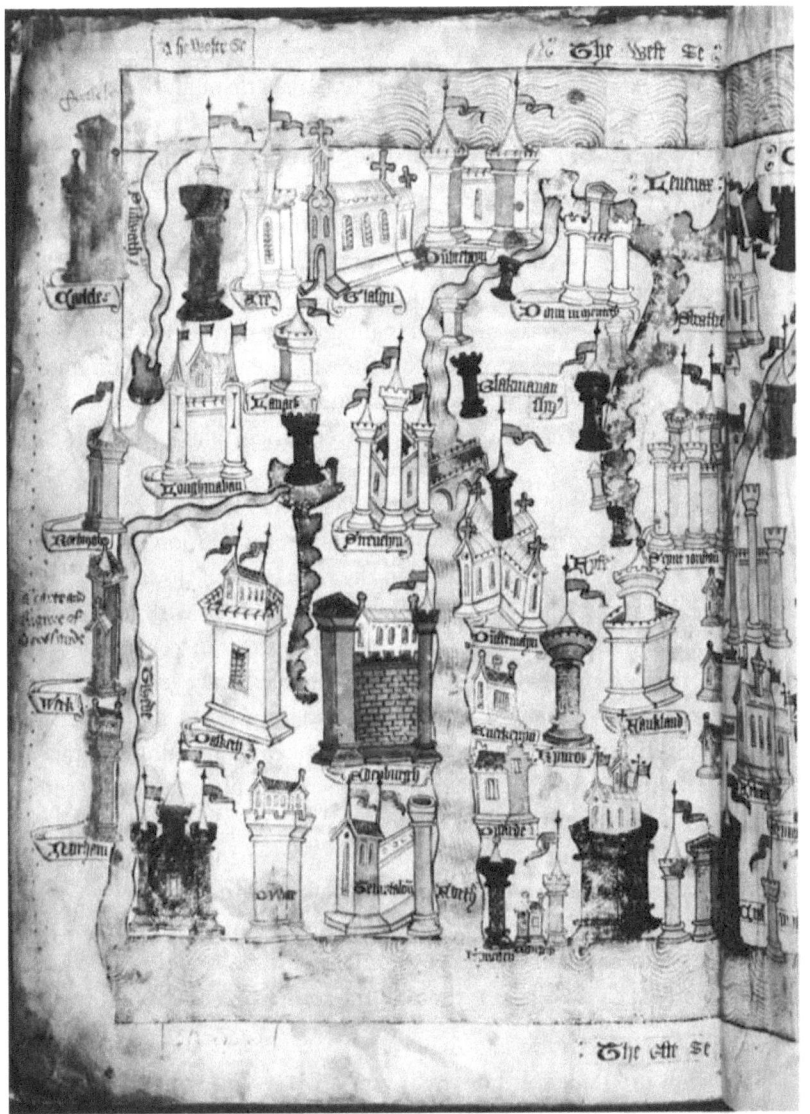

Fig. 5.1. Detail of Map of Scotland. John Hardyng's *Chronicle*. London, British Library, MS Lansdowne 204, fol. 226v. By permission of the British Library.

choice at least by the fifteenth century.) The verses that accompany the map provide the key to deciphering it; in fact the map makes little sense without the accompanying narrative to serve as an orientation. So, for instance, as it passes through the section of the map reproduced here (figure 5.1), the text directs an imagined army to pass through Berwick in the southeast (lower left corner), move due north twenty miles to Dunbar (to the right), and proceed twenty-four miles northwest to Edinburgh (brick castle). From there they would go due west to Stirling (Strevelyn), "Besouth Foorth, that ryuer principall," where they would cross the River Forth at the bridge to enter Blackmananshire. Here Hardyng sends them north to Falkland—"from the doun (down of Menteth) you have a fair way throughout Monteth and Clakmannanshire through Fife to Falkeland"—and then northwest to St. Johnstown. The map offers no kind of scale. It indicates neither the relative size and importance of various towns (except pictorially) nor the distances between them. This information is conveyed only by the accompanying verses.

The map included in BL MS Harley 661 is less lavish than the Lansdowne map, but no less interesting in its representation of Scotland. Drawn in black ink with red lettering, the map runs to three folio pages. Unlike the Lansdowne map, the Harley map is oriented with north at the top, perhaps the influence of thirteenth- and fourteenth-century navigational or Portolan charts. Like the Lansdowne map, however, it is still not meant to be read aerially but sequentially from the ground. In fact, because of its length (three folio pages) it cannot be taken in at a single glance so that it really ceases to be a map at all but a set of explanations that repeat the accompanying text that overwhelms it.

Perhaps the most curious feature of the Harley map occurs on folio 188 where fully three quarters of the page is taken up with a description of the lands north of Scotland. Dividing the northernmost part of Scotland—Catenesse—is a square bordered by four seas: Styx, Cochiton, Acheron, and Phlegethon, in classical mythology the four rivers of the underworld.

> Stix Fflegiton Cochiton and Acheron
> Tho ben foure flodes withouten any rest
> Ever flowynge & ebbynge the see upon
> With wynde & wawes of the boriales west
> Blowyng mysrule thorowe Scotland al & sum
> As Scripture seith *a borea omen malum*
>
> Betuene þe see of the west occioun
> And the hilles of Scotlande occident

The wilde Scotrie have their propre mancion
Which dispose theym noone with an oþer assent
And the wilder thei been withoute regyment
The soner muste þei be meked & tamed.⁹

The conservative geography is still apparent in the late fifteenth century in the view of the north as the "realm of Lucifer." However, that Hardyng locates Scotland just south of hell suggests the extent to which Scotland in the fifteenth century was still thought of as uncivilized "wild" territory. The northern winds blow "mysrule" throughout Scotland, so that, naturally, the "wilde Scotrie" must be "meked & tamed" by their English overlords. The Scots clearly represent a different kind of threat than, say, the French, with whom the English had simultaneously been engaged in dynastic warfare during the Hundred Years' War.¹⁰ The barbaric and uncivilized Scots are cast as the barely human "other" of postcolonial discourse, legitimizing invasion from the south as a means of restoring proper order to a wilderness.

The invasion maps included in the Hardyng manuscripts, then, participate in a visual program predicated on a paradigmatic grammar of sequence in which, like the manuscripts cited at the opening of this chapter, one thing follows the next in a hierarchical order. The visual programs of the luxury manuscripts, which include maps, genealogies, and heraldry, carry out the cultural work of legitimation within a framework of patronage and feudal relations.

Foundation Myths

The obsessional repetition of sequence as a structural device in Hardyng's *Chronicle* calls attention to its ideological agendas as much through its failures as through its successes. Sequentiality signals a need to identify a founding moment, an *arché*, that sets the sequence in motion and a teleological endpoint that concludes it (that shows history leading logically to the current state of affairs). As such, it suggests ways in which the political communities emerging in Europe by the fifteenth century still imagined their communal ties somewhat differently from those of the modern nation-state. More than language or common territory, descent from a common ancestor, the so-called *origines gentium* (Reynolds, *Kingdoms and Communities*, 258), not necessarily conceived as biological continuity, was the core around which imagined "ethnic" communities differentiated themselves in the Middle Ages,¹¹ the ways in which the English, for instance, differentiated themselves from the Scots, Welsh, Irish, or French, even while their laws, property claims, business dealings, alliances, marriages, and patronage networks brought them into close, if often conflicted and tangled, relations with one another.

As we argued above, both the narrative structure of the *Chronicle* and the visual programs of the luxury manuscripts create the illusion of an unbroken lineal succession that begins with the first ancestor and leads up to and legitimates the monarch currently sitting on the throne. However, the foundational myths Hardyng's text relates are noteworthy almost exclusively for the destabilizing effect they have on the subsequent narrative. At the very moment of Britain's founding, Hardyng introduces narrative elements that subvert the simple lineal genealogy implied by the *Chronicle* and its visual apparatus of seriality. To the traditional tale of the founding of Britain by the Trojan Brutus, Hardyng's *Chronicle* tacks on a more recent, but chronologically prior founding tale, the story of Albina and her sisters, the eponymous inhabitants of the island who discovered it more than a hundred years before Brutus and gave it the name Albion.

Hardyng begins with Dioclesian, king of Greece and Syria,[12] and his thirty daughters whom he married "to there degree / to kynges all of greate nobilitee" (ed. Ellis, 25). These daughters

> ... fell in pryde and hye elacioun,
> Thynkyng to be in no subieccion
> Of husbandes more, ne dominacion,
> But only, by a fell conieccion,
> Toke hole purpose and full affeccion,
> To kyll there lordes slepyng sodaynly,
> Soueraynes to be, and lyue all seuerally. (25)

The youngest daughter exposes the plot. As punishment the sisters, like Constance in the *Man of Law's Tale*, are put to sea in a boat and after much misadventure land finally on "this ysle / That then was waste, as chronicles do compile" (26). The eldest, Albina, assumes overlordship of the island and names it Albion after herself. The sisters then learn hunting and fishing. Once their material needs are met, they desire to "haue comforte of mennes consolacion" (29). There being no men on the island, they turn to incubi to satisfy their sexual appetites, producing a race of giants who, in turn, reproduce through further incestuous unions.

One effect of including this material is to expose the arbitrariness of all origins. It suggests, first, that one can always imagine an earlier act of founding in a process that is, theoretically, endless. Beyond that, however, Hardyng's handling of his material at the very beginning of his *Chronicle* perhaps unintentionally directs our attention to the arbitrary nature of all beginnings—whether of books or political communities.

In a text so concerned with establishing English hegemony over Scotland, why does Hardyng risk troubling the simpler account of the Trojan Brutus's founding of Britain with an earlier founding that undoes that account? The story of Albina's discovery of Britain does not appear before the fourteenth century and its provenance seems to be Anglo-Norman rather than English (suggesting that even at this late date language is still not a marker of national identity). The earliest known version is the Anglo-Norman *Des Grantz Geanz*. After the fourteenth century, this story sometimes prefaced copies of the *Brut* in Anglo-Norman, Latin, and English; it was even incorporated into some manuscripts of the *Historia Regum Britanniæ*.[13] Hardyng may have encountered the tale in any one of these texts and may simply have felt compelled to include it to be thorough. But the story may have served other purposes as well. Lesley Johnson and Susan Reynolds suggest that the eponymous story of Albion's origins may have been a response to the revival of interest in Scottish origins in the fourteenth century (Johnson, 25; Reynolds, "Medieval 'Origines Gentium,'" 377). Since Nennius, Scotland had traced its roots back to Scota, the daughter of an Egyptian pharaoh (Kennedy, 192), offering the Scots an older and more venerable foundation narrative than the English story about Brutus.[14] The Albion story may have been of interest to Hardyng for the cultural capital it could provide in the conflicts between the English and Scottish monarchs over Scottish sovereignty. Scotland's claim to Egyptian, even pharaonic, origins testifies to its antiquity and ties it to an ancient and exotic Near Eastern civilization. The story of Albion's founding provided the English with a foundational history to rival Scotland's, one rooted, like Scotland's, in the older and more advanced civilizations of the East (Syria), civilizations that in the late Middle Ages were both feared and admired.[15]

Even as he relates the story of Britain's first founding, however, Hardyng calls attention to one of the major themes of *King Arthur and the Myth of History*—the textuality of all history. Hardyng's narration of the Albion story is continually crosscut and fragmented by his own metacommentary on the writing of history. At the end of the first chapter, Hardyng brings his narrative to a screeching halt to inform his readers that "I dare saye this chronicle [the one he has just related] is not trewe" (ed. Ellis, 26).

Already at the very beginning of this massive history, Hardyng has asserted that his own authority as a historian derives only from the books that he has read and that texts are a precarious source of legitimation because they never speak with a single voice. If, as we argue in chapter 1, history as a genre is marked by its claims to relate "what really happened," this proclamation that his sources are false moves us from the genre of history to that of historiography, a critique of the information he has just given us as historical fact. Hardyng argues that at this time there was no king in Syria so the facts as related in his sources must be in error. In a prose note prefacing the next chapter, Hardyng cites Hugh de Genesis, a Roman historiographer, as offering proof of the inaccuracy of the first source.[16] Hugh writes instead of a king of Greece named Danays who had fifty daughters whom he married to the fifty sons of his brother, the king of Egypt. It was these daughters who slew their husbands and ultimately founded the island of Albion after they were exiled. Hardyng's repeated insistence on the inaccuracy of his first source has the effect—whether intentional or not—of highlighting the discursive nature of all history, calling attention to the indeterminacies textuality entails. It foregrounds history's tendency to be always caught in the gap between "what really happened" and the need to relate a coherent and compelling narrative.

Hardyng vacillates anxiously between declaring Hugh's narrative the "chronicle trewe" and denouncing the inaccuracy of his other textual source:

> That chronicle should not bee desired,
> Seying that it is not trew ne autenticke,
> By no chronicle vnto the trewth oughte like.
> I dare well saie he sawe neuer Hugh Genesis,
> Ne he redde neuer the chronicles of Surry,
> Of Israell, Inde, ne of Egipciis, etc. (ed. Ellis, 27)

He then goes on to quote still another explanation for the name Albion from Bartholomaeus Anglicus's *De Proprietatibus Rerum* that "this ysle of Albion had name / Of the see bankes full whyte, all or sum, / That circuyte the ysle," hedging his bets by claiming that "Both two [stories] myght be together clere and trewe" (30). Hardyng is scholar enough to feel compelled to include all the sources he has read but not writer enough to synthesize them or to compile them into a coherent account by weeding out inaccuracies for his reader. Most likely Hardyng did not consciously choose to write a metacommentary on the writing of history; instead his incompetence compelled it. The incoherence of the narrative reminds us that history relies entirely on texts, indeed is constituted by them. This breakdown of historical transparency, however, has larger repercussions for Hardyng's project. His claim of English rule over Scotland rests entirely on readers' judgments about the authenticity of the various documents (most likely forged) claiming English sovereignty over Scotland that he appends to his manuscripts. Having impugned the veracity of the very first source he cites, he seems to invite historiographic examination of the rest of his text.

Hardyng's story of Albina and her sisters provides a postcolonial moment at the very threshold of colonial encounter. Since Geoffrey of Monmouth, the story of Brutus's founding of Britain had provided English history with a tale of common descent, a colonial myth in which the colonizers (the Trojans) bring civilization to a previously barbaric and nearly uninhabited outpost, in this case an England populated entirely by giants whose savagery, at the moment of colonial encounter, has brought them to the point of extinction. The Albion story suggests that Brutus colonized not a barbaric or empty wild space, as Geoffrey's Trojan story does, but a land with historical ties to a highly developed Near Eastern civilization as prestigious as that Brutus will later bring and of greater antiquity.

Colonization in Hardyng's opening moves from the settled Islamic East to the presumably empty wild spaces of the West, the opposite of the ideological trajectory of nineteenth-century colonialism. In adapting contemporary postcolonial theories to medieval histories, we must be careful not to read into these histories an anachronistic orientalism of the kind Said attributes to the nineteenth century. Europe did not occupy the same central space in the world system of the Middle Ages that it did during the nineteenth century. Medieval Europe, as Janet Abu-Laghod has argued, was a marginalized cultural backwater in comparison to the great civilizations of the Far East or even the more proximate Muslim world (15–20). This position tended to temper Christian hostilities toward Europe's non-Christian neighbors whom they both admired and feared. Albina and her sisters bring their superior civilization to a land described as "waste" (ed. Ellis, 26), introducing skills like hunting and fishing and imposing on the island a recognizable political organization based on vassalage. At the same time, however, the Eastern civilization that produced Albion's first inhabitants is seen as perversely flawed, even dangerously feminized. If Hugh's version of the story is correct, the sisters' marriages to their cousins already carry the stigma of incest. The murders of their husbands upset the normal patriarchal order as the sisters substitute their desire for "sovereignty" for the "submission" of wives to their husbands required of patriarchy. Subsequent actions including sexual intercourse with devils and further incest, both of which produce an increasingly monstrous community, bring the inhabitants of the island to near extinction and seem to require the intervention of Brutus's invasion (once again from the East) to restore order.

From the beginning, however, Hardyng defuses the potential link between the sisters' rebellion against their husbands' domination and the claims of colonized territories to political sovereignty by framing the sisters' desire as personal, situating it within the generic conventions of the romance. Deliberate echoes of Chaucer's *Wife of Bath's Tale*—"Note that women desyre of al thynges soueraynte, & to my conceypt, more in this land than any other; for they haue it of the nature of the saied susters" (ed. Ellis, 26)—recast what might be read as a political drama into a lurid romance. The exile of the daughters does not so much restore the disturbed political order of Syria as provide scope for the sisters' exercise of their own ambitions; it precipitates a quest. In what ways might we read their exile as resembling that of the dispossessed younger sons of Europe who from the eleventh century on set off in the opposite direction on Crusades in hopes of winning the lands they could not inherit at home (Bartlett, *Making of Europe*, 24–56)? Hardyng's conservative agenda in the *Chronicle* works to affirm the ancient lineage of the English crown without empowering the rebellion of those disinherited by it.

Seeking the Grail

Hardyng's incorporation of the quest for the Holy Grail into the Arthurian section of his *Chronicle* provides another narrative about origins highlighting the antiquity of British imperialist claims. There is no precedent in the chronicle tradition for this material; Hardyng is the first to include the Grail in his history of King Arthur, adapting it from the French romance, *La Queste del Saint Graal* (Kennedy, 188). As he encountered it in French romances like the *Queste* or the *Estoire del Saint Graal*, the Grail quest, which contrasts earthly and spiritual knighthood and explores the private and interior development of individual knights, the best of whom—like Galahad—must logically reject outright the chivalric and secular world of Arthurian romance, proves largely intractable to Hardyng's purposes. The style of his romance sources is leisurely, following several knights through a complex series of interlocking episodes. The narrative technique of interlace used to structure these romances is the antithesis of Hardyng's spare sequential style (Riddy, "Chivalric Nationalism," 406).

Hardyng, however, is not interested in the internal spiritual development of the knights of the Round Table; he is not interested in following their separate quests for perfection; he is not interested, as the romances are, in exploring the vagaries of signification, the difficulties of correctly interpreting signs in a deceptive world. The Grail fits into his scheme only insofar as it validates the antiquity of British institutions (in this case the British church) and establishes a paradigm for an earthly Christian monarchy, one that, as Valerie Lagorio has argued, is "a microcosm of Church and State in one, a unit of imperium reflecting the sovereignty of its master" (220).

The Grail provides Hardyng with a symbol that gives the secular preeminence of England a religious imprimatur and does so by using the same process of sequential serialization that is, as we argued above, the primary hallmark of Hardyng's style. Felicity Riddy notes that "for Hardyng, the Grail of the Quest is not a religious symbol but a heraldic emblem that harks back through history to Joseph of Arimathea, binding together the past rather than transcending history in the Eucharist" ("Chivalric Nationalism," 407). In Hardyng's hands the Grail unites heraldry, genealogy, religious mysticism, colonial expansion, and political idealism, giving a public face to the privatized landscapes of the French Grail romances. Those romances had already begun to link the Grail and its chief knight, Galahad, with the figure of Joseph of Arimathea, who in the New Testament is the owner of the tomb in which the body of Christ rested after the Crucifixion. Both Lagorio and Riddy argue that Hardyng shaped the Grail materials toward nationalistic ends, that he was creating symbols capable of forging an imagined community of the nation, "a comun signe, eche man to knowe his nacion / From enemies" (ed. Ellis, 85). Although the *Chronicle* is undoubtedly tinged throughout with Hardyng's chauvinistic and imperialistic agendas, we think it may be premature to attribute to Hardyng nationalism as we understand it. Throughout the *Chronicle*, its various manuscripts, and its visual programs, Hardyng displays a conservatism that harks back to older forms of imagined communities that preceded the nation.[17]

To understand the means by which Hardyng untangles the complex threads of the Grail story to create a simple serial sequence to serve his political agenda, we must turn briefly to a discussion of the environment in which Hardyng wrote. In particular we must understand the political stakes involved in joining material about Arthur, the hero king of the Britains, with Joseph of Arimathea, the saint responsible for bringing Christianity to Britain. There was precedent for the incorporation of material about Joseph of Arimathea in histories of the island. In the thirteenth century an anonymous monk of Glastonbury added to William of Malmesbury's history of Glastonbury Abbey a reference to Joseph's visit to England during the century after Christ's death. In the 1340s John of Glastonbury wrote a history of the abbey that included a detailed account of Joseph's arrival at Glastonbury during the reign of King Arviragus, a first-century contemporary of Emperor Vespasian. Joseph preached, founded a church, and was eventually buried there (along with those other famous residents of the Glastonbury cemetery—Arthur and Guinevere—whose remains were supposedly discovered there in 1191).[18]

Valerie Lagorio suggests that legends about Joseph's conversion of the Britains figured prominently in the conciliar movement of the early fifteenth century, a movement that attempted to decentralize the church by stressing local control over Roman rule (220–24). This attempt to strengthen the role of "national" churches, she argues, reflected the nascent nationalism of the age. During these debates English prelates sought to "prove their status as a Christian nation, on par with France, Italy, Spain, and Germany" (221). Lagorio's formulation suggests a concept of nationalism, much like our own, based on simultaneous serials. The English church in her view imagines itself as one national church enjoying equal status and power with other churches—French, German, Italian, Spanish. But closer inquiry into this material suggests that this is not how the arguments were framed in these councils. If the conciliar movement had imagined a nationalism based on simultaneous serials, the debates in the councils would have stressed the independence of all the various national churches from Rome (as, for instance, would happen during the Reformation a century later), the legitimacy of local control, and the equality of these independent churches. Instead the arguments Lagorio cites seem much more focused on the foundation of these churches. The key question appears to be which church can claim to be the oldest, the originary church; it is this church that deserves preeminence among all the other churches. Foundations by disciples closest to Christ himself constituted strong claims, but blood ties were even stronger. Rome's claim to prominence, for instance, was based on the claim that its church was founded by St. Peter, the apostle closest to Christ. Participants in this debate, however, seem able to imagine only one church as the originary, foundational church.

English prelates used the Joseph legend to bolster the English church's claims to precedence over all other churches, not merely its independence from Rome. In fact, Thomas Polton, arguing at the Council of Constance in 1417, seems much more interested in using the Joseph legend to prove the English church older than its French counterpart than in challenging Roman rule:

> Whereas they strain overmuch to exalt the realm of France above the realm of England and the length of time since it received the faith of Christ, from which it has never strayed, as compared with the realm of England, we reply that if they had noted the time when the realm of England first received the faith of Christ and when the realm of France first received it, and how the faith of Christ has stood unshaken in the realm of England to this day, although at intervals raging storms of infidelity have assailed it, and endeavored to destroy it in part, they would never have tried that argument. For immediately after the passion of Christ, Joseph of Arimathea, the noble decurion who took him down from the cross, came with twelve companions to labor in the morning in the Lord's vineyard, that is, in England, and converted the people to the faith. (Lagorio, 221–22)

The English arguments seem intent on establishing a sequential serial in which one church—the English church—proves itself the origin of Christianity, the oldest church, established by a disciple of Christ's and, incidentally, one in his bloodline. Such a church could claim precedence over all the other European churches.

Hardyng may have been interested in the Joseph legend insofar as it supported his arguments for British sovereignty over Scotland in the religious sphere. It countered Scottish claims to the antiquity of its church, described in Fordun's *Chronicle*, as based on their possession of the bones of St. Andrew as early as the second century A.D. (Kennedy, 191–96). Hardyng's account of Joseph's arrival in Britain quite specifically dates it earlier; in 76 A.D. Joseph had languished in prison for forty-two years after the death of Christ:

> But Vaspasyan, with his hoste full royall,
> And Ioseph also, came into Britayne,

> The yere of Christe was then accompte, in all,
> Seuenty and syxe, the sooth for to sayne. (ed. Ellis, 84)

This date, 76 A.D., would make the English church older than the Scottish church and thus establish its precedence.

Hardyng's treatment of Joseph's conversion of the British king Arviragus anticipates the development of the Grail materials during the later Arthurian section. This is perhaps the only instance in which Hardyng deviates from his relentlessly serial emplotment in which time moves only forward and one king follows the next. He foreshadows the trajectories of two symbols—the Round Table and the red cross arms—that will find their fulfillment during the reign of Arthur. A marginal gloss in BL MS Harley 661, most likely not authorial, explicitly links Joseph's sojourn in Britain with the Holy Grail.

> Also this Joseph brought into Britayne with hym parte of the blode of Criste / which is called Seyntgraal / the true sayinge is Sank Roiall / Also this Joseph made a Round Table for hym and for hys fellows in remembraunce of xii Apostolles / which Rounde Table kynge Arthure honoured and held (fol. 27r; cited in Riddy, "Chivalric Nationalism," 401).

In most of the manuscripts, Hardyng is content to make the connection between Joseph and the Grail through the symbols of heraldry. After converting King Arviragus and baptizing him, Joseph

> ... gaue hym then a shelde of siluer white,
> A crosse endlong and ouertwhart full perfect.

> Of his oun blode, whiche from his necke did rynne,
> He made that crosse in signyficacion
> Of Christes blode, that ranne out fro withynne
> Vpon the crosse at his expiracion:
> Whiche shelde, by Ioseph exhortacion,
> He bore on hym in feldes of were alwaye,
> And in his baners and cote-armour gaye,

> These armes were vsed through all Brytain
> For a comon signe, eche mane to knowe his nacion
> Frome enemies. (ed. Ellis, 85)[19]

For Hardyng, the red cross arms are the most significant symbol of Britain's religious legacy. These arms, which later Galahad will find in Avalon and take up as his own, are only metonymically linked with the Grail through the image of blood. The literal blood—Christ's blood—the Grail is supposed to contain is figured by the centrality of blood in genealogy. Lancelot and Galahad are of the blood of Joseph and, because Joseph was kin to Christ, of Christ. Writes Riddy, "the red-cross arms bring together the secular genealogy that Geoffrey of Monmouth developed when he linked Britain, through Brutus, to Troy and the religious genealogy of the Vulgate Grail texts that linked Britain through Joseph to Jerusalem" ("Chivalric Nationalism," 403).

The Grail, when it finally does appear in the Arthurian section, seems to have much less significance for Hardyng. It behaves not like the mystical symbol of the Vulgate romances, but more like the golden snitch in the Harry Potter game of Quidditch:

> So sodenly doores and wyndowes al clapped
> With hydeous noyce, farre passyng meruelous,
> Opened and sperred al by theim selfs fast rapped,
> For whiche thei trust of some cause meruelous;
> As with that noyse the saynt Graall precious
> Flowe thryse about within the hall full ofte,
> Flytteryng full fast aboue theim high on lofte. (ed. Ellis, 132)

Riddy suggests that the verb "flytteryng" calls to mind the Pentacostal image of the Holy Ghost as a dove ("Chivalric Nationalism," 405), but it also has a trivializing effect, undermining the solemnity of the scene. Galahad perfunctorily chases the Grail, discovering it finally in Wales, but the text seems far more interested in his discovery of the red cross arms in Avalon, perhaps because it is the arms, not the Grail, that establishes Galahad's genealogical link with Joseph of Arimathea and hence completes the lineal sequence prefigured earlier in the text.[20] Similarly the Round Table functions in Hardyng not as the material embodiment of the ideals of chivalry, as it will for Malory, but as the material embodiment of the principles of genealogy, of the sequential serial. Its only purpose in the *Chronicle* is to establish Galahad's credentials when he appears at King Arthur's court. There, after paying homage to the king and queen, he sits

> ... downe in the siege pereleous
> Of the table rounde, where none durst sitte afore
> But Ioseph, that was full religious,
> That made it so ere Galaad was bore,

> And kyng Arthure that satte therin therfore,
> And neuer moo that it had ought presumed,
> But they were brent therin, shamed & consumed. (ed. Ellis, 132)

Galahad becomes the fulfillment of a prophecy that is revealed only at the moment he fulfills it. Nothing is allowed to impede the narrative progress that establishes Galahad as the earthly exemplar of chivalry and good government. Hardyng eliminates virtually anything that gives the Grail romances their moral complexity. Most significantly, he expunges Lancelot's adultery. Galahad is not the perfect knight who springs from a flawed but noble father; rather he is the perfect knight "Lancelot gat, in very clene spousage, on Pelles doughter" (ed. Ellis, 131).

If Hardyng shows only the most mechanical interest in the actual quest for the Holy Grail, he is very interested in Galahad's post-Grail career. After achieving the Grail,

> Then rode he forth vnto the Holy Lande,
> Through God and holy inspiracyon,
> To God he gaue his seruyce, and hym bonde
> To chastyte, and greate contemplacyon;
> And kyng was made, by hole coronacyon,
> Of Garras[21] then, and duke of Orboryk,
> Of whome the people full well dyd theym lyke. (ed. Ellis, 135)

Galahad embodies not secular chivalry as service to a lady (as Lancelot does in the Grail romances), but chivalry as service to God. As such, he becomes the divinely inspired exemplar of secular government joined to religious service, becomes indeed the very embodiment of Crusade ideology, so it is perhaps fitting that his later career takes place exclusively in the Holy Land. This ideal is more explicitly elaborated in the earlier Lansdowne version than in the later manuscripts:

> Whose reule was this by Galaad constytute:
> To leue evermore in clennesse virginall;
> Comon profyte all way to execute;
> All wronges redress with batayll corperall
> Where law myght nought haue course iudicialle;
> All fals lyuers his londe that had infecte
> For to distroy, or of thair vice correcte.
>
> The pese to kepe, the laws als sustene,
> The fayth of Criste, the kyrke also protecte;

Widows, maydyns, ay whare fore to mayntene
And chyldre yonge, vnto thar age perfecte
That they couthe kepe thaym self in all affect. (fol. 78r; Riddy,
    "Chivalric Nationalism," 408)

As Riddy suggests, this rule almost exactly duplicates the Pentecostal oath sworn by Arthur's knights in Malory's *Morte Darthur*. Here, however, the ideal is safely distanced, removed from local British or even European politics by displacing it onto the Holy Land, the far-off land of the Crusades.[22] In fact, in the *Chronicle*, Galahad is never seriously held out as a practical model of kingship. His story functions more like hagiography, establishing a disembodied ideal that could not reasonably function in the secular world rather than a model to be emulated. Galahad's kingship can never be anything but temporary. His chastity removes him from the processes of feudo-dynasticism, which required the production of legitimate heirs, upon which secular governments of the time relied. Galahad's lands, however justly ruled during his lifetime, are left ungoverned after his death, and his lineage—the lineage of Joseph of Arimathea and ultimately of Christ—dies with him.

But Galahad's significance for Hardyng's political agenda does not end with his death. By way of conclusion, we might explore the ways in which the processes of memorialization enacted in Hardyng's narrative of Galahad's death appeal to symbols that would mobilize the specific political communities Hardyng's history was designed to serve. After Galahad's death, Percival and Bors return to Arthur's court bringing with them Galahad's heart "closed all with golde" (ed. Ellis, 135). Galahad's heart, transformed into a relic, is buried beside Joseph at Glastonbury. This striking image of glorification once again links Galahad both with English–Scottish politics and with the emblems of a specifically British Christianity. Kennedy suggests that Hardyng based this scene on the death of Robert the Bruce, as recorded in John Barbour's *Bruce*. After his death, Bruce's "heart was encased in silver, taken on a pilgrimage against the Saracens, and brought back to Scotland and buried with great ceremony at Melrose Abbey" (Kennedy, 205); similarly Galahad's heart is also brought back from the Holy Land and interred in a great abbey. Riddy argues that Hardyng would also have known, from his patron Sir Robert Umfraville, the story about St. George's heart, "which was presented to Henry V by the emperor Sigismund on the occasion of the latter's admission to the Order of the Garter in 1416" ("Chivalric Nationalism," 409).

In all three cases the forms of memorialization enacted in these events, although they do create symbols capable of mobilizing particular political communities, function differently from those forms of memorialization associated with the "official nationalism" of the twentieth century.[23] All three instances depend upon the physical presence of the individual being memorialized. The actual remains of the "saint" or hero are enshrined; it is not simply a representation of an absent presence. There is what Anderson calls an "aura"—inherited from the religious worship of relics—that surrounds the actual remains of the political hero: Galahad, Robert Bruce, St. George. According to Anderson, what marks the memorials of the heroes of the modern nation-state is their serialization. They are always replicas without an original; they can never be singular (*Spectre of Comparison*, 48).[24] They are always one in a series of such monuments that circulate easily through a variety of media (stamps, t-shirts, postcards, etc.). In Hardyng's *Chronicle*, the construction of the imagined political community is intimately bound up with specific personal relationships; the formation of community still requires some forms of physical presence.

Finally, then, Hardyng's book does not simply recount history. It participates in an exchange of patronage at the same time it creates legitimacy for a regime (the Yorkist regime) at a time when it was very much in doubt. The imaginative ties it constructs to both are not like the "deep horizontal comradeship" of the nation, but the hierarchical intimacies of patronage and feudal custom. In the next chapter, we will examine forms of emerging nationalism in Malory's *Morte Darthur*, written only a generation after Hardyng.

6

Patronage, Printing, and Symbolic Economies of Nationalism in Caxton's *Morte Darthur*

When Richard III charged that Henry Tudor was an upstart pretender with "no manner of right, interest, title, or colour" in the throne of England, Henry sent a commission into Wales that produced a report tracing his ancestry through Geoffrey of Monmouth's King Arthur back to Brutus, the Trojan hero who was the eponymous founder of Britain. Henry's first son and presumptive heir was christened Arthur and hailed as "Arturus secundus." He was born in Winchester, the "English Camelot," September 19, 1486, one year after William Caxton issued his printed edition of Sir Thomas Malory's Arthurian romance, the *Morte Darthur* (Millican, 16, 154; Parry and Caldwell, 89). Henry's strategy to legitimate his dynastic ambitions at the end of the Wars of the Roses, some three centuries after the first appearance of Arthur as a British cultural hero, attests to the potency of the figure of Arthur as a cultural signifier in the British politics of feudo-dynasticism. The publication of the *Morte Darthur* during the last months of the Yorkist monarchy, just before Henry Tudor's successful rebellion put an end to the Wars of the Roses, provides an opportunity to examine the "symbolic economies" (Goux, *Symbolic Economies*, 10) of patronage and exchange at work in the formation of national identity in early modern England. It enables us to explore the intersections between a feudal community in which relationships remained essentially private, defined by social and economic exchanges that involved both patrons and clients, and the imaginary, impersonal, and corporate community of the nation that Caxton's publications were just beginning to represent and, thus, to make possible. The antiquarian interests displayed by England's first printer enable us to examine the Tudor recuperation of the ancient Celtic past as a political reclamation that served particular nationalistic ends—the construction of a political mythology and a corporate identity, an imaginary representation of national identity that could bring an end to nearly a century of political turmoil and civil war.

Caxton's role in the production and circulation of Sir Thomas Malory's *Morte Darthur* has been shaped, and largely devalued, by nineteenth- and twentieth-century notions of the author-function that assume that the text is the production of a single controlling consciousness (see Foucault, "What Is an Author?"). The author is the sole creative genius, the source of the work and guarantor of its literariness. From this premise it follows that only authors can have creative intentions. Authors cannot make mistakes in their texts; only scribes, editors, and publishers can. Furthermore scribes, editors, and publishers can never have creative intentions (or any intentions for that matter); they can only produce error. This perception of Caxton as at best a popularizer and at worst a mutilator of Malory's work of art was exacerbated by the discovery in 1934 of the Winchester manuscript that held out the promise of a text closer to the poet's original intentions. Those who see Winchester as a closer reflection of Malory's artistic intentions—Eugène Vinaver and P.J.C. Fields, primarily—see Caxton's heavy editorial hand as a corruption and mutilation of Malory's writing. Even those who defend the integrity of Caxton's 1485 printed edition—William Matthews and James Spisak, for instance—resort to arguments that make Malory, not Caxton, the "author" of its revisions.[1] In this argument, Winchester becomes an early draft and Caxton's the revised edition. But in either case the central premise remains intact: both sides deny that Caxton's purposes in publishing the manuscript may be as significant as Malory's authorship to our understanding of the *Morte Darthur*.

We contend that the situation is rather more complex. In choosing to focus attention on Caxton's agency in publishing Malory's text we argue that the *Morte Darthur* is a space where competing social and political interests intersect in dialogical contestation over institutions, beliefs, values, practices, and even styles (Bakhtin, *Dialogical Imagination*, 272–73). If we leave aside issues of authorial and editorial prerogatives, Caxton's choice to publish the *Morte Darthur* in 1485 could not have been without a political significance that distinguishes Caxton's printed text from any manuscripts that may have preceded it. It may seem perfectly obvious that the Winchester manuscript and the 1485 edition of Caxton's *Morte Darthur* represent two very different media—manuscript and printed book; but as scholars have lost themselves in arguing for the priority of one or the other, they have forgotten that this difference has political and cultural implications for any reading of either text. Caxton's edition circulated within the institutions of late-fifteenth-century English culture in a number of ways, serving particular political, social, and ideological agendas that we have only begun to unravel and that will only fully unravel by examining the edition as a significant cultural event in its own right. In what follows, we unpack those agendas that led to the publication of Caxton's text.[2]

By publishing the *Morte Darthur*, Caxton chose to make available to the fifteenth-century reading public his preference for chivalric materials and his decidedly popularizing bent, aspects of Caxton's work that have been noted by almost all his biographers. These contradictory impulses—toward a private coterie audience of patrons and toward a larger and more popular public readership—suggest the ways in which Caxton's project looks both backward to a feudal economy of patronage relationships and forward to symbolic economies dependent upon representations of an English nation imagined as a corporate and sovereign entity. Caxton's preference for materials about chivalry that drew heavily from the Burgundian fashions popular during the reign of Edward IV would appeal to his royal patrons who had included, at various times, Edward's sister Margaret, duchess of Burgundy, his queen Elizabeth, her brother Lord Rivers, and the young Prince of Wales (Painter, 141–42). At the same time, Caxton's dissemination of this material through the printing press made it available to a much wider reading public than would have been possible in manuscript. This dual orientation toward the private tastes of aristocratic patrons and toward the public consumption encouraged by print capitalism must figure prominently in any discussion of the role of patronage, with its emphasis on networks of personal relationships, in the creation of the corporate relationships required for the formation of the "imagined community" of the nation.

The nation, as we argue throughout this volume, is not a self-evident or timeless concept. It has a history and its meanings have changed over time. In *Imagined Communities*, Anderson cites religious communitarianism and dynasticism as two important precursors of this "imagined community" of the nation, and undoubtedly this is so. But even more significant to his account of nationalism is the advent of print culture. Anderson associates nationalism, defined as identification with an imagined community that is both inherently limited and sovereign, with the rise of print capitalism, and this is why we think Caxton is a key figure in this representational shift at the end of the fifteenth century. According to Anderson, print capitalism encouraged nationalistic enthusiasms by (1) creating unified fields of exchange below Latin and above spoken vernaculars because dialectical differences that would make conversation impossible are flattened out in print; (2) stabilizing language over time, making it capable of virtually infinite reproduction; and (3) establishing new languages of power of a kind different from older administrative vernaculars, languages of power that drew upon a number of dialects (*Imagined Communities*, 47–48). Because, unlike the manuscript, the printed book can be endlessly replicated, readers of a printed book, say, the *Morte Darthur*, could imagine a large number of people they did not know reading the same book at the same time.[3] Because it was more likely that these imagined readers would be English speakers rather than, say, French speakers, the printed book—and later the newspaper, broadside, pamphlet, and periodical—provided the means of forging imagined communities while at the same time validating its own worth as a marker of national identity. "The printed book," Elizabeth Kirk writes, "distances author, reader, and text from each other in ways that raise troubling questions" (276); but that distance, in turn, also made it possible to imagine a new "mode of signifying" that could represent an abstraction like "English society" to itself, could create symbolic registers to represent the monarchy, the nation, and history itself.

Anderson's focus on the imaginary and representational shifts that accompanied the advent of printing in late-fifteenth-century England, however, ought not to obscure the participatory and material relations among the producers and consumers of printed books that fueled such imaginative shifts. The book, as Natalie Zemon Davis has pointed out, is not merely a receptacle for ideas; it is also a "carrier of relationships" (*Society and Culture*, 192). Because the introduction of the printing press into England at the end of the fifteenth century brought about specific changes in the mode of production of written texts—not only of literature or devotional texts, but of political discourse as well—it also created specific changes in social relations. As a printer, Caxton had to orient the works he chose to publish in two different directions; he had to please two very different audiences with different tastes. He had to look to the patrons who provided both symbolic and real capital to finance his ventures and to the larger popular audience of potential book buyers who would make the venture financially profitable. This dual orientation explains Caxton's preference in his publishing for chivalric materials (like the *Morte Darthur*) that would please his royal patrons and those whose wealth enabled them to purchase books, that is, those who might possess aristocratic pretensions.

The patronage networks that marked feudal relationships dominated by the exchange of "gifts" were still the primary means by which those outside of the aristocracy negotiated their relations with it. Caxton's reliance on the patronage of his Yorkist benefactors is obscured in the preface to the *Morte Darthur*, which was printed after Edward IV's death and the execution of Caxton's principal patron, Lord Rivers. But dedications of earlier works to Margaret, duchess of Burgundy, and to Lord Rivers, as well as a later dedication to Henry VII, make clear Caxton's indebtedness to these royal patrons. As Russell Rutter has argued, Caxton was "a man of business, a prosperous merchant, a successful administrator, and a sometime diplomat" engaged in the high-risk endeavor of attempting to derive profit from a relatively new technology (469–70). But he was by no means a full-blown capitalist whose only responsibility was to a mass-market readership; the feudal system of patronage minimized Caxton's financial risks, even if his patrons could not supply all his capital needs. What they offered instead of money was "symbolic capital," forms of prestige, status, and social control that Caxton could convert into material wealth (Bourdieu, 178). Caxton's patrons provided access to markets and to the foreign labor necessary for printing, as well as protection from enemies and competitors. In many of his prefaces Caxton gratefully acknowledges those supporters who offered both material and symbolic capital.[4]

The social relations of patronage that provided the capital for the spread of print culture must also figure into any account of English nationalism. The new technology of printing, because it greatly expanded the audience for books, altered significantly the interpersonal, dyadic relationship between patron and client that marked manuscript culture, creating the possibility of representing new kinds of corporate relationships. Because it was produced during a period of political upheaval during which Caxton's patronage was uncertain, the preface to the *Morte Darthur* provides a glimpse of these emergent identities.

In the preface to the *Morte Darthur*, Caxton is at once self-deprecating in his relationship to his patrons and appreciative of how his printed text will serve to reclaim the past for those living in England. He writes of the "many noble and dyuers gentylmen of thys royame of Englond" who "camen and demaunded me many and oftymes" and "instantly requyred" that he print the "noble hystorye of the Sayntgreal and of the moost renomed Crysten kyng, fyrst and chyef of the thre best Crysten and worthy, Kyng Arthur, whyche ought moost to be remembred emonge vs Englysshemen tofore al other Crysten kynges" (Malory, *Caxton's Malory*, 1:1). Caxton offers, in his preface, an overview of the English chronicle tradition, weighing the truth value of those texts that omit mention of Arthur and those, like Malory's, that tell "the noble and ioyous hystorye of the grete conqueror and excellent kyng" (1:40). However Malory may have intended his compilation of Arthurian materials—and however we may now read Malory's writings—for Caxton they function not as a romance, but as a "hystorye," a chronicle, comparable to others in the genre, "whyche copye Syr Thomas Malorye dyd take oute of certeyn bookes of Frenssche and reduced it into Englysshe" (2:2).[5] Arthur is positioned in the preface not only as one of the three Christian "worthies," but more specifically as an English worthy. The question remains, however, whose past is Caxton reclaiming in celebrating the "fyrst and chyef of the thre best Crysten and worthy." Curiously, although he singles out one in particular, he does not name any of his patrons, these "gentylmen," thus seemingly depriving them of the symbolic capital that would repay their patronage. Caxton's omission of his patrons' identities can only be explained by the political situation at the end of the Wars of the Roses.

The *Morte Darthur* made its appearance only one month before the Welshman Henry Tudor defeated Richard III at Bosworth Field. While evidence indicates that the Winchester manuscript may have been in Caxton's shop from as early as 1480, Caxton's printed book was most likely planned and executed during the two years Richard held the throne, a period of continual rebellion and political uncertainty. As Lotte Hellinga notes, "Fickleness in human behavior apart, the turbulence of the times may go a long way to explain the manuscript's lingering in Caxton's premises" (134). Caxton's silence—not only his refusal to name his patrons, but also his omission of Richard III's regnal year (or indeed any mention of the reigning monarch)—has been attributed by most biographers to Caxton's close ties of patronage with Richard's brother Edward and the now disfavored Woodville family, which included Edward's widow (Painter, 146–47). Caxton's proximity to the dowager queen during this time—both were housed in the precincts of Westminster Abbey through the offices of its abbot, John Eastney—suggests that Caxton's ties with this family did not end with Edward's and Rivers's deaths. It is not inconceivable that Caxton carried out this project as a favor to the Woodville family, which was scheming to marry Edward's eldest daughter, Elizabeth, either to Richard or Henry Tudor, whoever was victorious (146).

Still the project must have struck Caxton as a double-edged sword at best. The circulation of stories about Arthur might well appeal to Henry, as our anecdote at the beginning of this chapter would suggest, but they would certainly anger the king. This would explain Caxton's professed reluctance to certify the Arthurian material as history—to give it the imprimatur of absolute truth—a reluctance not evident in earlier works published by Caxton, such as the 1482 *Polychronicon* or the *Order of Chivalry*, possibly published in 1484 and dedicated, unsuccessfully one would imagine, to Richard (Higden, 337, and Caxton). In the preface to the 1485 *Morte Darthur*, Caxton says that "dyuers men holde oppynyon that there was no suche Arthur, and that all suche bookes as been maad of hym ben but fayned and fables, bycause that some *cronycles* make of hym no mencyon ne remembre hym noothynge ne of his knyghtes" (Malory, *Caxton's Malory*, 1:1).

It is perhaps not all that surprising that Caxton might want to create plausible deniability by dissociating himself from the cultural hero whose descendent and rightful heir a Welsh pretender was claiming to be.[6] Caxton's analysis of the historicity of the Arthurian stories vacillates between reluctant disbelief and reluctant belief. He allows himself to be convinced by "one in specyal," whom many take to be the late Rivers, "that in hym that shold say or thynke that there was neuer suche a kyng callyd Arthur myght wel be aretted grete folye and blyndnesse" (1:2), and by abundant material evidence he cites for Arthur's existence, including his sepulcher at Glastonbury: "fyrst in the Abbey of Westmestre at Saynt Edwardes shryne remayneth the prynte of his seal in reed waxe closed in beryll, in which is wryton, PATRICIUS ARTHURUS BRITANNIE GALLIE GERMANIE DACIE IMPERATOR. Item in the Castel of Douer ye may see Gauwaynes skulle and Cradoks mantel; at Wynchester, the Round Table; in other places, Launcelottes swerde, and many other thynges" (1:2). Yet at the end Caxton feels compelled to include one final disclaimer: "And for to passe the tyme thys book shal be plesaunte to rede in, but for to gyue fayth and byleue that al is trewe that is conteyned herin, ye be at your lyberte" (1:3). Caxton seems simultaneously to assert the possibility of reading the Arthurian story historically and to deny it, thereby satisfying his patrons and potential patrons (Henry Tudor) with a narrative that aggrandized their dynastic ambitions at the same time it placated the ruling monarch by questioning the story's truth value.

Thus, the publication of the *Morte Darthur* may have served an agenda amenable to Caxton's unnamed patrons, while shielding him (and them) from the displeasure of the reigning monarch. But Caxton did not print the work only for a small, select group of patrons. Indeed, among the arguments for publication incorporated by Caxton's patrons was that there would be a wider audience interested in and willing to purchase this history of England's triumphant past. Between three hundred and six hundred copies were likely produced by Caxton's press and commercially marketed (Rutter, 443). Caxton explains that his patrons demanded he publish a book about Arthur because, "I ought rather t'enprynte his actes and noble feates than of Godefroye of Boloyne or ony of the other eyght [worthies], consyderyng that he was a man borne wythin this royame and kyng and emperour of the same, and that there ben in Frensshe dyuers and many noble volumes of his actes and also of his knyghtes" (Malory, *Caxton's Malory*, 1:1). Caxton's printing the history of Arthur would serve, according to these gentlemen, not merely to claim a national past, but to reclaim it from foreigners who have co-opted it:

> For in al places Crysten and hethen [Arthur] is reputed and taken for one of the IX worthy and the fyrst of the thre Crysten men. And also he is more spoken of beyonde the see, moo bookes made of his noble actes, than there be in Englond: as well in Duche, Ytalyen, Spaynysshe, and Grekysshe, as in Frensshe. And yet of record remayne in wytnesse of hym in Wales, in the toune of Camelot, the grete stones and meruayllous werkes of yron lyeng vnder the grounde, and ryal vautes, which dyuers lyuyng hath seen. Wherfor it is a meruayl why he is nomore renomed in his owne contreye, sauf onelye it accordeth to the word of God, whyche sayth that no man is accept for a prophete in his owne contreye. (1:2)

Although he is an English hero, Arthur is more honored in other places than in his own land. In these passages, Caxton stresses what Arthur has in common with the readers of his book: they are Englishmen, and the exploits of a hero-king like Arthur remind them of their membership in the larger community of the realm ("royame"). They point to an extended community beyond the small circle of patrons and clients, toward a nation properly headed by a legitimate monarch. The emergence of something like national feeling out of earlier, more heterogeneous and shifting social relations of patronage depended upon the stabilization of that heterogeneity around what Jean-Joseph Goux has called a "general symbolic equivalent," an idealized standard and measure of value that exists in an imaginary relationship of privilege and exclusion to all other elements that it governs and represents. In *Symbolic Economies*, Goux locates in the accession of money as the privileged bearer of value in the economic sphere a "mode of signifying" that can account for the "symbolic economies"—regulated processes of exchange and substitution—that "cut across separate registers of the social body," including the political, linguistic, religious, and psychosexual (10). He describes an interconnected social dynamic by which the "majority of signs" are placed under the "command of a select few among them." Some equivalent sign had to be vested with the power to make things that are different appear the same for the purposes of exchange. "Value," he writes, "seems to gather, capitalize, centralize itself, investing certain elements with a privileged representativeness and even a monopoly on representativeness within the diverse set of which they are members." The mysterious genesis of this monopoly is then erased, leaving the monopoly absolute (26). This radical conception of exchange imagines the centralization of various forms of power (state, economic, patriarchal) not simply as the application of brute force to the social body, but as symbolic investment and structuration.

In the realm of the state (at least as it was emerging in fifteenth-century England), the monarch functions as the general symbolic equivalent, the privileged representative and embodiment of the nation, just as in the realm of economics it is money and in the realm of signs it is language. Caxton's *Morte Darthur* describes a process by which the multiplicity of patronage relationships can be reduced to a single relationship, that between the monarch and his subjects, with the monarch—Arthur—as the privileged and excluded bearer of all value. Language, eventually unified and standardized through the efforts of print capitalism, becomes the privileged medium for this process, whose completion is thus "imagined" as a representation—even during the turmoil of the Wars of the Roses—long before it ever existed as a political reality.

Seen in this light, Caxton's presentation of Malory's text as a single volume of twenty-one books and 503 chapters seems less a "mutilation" or corruption of Malory's original "intention," as several critics, most prominently Eugène Vinaver, have contended (see Malory, *Works*, 1:xxxv–lvi), than a conscious program designed to represent to a larger reading public the aesthetic tastes and political needs of his patrons, the unnamed "noble and dyuers gentylmen of thys royame of Englond" who commissioned the work. Twentieth-century Malory criticism has been reluctant to read in Caxton's structuring of the *Morte Darthur* an overtly political agenda. The tiredest controversy imposed upon Malory scholarship is the question of whether the *Morte Darthur* is one book or eight. This question has, since the appearance of Vinaver's edition, been debated exclusively on aesthetic grounds. Thus Vinaver writes, "We take it for granted that unity is not only a supreme artistic merit, but a feature without which no work of literature, regardless of its date and character, has any claim to recognition. To show that the *Morte Darthur* was 'one book' and not several was therefore not simply to add to its value: it was to establish its existence as a work of art" (1:xliv). Vinaver's critics accused him of destroying an English classic; it had been "pulled to pieces by an insensitive critic whose ear was not attuned to the inner harmonies of the text" (1:xliv). For his part, Vinaver saw Malory not as the inventor of the novel, but of the novella, thus imposing a different standard of artistic unity and appreciation on the text. Seen as a single entity, the *Morte Darthur* is riddled with inconsistency, but in a series of discrete romances, such inconsistencies become irrelevant. All of these remarks imply that if we could just get close to Malory's original intention we would also have the version that is most aesthetically pleasing. The argument is a spectacular example of the circularity Foucault describes in "What Is an Author?": because a particular version is closest to Malory's intention it is aesthetically pleasing and because it is aesthetically pleasing it is closest to Malory's intention. The "author-function" becomes the guarantor of the text's unity and value.

Instead, we might think about the very different purposes served by the Winchester manuscript and Caxton's 1485 printed edition and the different modes of circulation between them. If we grant hypothetically, at least, Vinaver's argument that Malory composed a series of discrete romances (a proposition not accepted by all Malory scholars), why does Caxton need the *Morte Darthur* to be one comprehensive story about Arthur? The answer might simply be that to serve as a political legitimation of English national ambitions it has to be a complete historical text—a *chronicle*. More importantly, to serve as a history of an emergent English "nation" the events recorded need to be more or less homogeneous, more or less equivalent in weight and emphasis. This is exactly the effect Caxton achieves by dividing the book into 503 chapters. The sprawling and episodic narrative style of the romance as a genre is (with only partial success, to be sure) brought under the command of the chapter, which functions as the unit of organizational structure within the romance narrative.

Concomitant with this narrative reorganization is a simplification and standardization of language designed to create a single linguistic standard for the English language that would be comprehensible to all speakers. The language in which those events are recorded must also be homogenized so that the book would be intelligible to the wider audience Caxton sought to reach. In a famous passage from his preface to the *Eneydos* (1490), dedicated to Arthur, the Prince of Wales, Caxton complains of the lack of just such a standard for English:

> And certainly our language now used varyeth far from that which was used and spoken when I was born, for we Englishmen been born under the domination of the moon, which is never steadfast but ever wavering, waxing one season and waneth and decreaseth another season. And that common English that is spoken in one shire varyeth from another. Insomuch that in my days happened that certain merchants were in a ship in Thames for to have sailed over the sea into Zeeland. And for lack of wind they tarried at Foreland and went to land for to refresh them, and one of them named Sheffelde a mercer came into an house and asked for meat and specially he asked after eggs. And the good wife answered that she could speak no French, and the merchant was angry for he also could speak no French, but would have had eggs, and she understood him not. And then at last another said that he would have eyren; then the good wife said that she understood him well. Lo, what should a man in these days now write, eggs or eyren? Certainly it is hard to please every man by cause of diversity and change of language. (108)

A people who cannot even understand one another's simplest communication cannot imagine the kind of communal bond necessary to identify as a nation. Mutual incomprehensibility in a print culture is a sign of social disintegration and conflict. Caxton's solution to this linguistic babel is to impose a standardization that, while claiming inclusiveness, actually is formulated in the exclusivity of the published text. He writes:

> this present book is not for a rude uplandish man to labour therein nor read it, but only for a clerk and a noble gentleman that feeleth and understandeth in faytes of arms, in love and in noble chivalry, therefore in a mean between both I have reduced and translated this said

book into our English not over rude nor curious, but in such terms as shall be understood by God's grace according to my copy. And if any man will engage in reading of it and findeth such terms that he cannot understand, let him go and learn Virgil or the Epistles of Ovid, and there he shall see and understand lightly all if he have a good reader and informer. (109)

Language had to standardize around a universal equivalent capable of becoming a sign of Englishness, which, Caxton claims, consists of a "golden mean" between a rude and gentle speech, a mundane and "curious" language, but which must, in fact, be constructed almost exclusively with reference to a standard derived from the written texts of learned "authorities" like Virgil and Ovid.

Perhaps nowhere in the *Morte Darthur* is Caxton's hand in creating a linguistic standard for English more apparent than in the section describing Arthur's Roman wars. Nor does any other section of the *Morte Darthur* convey a more openly nationalistic—indeed imperialistic—agenda. The portion of the Winchester manuscript to which Vinaver refers as "The Noble Tale of King Arthur and the Emperor Lucius" follows its primary source, the fourteenth-century Alliterative *Morte Arthure*, in a number of ways, replicating not only the rhythms but dialectical idiosyncrasies as well. In the Caxton text, both the form and the language are "standardized," made consistent with the remainder of the *Morte Darthur*. The aesthetic result of this standardization process is the illusion of seamlessness, the illusion of the *Morte Darthur* as a "whole book," which tells, as Caxton promises in his preface, the "noble hystorye . . . of the moost renomed Crysten kyng, fyrst and chyef of the thre best crysten and worthy, Kyng Arthur, whyche ought moost to be remembred emonge vs Englysshemen tofore al other Crysten kynges." The political implications are likewise significant. For an England ravaged—brought nearly to the point of chaos—by political and social disintegration, Caxton's version of Arthur's wars with Lucius provides the foundation for the imagined community desired both by the publisher's wealthy patrons and his reading audience.

Unlike other scholars who have dealt with this episode, we are concerned not with who made the revisions but with the widespread shifts in the signifying practices of late medieval English culture that this portion of Caxton's printed book reveals.[7] In particular we are interested in those shifts that manifest a tendency toward a centralization and stabilization of exchange around a universal symbolic equivalent, whether this occurs in the realm of language through the emergence of a standardized English or in the realm of political relations through the representation of Arthur as monarch. In the Winchester manuscript, Arthur functions primarily as a patron, his association with the action, or those performing the action, is direct and personal in the ways that patron–client relations are direct and personal. Lucius sends his messengers "unto Arthur . . . commaundynge hym for to pay his trewage that his auncettryes have payde before hym" (Malory, *Works,* 1:185). Upon hearing the ambassadors, Arthur "loked up with his gray yghen and angred at the messyngers passyng sore" (1:185). In Caxton's book, Arthur's role as patron becomes ambiguous, his involvement with action is much more impersonal and indirect. Lucius's ambassadors demand that Arthur pay "the truage due of this royamme vnto th'Empyre" (Malory, *Caxton's Malory,* 1:121), and the king betrays no emotional response whatsoever. In the Winchester manuscript Arthur is called upon to pay "his trewage"; in Caxton's text it is the "truage due of this royamme." The Winchester manuscript represents Arthur as a man who happens to be the ruler of certain lands and patron to a group of warriors. In the *Morte Darthur,* he becomes England—or at least the corporate representative of its obligations.

The length of "The Noble Tale of King Arthur and the Emperor Lucius" is approximately halved in Caxton's *Morte Darthur.* What is most often left out is Arthur's involvement in the accumulation and dispensation of wealth and symbolic capital. For instance, the Winchester manuscript, in the following long passage, relates Arthur's campaigns following the defeat of Lucius:

> Now turne we to Arthur with his noble knyghtes that entryth streyghte into Lushburne and so thorowe Flaundirs and then to Lorayne. He laughte up all the lordshyppys and sytthen he drew hym into Almayne and unto Lumbardy the ryche, and sette lawys in that londe that dured longe aftir. And so into Tuskayne, and there the tirrauntys destroyed, and there were captaynes ful kene that kept Arthurs comyng, and at streyte passages slew muche of his peple, and there they vytayled and garnysshed many good townys.
>
> But there was a cite kepte sure defence agaynste Arthure and his knyghtes, and therewith angered Arthure and seyde all on hyght, "I woll synne this toune other ellys many a doughty shall dye!" And then the kynge approached to the wallis withoute shelde sauff his bare harneys.
>
> "Sir," seyde sir Florence, "foly thou workeste for to nyghe so naked this perleouse cite."

> "And thou be aferde," seyd kyng Arthure, "I rede the faste fle, for they wynne no worshyp of me but to waste their toolys; for there shall never harlot have happe, by the helpe of oure Lord, to kylle a crowned kynge that with creyme is anoynted." (Malory, *Works*, 1:227)

The *Morte Darthur* abbreviates this section, at the same time shifting its emphasis significantly:

> Now torne we vnto Kynge Arthur and his noble knyghtes, whiche after the grete batayle acheued ageynste the Romayns entryd into Lorayne, Braban and Flaunders, and sythen retorned into hault Almayn, and so ouer the montayns into Lombardye, and after into Tuskane, wherin was a cyte whiche in no wyse wold yelde themself ne obeye. Wherfore Kynge Arthur biseged it, and lay long aboute hit, and gaf many assautes to the cyte, and they within deffended them valyauntly. (Malory, *Caxton's Malory*, 1:131)

While the geography is more or less the same in Caxton's text, the abbreviations have flattened out the language considerably, ridding the text of its alliteration—"sette lawys in that londe that dured longe aftir," "doughty shall dye"—and of its more provincial vocabulary, words like "laughte," "garnysshed," and "harlot."

Arthur's ability to amass capital and dispense gifts to royal retainers is subsumed in Caxton's text into a more generalized description of the expansion of England's borders. The passage in which Arthur explains his refusal to take up a shield for protection in his siege of a town because no one would dare assault "a crowned kynge that with creyme is anoynted" is dropped from the Caxton version, drawing our attention away from the intensely personal relations of clientage between the king and his closest subordinates, which lose significance as wealth itself becomes mystified in the creation of the nation as an imagined community.

At the conclusion of "The Noble Tale of King Arthur and the Emperor Lucius," Arthur ceremoniously rewards his best knights, his clients. Lancelot and Bors are given both land and advice concerning their new role as patrons: "Loke that ye take seynge in all your brode londis, and cause youre lyege men to know you as their kynde lorde, and suffir never your soveraynte to be alledged with your subjectes, nother the soveraygne of your persone and londys" (Malory, *Works*, 1:245). Property is also given to the recent Christian convert Priamus, and "Thus the kynge gaff many londys. There was none that wolde aske that myghte playne of his parte, for of rychesse and welth they had all at her wylle" (1:246). In the *Morte Darthur,* the apportioning of gifts is not so particularized. The institution of the patron–client relationship seems to be replaced by a more complex relationship between the king and the nation, in which rules concerning accumulation and dispensation of wealth become both more informal and vaguer. In the *Morte Darthur,* the king "gaf londes and royaummes vnto his seruantes and knyghtes, to eueryche aftir his desert, in such wyse that none complayned, ryche ne poure" (Malory, *Caxton's Malory,* 1:136). The Caxton text's shift in the depiction of Arthur, from patron to general symbolic equivalent of the nation, is subtle and not always complete. It is, we would like to suggest, reflective of transitions in the culture of late-fifteenth-century England. Sir Robert Filmer would argue in the seventeenth century that the patriarchal and paternalistic bonds of patron and client would form the basis for the nation and for the divine right of kings (23); however, for this to happen the patronage relationship had to be expanded to include the more corporate and generalized relationship between monarch (as universal equivalent) and his subjects (most of whom the monarch would never meet or know), and at the same time the particularity, the close interpersonal dynamic, and the multiple loyalties that marked patron-client relations had to be suppressed.

What is it about Arthur specifically that makes him suited to serve as a model of the monarch as a general symbolic equivalent? Arthur is a figure from England's Celtic prehistory who plays an ambiguous role as a historical figure. He is caught between the chronicle tradition with its claims to historical veracity and a more fabulous romance tradition inherited from the French. He is at once both historical precursor and legendary romance hero. Both Caxton and his patrons were acutely aware of Arthur's historical ambiguity, as Caxton suggests in the preface: "dyuers men holde oppynyon that there was no suche Arthur, and that all suche bookes as been maad of hym ben but fayned and fables"; yet others hold that "there can no man resonably gaynsaye but there was a kyng of this lande named Arthur" (Malory, *Caxton's Malory,* 1:2). Negotiating this ambiguous ground between history and fable, Arthur serves, as Patricia Ingham suggests, as a "sovereign fantasy" (*Sovereign Fantasies,* 7).

This ambiguity is critical in creating the role of the monarch as general equivalent within the symbolic economy of the nation precisely because it enables Arthur to fulfill Goux's three main requirements for a general equivalent. First, as king, Arthur is privileged and set apart from all others.

Second, he is invested with a certain superfluity; he is surplus value. As king, he must be excluded from participation in exchange. By establishing patronal relations with his knights—by giving them land—Arthur is able to impose a structure on the martial violence of his knights based on the exchange of violence in the form of the Pentecostal Oath in which he charges them "neuer to doo outragyousyte nor mordre, and always to flee treason. Also by no meane to be cruel, but to gyue mercy vnto hym that asketh mercy, upon payn of forfeture of their worship and lordship of Kyng Arthur foreuermore, and alweyes to doo ladyes, damoysels, and gentylwymmen socour vpon payne of deethe. Also that no man take noo batails in a wrongful quarel for no love ne for noo lawe, ne for noo worldes goodes" (Malory, *Caxton's Malory*, 1:92).[8] Note that this oath attempts to bring violence under the control of official institutions, to render it a form of exchange, not to eliminate it. This reformulation of the patron–client relationship around the general symbolic equivalent of the king, however, demands the exclusion of the monarch from participation in exchange—especially the exchange of violence. While violence escalates with various knights competing with one another for recognition, Arthur, once he has established his authority, retreats further and further from the action—at least until the end. This distinguishes him from the Arthur of the chronicle tradition who is almost always at the center of the action. In the *Morte Darthur*, as that which gives value to his subjects—the Knights of the Round Table—Arthur cannot himself be involved in the pursuit of value, but must be excluded.

Finally, he is imaginary. Just as the image of gold, not gold itself, gives value to commodities in the economic sphere (Goux, *Symbolic Economies*, 20), so the image of the king, not necessarily the king himself, gives value to his subjects. This process, as Ernst Kantorowicz has argued, is the essence of the medieval political theory of the King's Two Bodies, in which the king's "body politic" is imagined as separate from his natural body and impervious to the imperfections and shortcomings of a body subject to aging, decay, disease, and death: "this Body is utterly void of Infancy, and old Age, and other natural Defects and Imbecilities, which the Body natural is subject to, and for this cause, what the king does in his Body politic, cannot be invalidated or frustrated by any Disability in his natural Body" (7).[9] The "body politic" is whole, perfect, immortal, static, and unchanging.

Kantorowicz's analysis of the way in which the Middle Ages represented kingship to itself is suggestive, but incomplete because it focuses primarily on medieval idealizations of kingship, its ideology, without taking into account the contradictions endemic to such ideologies. It imagines that representation as structured by a binary opposition between the corrupt human body and an incorruptible, immutable body. This opposition might be represented as a Hegelian dialectic whose synthesis will be the body politic:

corruptible body (thesis) incorruptible body (antithesis)

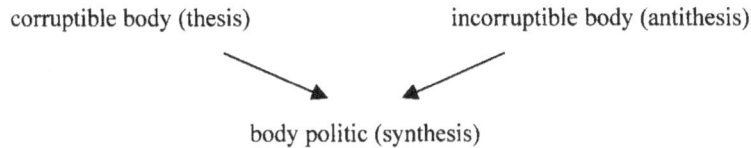

body politic (synthesis)

According to Elizabeth Pochoda, in the fifteenth century, the "'body politic' was no longer defined simply as the king's person in his official or public capacity, but as a corporation: the actual body had the king for its head and his subjects as members" (39). Christine de Pizan in her *Book of the Body of Policy*, which was translated into English during the fifteenth century, perhaps by Caxton's patron, Anthony Woodville, Lord Rivers, describes just such a body politic when she likens the three estates to

> a living body . . . of which the prince or the princes hold the higher place of the head in as much as they should and ought to be sovereigns and from them should come the particular institutions just as out of the understanding of men springs forth the deeds that the limbs achieve. The knights & the nobles hold the place of the hands and arms. For as the arms of a man are strong to endure labor and pain so they ought to have the charge to defend the rights of the prince and the commonwealth. And they also are compared to the hands for as the hands put away the annoying things, so they should put away all things that are evil and unprofitable. The third estate of the people are like the belly, the feet, and the legs. For as the body receives all things that comfort the head and the limbs, likewise the exercise of the princes and nobles ought to return to the public good . . . and as the legs and feet bear the weight of a man's body, so the laborers sustain all other estates.[10]

Christine de Pizan imagines the body politic as a single unified entity, analogous to the human body, but without its mutability. While hierarchy still dominates the relations between the three estates, individuals are encouraged to see themselves as vital parts of a whole, as horizontally as well as vertically bound with others. The metaphor of the body, drawn from medieval representations of the church, but secularized, is designed to remind the reader that the body politic is one entity that requires the health of all its members to function properly: "For just as the body of a man is defective and deformed when he lacks any of his members, likewise the body of the polity may not be perfect or entire if these estates are not well joined and assembled all in one so that each of them holds the others" (m.v).

What Christine imagines as the creation of the body politic, Caxton's printed text performs by transforming Arthur into the general symbolic equivalent of the nation that can be read in a standardized English ostensibly comprehensible to all (at least that is the fiction). However, "fetishism (of gold, of the phallus, of the king) originates in *the erasure of a genesis, the obliteration of a history*" (Goux, *Symbolic Economies*, 33; emphasis in original), and we must pay attention to what this narrative attempts to erase. Because Arthur is a figure from ancient prehistory, history, especially the most violent recent history with its chaos, civil war, and divided loyalties, must be—but never entirely is—erased at the same time a pristine myth of origin can be substituted. What Ernst Kantorowicz describes in the medieval political theory of the King's Two Bodies, then, is the ideal, an ideal Arthur embodies for Caxton's "diverse gentlemen." We must, however, pay attention to what is occluded by the process of idealization. The synthesis suggested by the body politic is always haunted by its own instability, by desires that undermine the synthesis of the corrupt and incorruptible body. This instability suggests, as the semanticist A. J. Greimas notes, "the existence, beyond the realm of the binary, of a more complex elemental structure of signification" (Schleifer, 25). Greimas attempts to map the dynamic relationships of this "complex elemental structure" that troubles the logic of opposition in the semiotic square, which, if we understand it as a heuristic device rather than a prescriptive structure, may assist us in mapping the complexities involved in the *Morte Darthur*'s construction of the imagined community of the nation.

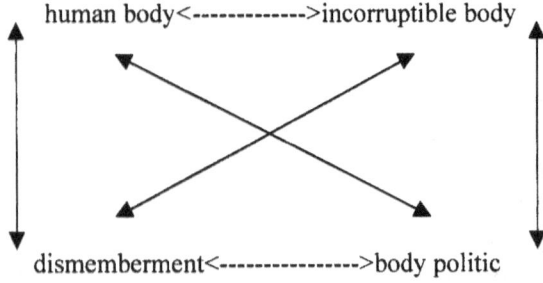

This square suggests that the "contrary relationships"—in this case the opposition between corruptible and incorruptible bodies—engenders and is engendered by a more complex structure of signification. The lower right-hand position represents the "positive term," the synthesis of the Hegelian dialectic, the body politic. But this gesture toward transcendence invariably produces the "contradictory relationship" that leads to the "negative complex term" in the lower left-hand corner. Kristeva refers to this position, the fourth term of the Hegelian dialectic, as "that which remains outside logic . . . , what remains heterogeneous to logic even while producing it through a movement of separation or rejection" (141). Slavoj Žižek calls this "radical negativity" that resists symbolization, this "traumatic point" that "persists as a surplus and returns through all attempts to domesticate it," the "anamorphotic" blot (*Looking Away*, 91).

In our square we have represented the negative complex position as the dismemberment of the body politic, by which we mean to imply the destructive violence—the dismemberment of physical bodies—necessary to get and maintain power. It is important to keep in mind that we cannot keep both the idealized Hegelian structure of the first three terms in focus at the same time as the fourth position. That's why it is anamorphic.[11] The *Morte Darthur* oscillates between two mutually exclusive views of the violence required to maintain the body politic (see Finke and Shichtman). In the one view, despite a tendency to link it with random, impulsive, and unreflective behavior, violence has a structure, one that is oriented toward a purpose, in this case the construction of a centralized monarchy based on martial prowess. Such institutionalized forms of violence (state-sanctioned violence) are structured through a yoking of physical injury—bodily dismemberment—to some form of contest in the service of some officially sanctioned goal. In the classical medieval romance, violence is carefully contained by well-established rules governing its application (one thinks here for instance of the Beheading Game in *Sir Gawain and the Green Knight*). These rules—evident in such medieval institutions as warfare, the hunt, the joust, single combat, and juridical situations (trial by ordeal, trial by battle)—govern the times and places at which violence can occur, the individuals who can participate, and the means by which violence may be applied. The *Morte Darthur* does not deviate significantly from other romances in this regard. Physical violence provides the foundation for an elaborate structure of exchange that determines sociopolitical hierarchies among men; it functions as a form of what anthropologist Pierre Bourdieu refers to as symbolic capital, a system of social exchange in which such intangibles as prestige, status, social control, and (in this case) violence serve as institutionalized (if unspoken) means of acquiring economic wealth and social power.[12] In such a system, violence serves to stabilize the social order represented by Arthur and the Round Table, an idealized social order—a body politic—whose purpose is to represent an emergent monarchical centralization.

Viewed from a different perspective, however, from the fourth position in our Greimas square, violence in the *Morte Darthur* frequently escapes these authoritative discourses of containment and creates a perverse kind of carnival in which the official goals of violence are subverted by the many competing voices of anarchy. Such moments are figured by the archaic imago of the fragmented body, including representations of castration, mutilation, dismemberment, dislocation, and the bursting open of the body. Critics have argued that such representations of arbitrary violence in the *Morte Darthur* reflect the cultural and political upheavals in England during the Wars of the Roses.[13] This reading has some merit, but it misses the extent to which such social anarchy is not exceptional to the social order of chivalry, a function of civil rebellion, but endemic to it, its "anamorphotic" blot. The foundation of a social order on the exchange of violence creates the very chaos it is designed to hold at bay. Whatever its immediate cause, the *Morte Darthur* represents violence not only as a centripetal force encouraging order, hierarchy, and political centralization, but also as a centrifugal force that creates disorder, contention, and sometimes unbearable chaos. It recognizes both violence's potential for carnivalesque disruption as well as the possibility that this potential may be co-opted and used to foster social control.[14] The maintenance of the imaginary symbolic equivalent requires the continued circulation of the very acts of violence that constitute it. Within the *Morte Darthur*, then, violence becomes a vicious oscillation, required to establish the rule of the monarch—even in his absence—and yet, in its carnivalesque excesses, destructive of centralized control of any kind.

We might explore this oscillation in more detail by turning to Malory's version of the quest for the Holy Grail. It seems to us no accident that the many "noble and dyuers gentylmen" who came to Caxton requested not only the story of King Arthur but "the noble hystorye of the Sayntgreal" as well (Malory, *Caxton's Malory*, 1:1). Of all the many well-known episodes in the Arthurian corpus, the only one they ask for specifically by name is the history of the Holy Grail. What kinds of cultural agendas might have been served by such a request? The medieval political formulation of the body politic as the synthesis of the King's Two Bodies derives its force from religious images of the Eucharist—literally the body of Christ, which is both mortal (it suffers death) and immortal. Christ is both mortal and immortal because he unites human and divine in one body, the "word made flesh." Malory's Grail story uses this religious mythology to create secular legitimacy for his notion of an idealized body politic. The theory of the King's Two Bodies substitutes for divinity a notion of a corporate body of the state that is vested in the individual (the king) but transcends any individual monarch's mortality. Malory's retelling of the Grail story locates the pristine body politic literally in the inviolable and unchanging body of his perfect Grail knight, Galahad.

Galahad is always already a knight. He arrives at Arthur's court armored ("in reed armes," Malory, *Caxton's Malory*, 1:430), and there is a place waiting for him at the Round Table. At first little distinguishes Galahad from the great knights—like his father, Lancelot, or Gareth—who have preceded him. Before Galahad appears at Arthur's court, the community of the Round Table has established a mythology of masculinity that deploys the image of the knight as uncorrupted and incorruptible, an impenetrable male body.[15] Fantasies of armor and martial prowess imagine the great knight protected, impervious to bodily harm. In fact, that which makes a knight is the armor, which becomes a reification of the political theory of the King's Two Bodies. The vulnerable and corruptible human body is encased in a second body that is invulnerable to penetration and durable enough to be passed from father to son, generation to generation.

Galahad is the apotheosis of this fantasy. In him, the two bodies merge so that he perfectly realizes the ideal body of medieval political theory. There is nothing arbitrary about Galahad's role as preeminent Grail knight. He is known as "THE BEST KNYGHT OF THE WORLD" (Malory, *Caxton's Malory*, 1:429)—an identification repeated throughout the Grail quest narrative—even before he has made his entrance into the arena of chivalric contestation. The predictors of Galahad's success reside within his somewhat imprecise genealogical history; his familial associations are traced, variously, as "of kynges lygnage and of the kynrede of Ioseph of Arimathye" (1:430); "of alle partyes come of the best knyghtes of the world and of the hyhest lygnage. For Sir Launcelot [Galahad's father] is come but of the viii degre from oure Lord Ihesu Cryst, and Syre Galahalt is of the nynthe degree from oure Lorde Ihesu Cryst" (1:432). The slippage here is interesting. While the first reference notes the Arthurian tradition of Galahad's descent from Joseph of Arimathea (see chapter 5), the second reference substitutes Christ for Joseph as the originary ancestor, despite an apocryphal tradition that specifies only an imprecise kinship link between Joseph and Christ. The Grail story raises the stakes for Galahad. It is not enough that he be descended from a holy man, a prophet, and a saint. Galahad's ancestral relationship to Jesus Christ points directly to his role as the messianic bearer of the king's two bodies.

What most distinguishes Galahad from his fellow knights is his militant virginity. As Martin Shichtman notes, "Galahad's virginity is not of the 'just say no' variety. It is an ostentatious, aggressive virginity that leaves ideological marks—and in this sense might even be described as phallic—on all who are touched by the knight, including readers of the quest narrative" ("Percival's Sister," 13–14). Whereas armor may protect Arthur's Round Table knights from martial violence, it fails to defend against other sorts of physical defilement ordinary mortals suffer—such as erotic desire. Even Arthur's best knight, Lancelot, is susceptible to various temptations of the flesh, which undermine his perfection. However, unlike the other knights—even Perceval—Galahad is never able to step out of his armor. Because his physical body and his armor are in a sense one and the same, Galahad's untroubled virginity becomes an emblem of his perfection. His virginity is phallic because ideologically he penetrates the body politic, shifting the meaning of knighthood, of what makes a good knight, a good citizen, and perhaps even a good king in Arthurian society. We have argued elsewhere that there are largely two trajectories for knights. They can either remain knights-errant, involved in martial adventures, most often in the service of a lady, or they marry and take upon themselves the bureaucratic obligations of kingship (Finke and Shichtman, 124–25). Galahad offers a third trajectory, which eschews the company of women and insists that both martial service and kingship advance a salvation theology. Once the Knights of the Round Table determine to set out in quest of the Holy Grail, this ideological shift in the meaning of chivalry is signaled by a message—brought, significantly enough, by "an olde knyght comen emonge them in relygyous clothyng," a knight who has renounced secular chivalry and taken up chivalry in the service of the Lord—from the hermit, Nacien: "that none in this queste lede lady nor gentylwoman with hym, for hit is not to do in so hyghe a seruyse as they labour in. For I warne you playne, he that is not clene of his synnes, he shal not see the mysteryes of oure Lorde Ihesu Cryste" (Malory, *Caxton's Malory,* 1:433). The obsession with fleshly purity associates questing knights with the object they seek, their new, substituted object of their desire, the emblem of the Eucharist, "the mysteryes of oure Lorde Ihesu Cryste"'s pure inviolate body, the Holy Grail.

At first glance the Grail quest may seem only slightly less preposterous than previous knightly quests involving, for instance, the search for a damsel's brachet. Amidst special effects that include the cracking of thunder, a beam of sunlight "more clerer by seuen tymes than euer they sawe daye," and the grace of the Holy Ghost, whatever that may mean, Arthur and his knights are granted a very limited vision of the Grail.

> Thenne ther entered into the halle the Holy Graile couerd with whyte samyte, but ther was none myghte see hit nor who bare hit. And there was al the halle fulfylled with good odoures, and euery knyght had suche metes an drynkes as he beste loued in this world. And whan the Holy Grayle had be borne thurgh the halle, thenne the Holy Vessel departed sodenly that they wyste not where hit becam. (1:432)

What seems preposterous in this vision is that despite all the pyrotechnics, the Grail delivers little more than sweet smells and a good home-cooked meal. In fact, those present do not actually get to see the Grail, "ther was none myghte see hit nor who bare hit." Instead what they see resembles nothing so much as the accouterments of the Mass—the chalice and patent covered by a cloth, the central symbols of the Mass that represent the miracle of transubstantiation. (In the Middle Ages the central moment of the Mass—the sacring—was hidden from the congregants behind an alter screen so this moment may have been more revealing than it at first appears.) The Grail has long been associated in Christian tradition with the Eucharist, the "body of Christ." It also functions as a political symbol that links the Eucharist with an emerging notion of corporate political sovereignty, offering the only kind of legitimation that counted in fifteenth-century England. Patricia Ingham suggests an intriguing political connection between the Grail and the increasingly mystical coronation rituals of fifteenth-century English kings, including a coronation Mass in which the newly crowned king received communion under both species—wine and wafer—a privilege usually reserved only for priests (*Sovereign Fantasies*, 217–18). She also notes that during the highest mysteries of these rituals the sovereign was also shielded from view by a white silk screen. "Sovereign sacramental moments figure as holy of holies, a spectacle visible only through its invisibility as a hidden and mysterious transaction" (218).

Both Grail vision and coronation ritual evince a similar dynamic that oscillates between spectacle and concealment, a strategy that may be designed to heighten the ineffability of the rituals but which may also compensate for their emptiness. The coronation rituals Ingham describes cover over the instability of the British monarchy during the fifteenth century, the fact that, in forty years, the crown changes hands six times (192). And Felicity Riddy has noted "the haunting possibility of the Sankgreal—that the Grail may yield no meaning beyond itself, that at the heart of light there is only silence—lurks beneath the surface of the book's orthodoxies" (*Sir Thomas Malory*, 138). The Grail functions as a complex symbol holding together the signifying structure of the imagined community (of the nation). It promises to synthesize the mutable and immutable human body, so that viewed from one perspective it may offer itself up as a sign of ineffable transcendence, an assurance of the continuity of the body politic. But shadowing these significations is the fourth term in our Greimas square, the "negative complex term," that we read as "dismemberment." The Grail as a symbol for the imagined community is also the "anamorphotic" blot that remains outside of symbolization ("ther was none myghte see hit") and that "persists as a surplus and returns through all attempts to domesticate it." The Grail destroys the very structures it seems designed to organize, bringing about the dismemberment of both human bodies and ultimately the body politic.

At the very heart of the mystery of the Eucharist is the belief that transcendence of human frailty can only be achieved through the transmutation of the holy body into a relic—the apportioning of the tortured body of the savior into wafer and wine. The deconstructive possibilities of the Eucharistic motifs used to support the agendas of the political community become startlingly clear in the somewhat lurid story of Perceval's sister, which occurs about two thirds of the way through the Grail quest. After Perceval's sister, who shares Galahad's aggressively militant virginity, has joined the company of the three primary questing knights—Galahad, Perceval, and Bors—the group arrives at a castle where they are accosted by a party of knights and a woman carrying a silver dish. They are apprised of a strange custom: "Ther is in this castel a gentylwoman . . . Soo hit befelle many yeres agone there fylle vpon her a maladye, and whanne she had layne a grete whyle she felle vnto a mesel, and no leche she coude haue no remedy. But at the last an old man sayd, and she myght haue a dysshe ful of blood of a mayde and a clene vyrgyn in wylle and in werke, and a kynges doughter, that blood shold be her hele, and for to anoynte her withalle" (Malory, *Caxton's Malory*, 1:492). Sixty maidens, they later discover, have already given their lives unsuccessfully to the custom of the castle, among them twelve king's daughters. Galahad, Perceval, and Bors want to resist the gruesome custom, even if it means all-out war, but Perceval's sister agrees to the bloodletting. Her Eucharistic gesture—the mutilation of her body—is supposed to result in healing. By allowing herself to be bled to death, Perceval's sister argues, she will bring honor to her family, safe passage for her companions, and, through the healing of the castle's lady, the restoration of its body politic. However, despite its Eucharistic trappings, Perceval's sister's sacrifice is an utterly pointless gesture. As soon as the knights depart the castle with her body, the castle and its occupants are obliterated by a sudden "tempeste and a thonder, layte, and rayne, as alle the erthe wold haue broken; soo half the castel torned vpsoo-doune" (1:493). The religious mythologies that transform a living girl into a collection of relics (Galahad's scabbard is woven from her hair) and a shrine (the knights launch her in a boat in which she will aimlessly float until she turns up in Sarras at the end) point toward a promise of transcendent community; in fact the reliquization of Perceval's sister leads directly to dissolution and destruction, prefiguring the destructive forces that continually haunt the Grail quest.

Instances of dismemberment, of violence directed toward human bodies, are legion throughout the quest for the Grail, as indeed they are throughout the *Morte Darthur*. But while the structured violence that precedes the Grail quest (with some important exceptions) serves to create and expand the political community of the Round Table, during the Grail quest this violence turns inward against the members of the body politic itself.[16] The Arthurian court is fragmented as its members suffer the violence of the quest prophesied by Nacien the hermit in his exegesis of the allegory of the bulls: "they were tho whiche at Pentecost atte the hyhe feest took vpon hem to goo in the quest of the Sancgreal. Withoute confession they myghte not entre in the medowe of humylyte and pacyence, and therefor they retorned into waste countreyes: that sygnefyeth dethe, for there shalle dye many off them. Eueryche of them shalle slee other for synne, and they that shalle escape shalle be soo lene that hit shall be merueylle to see them" (Malory, *Caxton's Malory*, 1:467).

The senseless slaughter of so many of Arthur's knights cannot fail to have serious consequences for the political community, something that Arthur seems to intuit even before the quest begins. Once Gawain has made the oath to seek the Grail—"I shalle hold me oute a twelumoneth and a day or more yf nede be, and neuer shalle I retorne ageyne vnto the courte tylle I haue sene hit more openly than it hath ben sene here" (1:432)—and most of the fellowship of the Round Table have followed him, Arthur laments:

> Allas, said Kynge Arthur vnto Sir Gawayn, ye haue nyghe slayne me with the auow and promesse that ye haue made, for thorugh you ye haue berafte me the fayrest felaushyp and the truest of knyghthode that euer were sene togyders in ony royalme of the world. For whan they departe frome hens I am sure they alle shal neuer mete more in thys worlde, for they shal dye many in the quest. And so it forthynketh me a lytel, for I haue loued them as wel as my lyf, wherfore hit shal greue me ryght sore, the departycyon of thys felaushyp, for I haue had an olde custome to haue hem in my felaushyp. (1:433)

Galahad's achievement of the Grail creates a moment of individual transcendence for the three successful Grail knights; it even allows for the creation of a kind of holy state in Sarras during Galahad's lifetime. But Galahad's virginity means that there is no one to take on the governing of the state when he dies, and Malory says nothing of the fate of Sarras after Galahad's death. His interest lies in the effects of the Grail quest on Arthur's realm—Britain. The dismemberment ("departycyon") of the fellowship of the Round Table, which Arthur imagines as a face-to-face community ("I haue had an olde custome to haue hem in my felaushyp"), precedes by only a small while the destruction of Arthur's polity as the violence that was once directed outward toward consolidation and expansion of the community of the realm is turned inward on the body politic.

This violence turned inward on the state, this sense of failure and loss, was the experience of fifteenth-century Englishmen, including the "dyuers gentylmen" who commissioned Caxton's book. Caxton's Malory offers, on the one hand, the "'fetishism,' of gold, of the phallus, of the king" (Goux, *Symbolic Economies*, 33). As the privileged, excluded, and imaginary bearer of value, Arthur presides over and gives coherence to the representations of violence, sexuality, and capital (wealth) within the narrative. His story, told in a language now standardized by the printed book, gives form to a newly realized sense of England as a nation. Amidst the political turmoil of fifteenth-century England, Caxton's Malory offers the stability of a powerful imagined monarch leading a cohesive imagined nation. Through the technology of the printing press, this vision was disseminated not only to those in authority, those of sufficient capital, both real and symbolic, to play the role of patron, but to a wider community of the less privileged. Caxton allowed his patrons the opportunity to claim their present status as the legacy of a glorious past, to validate their own privilege, while at the same time suggesting to a new audience of book purchasers that they also, as English men and women, possessed a magnificent and unifying heritage. But another fantasy also lurks within Caxton's Malory, the fantasy of a king's death and the dismemberment of the body politic. Caxton's "dyuers gentylmen" no doubt also desired this nightmare, this haunting narrative of disunity, disintegration, and despair that so resembled the world in which they lived. They no doubt understood that the dream and the nightmare are the same—the anamorphotic blot. In the final chapter we trace the progress of this anamorphotic blot through the nightmares of twentieth-century history.

7

Paranoid History

Nazis at the Round Table

In a 1970s brochure from the National Socialist White People's Party, found in the University of Michigan's Labadie Collection archive, there are advertisements for poster-sized pictures. Most of these posters have distinctly Nazi themes: German soldiers and pictures of Hitler; there is even a two-for-one deal, offering both a portrait of Hitler and a photograph of the door to his home. One of the posters appears, at first glance, unremarkable, resembling the kinds of pictures often gracing the walls of male teenagers—comic book drawings of heavy-metal muscle-men, and sometimes women, engaged in, preparing to engage in, or triumphantly returning from some sort of battle against a generally unspecified enemy. The National Socialist White People's Party poster portrays the profile of an armored man on horseback (see Figure 7.1). While not quite as Schwartzeneggerian in physique as the figures on some other posters, the knight is muscular, riding atop a mammoth horse that tramples the bones of those who have fallen in whatever battle he recently fought. He sits proud, magnificent, majestic, a figure from a distant past, nostalgically recollected. On the knight's shield there is a swastika, suggesting not so much his political position (could a medieval knight possibly have a modern political position?) but rather his Aryan racial heritage and identity; this "coat of arms," the National Socialist White People's Party would have us believe, places the knight among world conquerors, uncorrupted and incorruptible, *übermenschen*. The poster's caption reads "Victory and defeat lie in God's hands—but we are the masters of our honor." This poster is copied from a woodcut that originally appeared in *Die Kunst im Dritten Reich* (*Art in the Third Reich*), described by Anthony Rhodes as the "most elaborate" of the

Fig. 7.1. Knight with Swastika. Labadie Collection, University of Michigan Library.

Fig. 7.2. Knight with Swastika. From *Die Kunst im Dritten Reich* (*Art in the Third Reich*).

Fig. 7.3. The Flagbearer. Hubert Lanzinger. Courtesy of the National Museum of the U.S. Army.

art journals produced by the Nazi regime, "beautifully laid out, with paper and color plates of the highest quality" (Rhodes, 25; see Figure 7.2). It recalls Nazi artist Hubert Lanzinger's painting, "The Flagbearer," in which the Führer, likewise in profile, armored and on horseback, holds the large swastika flag of the Third Reich (Figure 7.3). How necessary is it for the swastika actually to be pictured in order that the knight function as a player in fascist fantasy?

Some might argue that when alienated white male teenagers with Nazi sympathies fantasize themselves in knightly dress, they debase a beautiful, noble, and innocent past—just as they would argue that Lanzinger debased that past in his painting. They might insist that this fantasy, which feeds a desire to see the male body as larger than life, this fetishizing of the body as armor and muscle, may be perverse, but the ideal—the chivalrous knight who pledged himself to honor, loyalty, and brotherhood—should not be tarnished by that perversion. This chapter, however, explores the possibility that there is, in all imaginings of the knight, always the potential for fascist desire.[1] It suggests that there may be an unsavory kinship between the armored warriors of medieval Europe—even the romanticized armored warriors of King Arthur's court—and the armored divisions of Nazi blitzkrieg. A fascist aesthetic is the darkness at the heart of Arthurian history, especially as it celebrates aggressive hypermasculinity mobilized in the service of a persecuting society intent upon world conquest.

In "Fascinating Fascism," chapter 3 of *Under the Sign of Saturn*, Susan Sontag argues that a "fascist aesthetic" flows from and justifies

> situations of control, submissive behavior, extravagant effort, and the endurance of pain; [it] endorse[s] two seemingly opposite states, egomania and servitude. The relations of domination and enslavement take the form of characteristic pageantry: the massing of groups of people; the turning of people into things; the multiplication or replication of things; the grouping of people/things around an all-powerful, hypnotic leader-figure or force. The fascist dramaturgy centers on the orgiastic transactions between mighty forces and their puppets, uniformly garbed and shown in ever swelling numbers. Its choreography alternates between ceaseless motion and a congealed, static, "virile" posing. Fascist art glorifies surrender, it exalts mindlessness, it glamorizes death. (91)

Such an aesthetic is ahistorical, Sontag argues, and by no means confined to the politics of the radical right. It can be found, for instance, in Walt Disney's *Fantasia*, Busby Berkley's *The Gang's All Here*, and Stanley Kubrick's *2001* (91), as well as in movements as diverse as "youth/rock culture, primal therapy, anti-psychiatry, Third World camp-following, and the belief in the occult" (96). Furthermore, "features of fascist art proliferate in the official art of communist countries.... The tastes for the monumental and for mass obeisance to the hero are common to both fascist and communist art, reflecting the view of all totalitarian regimes that art has the function of 'immortalizing' its leaders and doctrines" (91). The attraction of the "fascist aesthetic" resides in its idealism: "the ideal of life as art, the cult of beauty, the fetishism of courage, the dissolution of alienation in ecstatic feelings of community; the repudiation of the intellect; the family of man (under the parenthood of leaders)" (96). Although obviously medieval knights could not possibly have conceived of themselves as fascists, they embraced an aesthetic that would later be adopted and, arguably, perfected by totalitarian regimes of the twentieth century. It should, therefore, come as no surprise that Nazis would find points of identification in medieval chivalry.

The patronage of Arthurian history, as we argued in chapter 3, reached its zenith during the aristocratic diaspora of the twelfth and thirteenth centuries—the age of the great Crusades— when the aristocracy of western Europe embarked on a period of conquest and domination (see pp. 94–102). Though events like the Norman Conquest or the Crusades perhaps lacked the singularity of purpose that characterized Nazi expansionism (such singularity of purpose was perhaps, for reasons we argue in that chapter, not possible), they attest to the sometimes fanatical militarism of the High Middle Ages. This period, not surprisingly since it was a period in which political boundaries were changing, was also marked, as R. I. Moore and John Boswell have both noted, by a growing intolerance and even persecution of those who lay outside of the dominant hegemony. While Boswell documents growing state and church persecution of same-sex love, Moore explores the creation of the "persecuting society" in the High Middle Ages' treatment of heretics, lepers, and Jews. The literature of chivalry, patronized by the same aristocracy that was so intent on expanding its territories, could not have glorified the knight as the agent of official state and church persecution. It had to displace that persecution into fantasy. King Arthur could hardly achieve heroic stature by riding around the countryside dispatching bands of peasants, lepers, and Jews. As the representative of the forces of order and religion, Arthur must triumph over more menacing and hence more prestigious foes, as, for instance, when he defeats the Mont-Saint-Michel giant on his way to conquer Rome (see above, pp. 97–99). The events that Arthurian histories displace into such glorious exploits were much more mundane—and considerably more horrific. They included the persecution and massacre of defenseless heretics, lepers, Jews, sodomites, and anyone else who for whatever reason threatened the political security of the ruling classes or held possessions desired by them (Moore). We have argued in previous chapters that medieval aristocrats used the genealogies provided by historical narratives of King Arthur to justify and promote their own, often oppressive, exercise of power. The narratives of twentieth-century fascists similarly serve as markers of genealogical transmission and legitimation.

The writings of post–World War I Germany's ultraright point to this possibility. Erich Edwin Dwinger's memoir, *Die letzten Reiter* (*The Last Horsemen*), rhapsodizes, for instance, on the significance of the Freikorps, right-wing paramilitary groups that arose in Germany following its defeat in the First World War: "One last time the old days rose again with us; they rose again in three senses! In the military sense first; . . . One last time we fought as true cavalrymen, raising a scarcely remembered weapon, a lance of old, to gleam again. Second, in a material sense: one last time we lived in wide open spaces, spending many of our days with men who called princely estates their own. But the space was taken from us and the Baltic princes fell.... Third, in the spiritual sense: one last time each of us could be individual, with nothing to constrain his spirit" (Theweleit, 2:63–64). Dwinger, reading his text on several symbolic levels with the fervor of a medieval exegete, suggests that Freikorps "history" is not so much a perversion of the Middle Ages but rather a successor narrative, a continuation of the impulse to romanticize history in order to legitimate—and even glorify—masculine aggression marshaled in the service of state-sanctioned violence. Dwinger laments the "end of chivalrous soldiery" displaced by modernity, by the ascendancy of the masses "rolling toward us from East and West" (Theweleit, 2:64).

We might simply dismiss Dwinger's fascination with the antique past as an adolescent nostalgia for what never was, as Klaus Theweleit seems to do in *Male Fantasies:* "Not one of the qualities apostrophized by Dwinger in his story of 'one last time' has ever pertained to these men. Not the knight's lance, nor the prince's table, nor the broad 'territory of the world' has ever been theirs—nor, indeed, has the 'boundlessness of the individual spirit' (whatever that may be).... The only reality expressed here is that of the youthful dreams of the youth movement's boyish romanticism, ... their dreams of world conquest, fantasies of nobility and King Arthur's roundtable" (2:64). *Die letzten Reiter* offers, however, more than simple nostalgia. If the recollection of an idealized past brought comfort to those for whom the present held dangers and insecurities, it also held out the prospect of mobilizing fascist desire. Dwinger deploys the figure of the chivalric warrior in both his defensive and aggressive postures. For Dwinger, and his Freikorps associates, the knight stands protected from—above—a world reckoned as having spun seriously out of control, a world in which Germany has lost a major war, has been severely punished, humiliated by its conquerors, and has been betrayed both by bureaucratic profiteers—bankers and industrialists—and the masses, vulgar and easily manipulated by greed and self-interest. But the knight also stands prepared to reclaim, by force, all that is rightfully his, his inheritance; he is prepared to recapture all that belonged to him and his kind in "the old days," prepared to bring about the restoration of a time when men of chivalric orders ruled without question. Dwinger's knight is armored and armed, determined to repel the conquerors, crush the profiteers, and lead the masses in the direction of righteousness; he is Germany's salvation.

There can be little doubt that Arthurian histories played some part in the Third Reich's efforts to romanticize—perhaps even mythologize—itself. But it is difficult to determine whether those who fashioned the Third Reich genuinely believed themselves inheritors of knightly chivalric tradition or cynically invoked this tradition because it easily functioned to advance an ideology of conquest and hatred. A number of historians have attempted to force this differentiation—to determine whether Nazism transformed idealism into propaganda or was simply unable to distinguish between idealism and propaganda—and have found themselves uneasily positioned, reading Nazis as Nazis sought to read themselves (see Höhne, 153–55). For these historians—as with those who research the chivalric codes of America's Old South—there lurks a fascination with the efforts of sometimes monstrous men to reproduce an antique past we have idealized. However, we believe that this differentiation may be beside the point, that the figure of the knight is continuously at the heart of fascist desire because something akin to fascist desire was continuously at the heart of the figure of the knight, that there is a link between the organized, armed masculine aggression of the Middle Ages and organized, armed masculine aggression in the twentieth century.

We read, for instance, in Heinz Höhne's *The Order of the Death's Head*, of Heinrich Himmler's attraction to things Arthurian. Himmler, who had been a member of the Freikorps, was no doubt indoctrinated into its ideology, no doubt dreamed the same dreams as those recalled by Dwinger. But Himmler's embrace of the Middle Ages draws its strength from specificity rather than from Dwinger's generalized affection for the "old days." Himmler, as Höhne tells it, had a very particular agenda: he "had learnt that King Arthur had assembled about the Round Table his twelve bravest and noble knights, with whom he defended the Celtic creed and liberties against the invading Anglo-Saxons. Here was clearly a lesson for the SS. The tale of King Arthur must have impressed Himmler, for he never allowed more than twelve guests to sit at his table. And as King Arthur had chosen his bravest twelve, so Himmler appointed his twelve best Obergruppenführer to be the senior dignitaries of his Order" (151). Similarly, in Wewelsburg Castle, Himmler's headquarters—which Höhne calls his Camelot—"the chosen few would assemble around the Reichsführer's oaken table in a 100-foot by 145-foot dining hall, sitting in high-backed pig skin chairs, each carrying the name of its owner knight inscribed on a silver plate" (152). Höhne writes: "Contact with the past was supposed to instill into the SS Order the realisation that they were members of a select band, to lay the foundations of historical determinism, marking out the SS man as the latest scion of a long line of Germanic nobility. Himmler's 'basic features of the SS' laid down that the SS was on the march 'in accordance with immutable laws as a National Socialist Order of men of the Nordic stamp and as the oath-bound community of their clans'; it continued: 'We would wish to be not only the men who fought of old, but the forebears of later generations essential to ensure the external existence of the Germanic people of Germany'" (154). For Höhne, Himmler seems to straddle the fine line between a magnificent madness, imagining himself King Arthur surrounded by a knightly corps of SS commanders, and brilliance, devising an extraordinary propaganda device that allowed for both the historicization and romanticization of the SS—a propaganda device that located the SS's origin in the chivalric Middle Ages. Höhne's narrative argues that Himmler understood knighthood as an institution both located in the antique past and transcendent of historical period—knights could just as well exist in postdepression Germany as they did during the twelfth century. This construction of the knight connects the SS to the medieval past and projects it into the future. Himmler's fashioning of the knight therefore places this figure at the center of fascist ideology, embodying those qualities that differentiate the select few, the military elite, from all others, the masses. Like the knight, the SS man functions as the elite apparatus by which high culture is determined and transmitted. Theweleit writes: "The man of culture is defined as the man who knows the difference between first-lieutenant, major, and captain; a barbarian is a man who feels no love either for uniforms or death. And the 'highest' form of cultural celebration is war" (2:63). Himmler's SS officer saw himself as not only carrying on the tradition of knighthood, but also representing an evolutionary leap forward—with an eye toward the next soldierly paradigm.

Hitler's sentiments regarding the institutions of knighthood, at least as they are reported by one-time confidante Hermann Rauschning, echo Höhne's description of Himmler. Hitler's appropriation of the Middle Ages, however, supplements Himmler's, marshaling medieval images of knighthood as a means of legitimating genocide. Rauschning reports one conversation in which Hitler muses on the arguments of Joseph Arthur, comte de Gobineau, a racial "scientist" whose *Essay on the Inequality of the Human Races* (1853–55) predicted that racial mixing—and therefore racial decay—was inevitable. According to Rauschning, Hitler remarked: "How can we arrest racial decay? . . . are we to allow the masses to go their way, or should we stop them? Shall we form simply a select company of the really initiated? An Order, the brotherhood of Templars round the holy grail of pure blood?" (229).[2] The contradictions implicit in this invocation of the Knights Templar and the Holy Grail by an erstwhile unemployed postcard painting, flop-house dwelling, beer hall brawling corporal in a defeated army are smoothed over by Hitler's rereading of Gobineau and racial science. The images of cultural power conjured up by Hitler's references to the Grail and the Knights Templar do not speak to his or his audience's experiences; they are alien and tantalizing. He addresses not aristocrats seeking to confirm their privilege, but those who perceive themselves as modernity's victims, whose conception of the future has been shattered by political and economic hardship. In place of the hard lessons of war and depression, Hitler offers a fantasy in which a dispossessed underclass could fashion itself as a new aristocracy, tracing its roots back to an old medieval aristocracy not through the patrilineage we describe in previous chapters but through the affinity of blood, through the doctrines of a racial science simultaneously mythologized and historicized.

Hitler's reading of the Middle Ages is mediated by Richard Wagner, whose music drama, *Parsifal*, is the subject of the Führer's lecture. Like Wagner, Hitler transforms Arthurian romance into an originary historical moment. In *A Communication to My Friends*, Wagner writes: "My studies thus bore me, through the legends of the Middle Ages, right down to their foundation in the old-Germanic Mythos; one swathing after another, which the later legendary lore had bound around it, I was able to unloose, and thus at last to gaze upon its chastest beauty. What here I saw, was no longer the Figure of conventional history, whose garment claims our interest more than does the actual shape inside; but the real naked Man . . . the *true human being*" (1:358). Seeking "chastest beauty," Wagner must move beyond romance, "the later legendary lore," to find "the old-Germanic Mythos." He is not interested in "conventional history"—the studies that bore him—but rather the Truth, origin, "the real naked Man." For Wagner, *Parsifal* embraces history only to transcend it; the music drama looks to the past to find "the *true human being*."

Hitler mythologizes and historicizes his understanding of race through an exegetical reading of *Parsifal*, which he understands as a historical rendering of the Middle Ages. Hitler, at least as Rauschning reports it, maintains that a fascist reading of the text, like Wagner's, would be a historical one that would strip it "of every poetic element," to reveal the truth concealed from the uninitiated: that "a world-wide process of segregation is going on before our eyes" (230).

> We must interpret 'Parsifal' in a totally different way to the general conception, . . . Behind the absurd externals of the story, with its

Christian embroidery and its Good Friday mystification, something altogether different is revealed as the true content of this most profound drama. It is not the Christian-Schopenhauerist religion of compassion that is acclaimed, but pure, noble blood, in the protection and glorification of whose purity the brotherhood of the initiated have come together. The king is suffering from the incurable ailment of corrupted blood. The uninitiated but pure man is tempted to abandon himself in Klingsor's magic garden to the lusts and excesses of corrupt civilization, instead of joining the elite of knights who guard the secret of life, of pure blood. All of us are suffering from the ailment of mixed, corrupted blood. How can we purify ourselves and make atonement? (229–30)

Like Wagner, Hitler does not conceive of Arthurian romance as mere fiction. But whereas Wagner may have only suggested, as Martin Shichtman argues, that *Parsifal* is "about a purging of impurities and a return to the happier spiritual days of the past, not only for those who live in the Grail kingdom but also for those in nineteenth-century Germany" (Shichtman, "Wagner and the Arthurian Tradition," 142), Hitler's interpretation is more overt; he insists that the poetic fiction conceals actual historical truths about racial struggle. In this sense he performs a medieval reading of medieval history, an exercise in *allegoresis*. For Hitler, as for the medieval historian, empirical reality is beside the point. What is important is the manner in which history moves—and moves its readers—toward a transcendental objective (see chapter 1). Of course, Hitler's transcendental real was not, as it was for Augustine, *caritas*—divine love—but rather the "pure noble blood" of the Aryan race.

Rauschning's Hitler offers a Grail fantasy as a corrective to Nazi anxieties about "racial" contamination, about the corruption of "pure" blood lines. According to Hitler's interpretation of the Grail legend, Anfortas is suffering from an "incurable ailment," "corrupted blood"; indeed, all endure "the ailment of mixed, corrupted blood." Klingsor's magic garden reproduces, as the Führer tells it, the modern world's "lusts and excesses of corrupt civilization." In opposition to the contaminated, Hitler places his brotherhood of Grail knights. Only by correctly interpreting the old narratives and following the canons of behavior set down by the aristocracy of the antique past can twentieth-century Aryans create a new paradigm to counter the decadence of modernity: "The eternal life granted by the grail is only for the truly pure and noble! . . . Only a new nobility can introduce the new civilisation to us. . . . Those who see in the struggle the meaning of life, gradually mount the steps of a new nobility. Those who are in search of peace and order through dependence, sink, whatever their origin, to the inert masses. The masses, however, are doomed to decay and self-destruction" (Rauschning, 229–30). The redundancy in Hitler's discourse points, dramatically, we think, to the obsessiveness of his program to promote a new kind of man, an elite warrior, "a select company of the really initiated," "a new nobility."

Hitler speaks of "pure, noble blood, in the protection and glorification of whose purity the brotherhood of the initiated have come together." Purification must come, Hitler tells us, from "selection," "segregation," "leaving the sick person to die" (230). Can there be any doubt here about the identity of the impure to whom Hitler refers? The language used to separate the elect from the diseased is precisely the language the Nazis used to differentiate those who would live and those bound for the gas chambers. A 1926 speech by Julius Streicher, editor of the *Sturmer*, an early, anti-Semitic, pro-Nazi newspaper, isolates the source of the pollution about which Hitler speaks: "There are three types of parasitic Jews. You will be familiar with the first type: their home is the bank, from whence they practice their economic extortions on their host nations. The second variety is equally widely known. These are the Jews one invariably sees sitting with blonde German girls in bars and cafes, sapping the sexual and racial strength of their host people and destroying them. But there is also a third type of Jew—the kind who quite literally sap the blood of Gentiles and their children. They do so not for religious reasons, but because their own chaotic blood is in danger of decomposition; it is only in sucking the blood of other peoples that they can preserve their own life" (Theweleit, 2:9–12). In this speech Jews are portrayed as vampires who survive by contaminating others—economically, sexually, and racially. They are a disease that infects their host.[3] Hitler, according to Rauschning's recollection, fantasizes about a new Grail knight who will purge such pollution from the system of the state; he will cleanse the organism.

How much different is this Nazi knight from his medieval counterpart? The introduction of the Holy Grail into Rauschning's eyewitness account reminds readers of medieval literature that romances such as Chrétien de Troyes's *Conte du Graal,* Wolfram von Eschenbach's *Parzival,* and the *Queste del Saint Graal* contain numerous references to Jewish responsibility for the Crucifixion of Christ. While these references seem largely gratuitous, their repetition suggests that the authors of these texts were not only unreflectively mimicking medieval church doctrine. In glorifying the values of their knightly patrons by placing Christian chivalry in opposition to Jewish collective guilt, they reinforced popular beliefs about Jewish contamination—that Jews polluted wells and caused diseases like the plague, that, vampirelike, they murdered Christian children for their blood—and advanced a political agenda in which the condemnation of an already disenfranchised minority served to reinforce the power and authority of a hypermasculine military ruling class. Norman Cohn, in fact, argues that the twelfth century brought about a significant shift in European anti-Semitism: "It was in the twelfth century that [Jews] were first accused of murdering Christian children, of torturing the consecrated wafer, and of poisoning the wells. . . . But above all it was said that Jews worshipped the Devil, who rewarded them collectively by making them masters of black magic; so that however helpless individual Jews might seem, Jewry possessed limitless powers for evil" (22).

Throughout the twelfth century—at the height of the production of both Arthurian history and romance—persecutions against Jews were carried out across Europe. Guibert of Nogent writes of the massacre at Rouen, where crusaders "herded the Jews into a certain place of worship, rounding them up either by force or by guile, and without distinction of age or sex put them to the sword" (Moore, 29). Other massacres occurred in such places as Mainz, Cologne, Trier, Metz, Bamberg, Regensburg, and Prague. In many of these cities, townspeople, at least initially, supported Jewish neighbors and assisted them in protecting property. As Moore notes, the massacres "were not the work of 'the people' but of crusading armies composed of mounted knights and led by nobles" (117–18). The massacres were the work of those who commissioned Arthurian history and romance. Like their medieval predecessors, Nazis produced their own strategies for displacing their excesses into chivalric adventures. For Dwinger, Himmler, and Hitler, knighthood promoted a genealogy of the blood and demanded the ruthless destruction of all those who posed the threat of contamination. Their notion of a knightly response to Jews—whom Hitler, even as he prepared for suicide, inveighed against as "the universal poisoner of all peoples"—and other "undesirables" included gas chambers and crematoria (Berenbaum, 191).

King Arthur and the Lunatic Fringe

While Höhne's "objective" journalism, Theweleit's cultural theory, and Rauschning's eyewitness accounts have provided the sorts of materials that have largely dominated debate among scholars concerning the Third Reich's appropriation of the medieval past (insofar as there has been any discussion at all on this matter), popular interest in the subject has been controlled by a number of pseudohistories that might well call to mind the excesses of a Geoffrey of Monmouth. Among those that consider Nazi Germany's interest in the Middle Ages are *Spear of Destiny: The Occult Power Behind the Spear which Pierced the Side of Christ* by Trevor Ravenscroft and *The Occult and the Third Reich: The Mystical Origins of Nazism and the Search for the Holy Grail* by Jean-Michel Angebert (two authors writing in collaboration, to whom, for the sake of convenience, we will refer as Angebert). We turn to these pseudohistories because, like the medieval chronicles we discussed in previous chapters, they have been widely accepted, at least within popular culture, as containing some "truth" value and because they have been successful in keeping public attention focused on the Arthurian legend. They function for twentieth-century readers much the same way Geoffrey's *Historia Regum Britanniæ* served the needs of its twelfth-century audience, supplying a myth of origin that glosses over twentieth-century anxieties about violence and political crisis.

According to Jean-Michel Angebert's *The Occult and the Third Reich*, on May 2, 1945, "a small group of select SS officers took possession of a heavy lead chest, following a short torchlit ceremony. The mysterious load now committed to their sole trust, they took the path leading to the Schleigeiss glacier at the foot of the 3000-meter-high Hochfeiler. It is there, in a ledge of snow at the precipice, that the object was buried: the Grail of Montségur, in all likelihood" (258). No one has recovered the Holy Grail since this interment, and all seekers have inexplicably suffered horrible fates, most "found horribly mutilated, as were for example, the Austrian lieutenant Franz Gottliech, the would-be 'Alpine climbers' Helmuth Mayr and Ludwig Pichler, or even decapitated, as was Emmanuel Werba in 1952" (258). Trevor Ravenscroft's *Spear of Destiny* renders the ultimate result of Adolf Hitler's acquisition of the Grail objects somewhat differently. Ravenscroft claims that, following Hitler's suicide, the American Seventh Army discovered, quite by accident, a bunker in Nuremberg's Oberen Schmied Gasse. Inside this bunker, "Resting on top of an intricately carved ten-foot-high altar, which had been looted from the historic Church of St. Mary in Krakow, Poland, stood an ancient leather case. Within the case, still resting on its faded red velvet dais, was the Spear of Longinus," the spear of the Grail (346–47).[4] Of the American occupying force, only General George S. Patton, who, Ravenscroft tells us, "had a historically oriented cast of mind, believed in reincarnation and had made a study of the search for the Holy Grail . . . realised the true significance of the fact that the USA were now the official possessors of the Spear of Destiny" (349). As Ravenscroft relates, despite Patton's objections, the government of the United States relinquished control of the relic, returning it to Austria, and "Today the Spear of Longinus is back in the Weltliche Schatzkammer of the Hofburg. The talisman of world historic destiny stands on a faded red velvet dais within an open leather case in exactly the same spot in the Treasure House where Adolph Hitler first beheld it in 1909. It is on view to the public from Monday to Saturday from 9 a.m. to 6 p.m. Admission is free" (353).

What interests us about texts like those of Angebert and Ravenscroft is the manner in which they offer to update the Arthurian narrative. They testify to the vibrancy of the Arthurian story as history even in the cynical twentieth century, to the ability of objects like King Arthur, the knight, or the Holy Grail to function as potent but empty social signifiers capable of masking even the cultural anxieties of postwar generations. These books purport to be objective histories, revealing a truth hidden from the public by various official conspiracies. Angebert blames the failure of historians to explain the "enigma" of the Third Reich on "conformist" practices, but also notes that information about the secrets of Hitler's rule has been hardly forthcoming (xv–xvi). Specifically, Angebert notes that important Nazi documents were either hidden or destroyed by Allied forces determined to suppress the truth. For a reader "tired of lies and pseudo-historical frauds," however, Angebert is willing to chance being branded sensationalist, to claim that "occult forces confront one another in the shadows, while on stage, impassive performers quietly act out an immutable drama under the very eyes of an unseeing public" (xix). Ravenscroft maintains that his book presents material so sensitive that "Sir Winston Churchill himself . . . was insistent that the occultism of the Nazi party should not under any circumstances be revealed to the general public" (xiii). Similarly, according to Ravenscroft, judges at the Nuremberg trials conspired to hide their findings about Nazi war criminals because to "have admitted even for an instant what their defeated enemies were really like, to have lifted the veil to reveal the real motives for such an astonishing reversal of values, might have opened millions of people to the risk of terrible corruption" (xiv). For Jean-Michel Angebert and Trevor Ravenscroft, writing history is a risky business.

Despite these wild claims, *The Occult and the Third Reich* and *Spear of Destiny* are handsomely produced books, filled, like Geoffrey's *Historia*, with all the trappings of scholarly exposition: prefaces, acknowledgments, footnotes, bibliographies, and indexes. They buttress their claims with an intellectual apparatus that cites *auctores* both medieval and modern: philosophers and intellectuals like Dante, Augustine, Bernard of Clairvaux, Wolfram von Eschenbach, Plato, and Plotinus; Nietzsche, Schopenhauer, Hegel, Kant, Marx, and Jung. Among the contemporary historians they cite are Hugh Trevor-Roper, Allen Bullock, Arnold Toynbee, and Norman Cohn. *The Occult and the Third Reich* received the imprimatur both of a major American publishing firm, Macmillan—also the publisher of Hugh Trevor-Roper's groundbreaking Hitler biography, *The Last Days of Hitler* (1947)—and an acknowledged scholar. Lewis A. M. Sumberg, academic, medievalist, founder and editor of the learned journal *Tristania*, both translates the book from its original French and provides a preface, in which he praises the authors' historical methods: "The present work is by two of the most resourceful, intuitive, and tenacious minds yet to approach the subject. It sees Nazism as only the most recent manifestation of a militant neo-Paganism locked in a death struggle with its arch-enemy, traditional Christianity, a struggle which will go on until the end of time. Its most recent roots go back to the Middle Ages, when the neo-Gnostic heresies, particularly Catharism, forcefully challenged the Church's spiritual authority everywhere in Europe" (Angebert, x). And yet these books' appearance in the 1970s was met with resounding silence from recognized historians. We were hard pressed to find a single review of—or even a reference to—either book in any mainstream publication of that decade. If there were any reactions to these histories in the 1970s they were circulating among marginalized small presses or through word of mouth. Yet both books have enjoyed a continuous readership: screenwriter Phil Kaufman's reading of *Spear of Destiny*, which remains in print to this day, influenced the screenplay for Steven Spielberg's 1981 *Raiders of the Lost Ark* (Pollock, 222). Both books have recently taken on a new life on the Internet among conspiracy theorists and New Age enthusiasts.

Why have historians so thoroughly neglected these two histories, not even bothering to denounce them? It seems to us that this is not merely a rhetorical question; answering it enables us to reprise many of the themes of this book. We have been concerned in our analyses of medieval histories with the slippage in historical writing between objectivity and referentiality, on the one hand, and belief and narrative, on the other; we have explored the contradictory claims of history to record "what really happened" and to create a "useable past." Presumably "serious" historians would dismiss Angebert and Ravenscroft because they fail to distinguish reality from fiction. This tension between reality and fiction, between truth claim and compelling narrative has been the subject of our study of Arthurian history. To argue that Angebert and Ravenscroft play fast and loose with their facts would be to buy into the belief that history is nothing more than a collection of facts, dates, and events that refer transparently to some preexistent reality. If Angebert and Ravenscroft fail as historians, however, it is not because they neglect facts. On the contrary, they literally overwhelm their readers with evidence: details, dates, names, events, as well as references to authorized histories. Instead, Angebert and Ravenscroft produce what Richard Hofstadter has called "higher paranoid scholarship," conspiracy theory. Such scholarship, as Daniel Pipes notes, does not ignore the facts: "[n]o less than conventional historians, [conspiracy theorists] steep themselves in the literature of their subject and become expert in it" (33).[5] In our analysis of medieval Arthurian histories, we have argued that the facts—"what really happened"—can only be formulated within a narrative logic that demands that "the facts" be organized into a coherent "story," agreeable to both writer and audience. If Angebert and Ravenscroft are to be differentiated from conventional historians—as Pipes insists conspiracy theorists must be differentiated from conventional historians—"the difference lies in their methods; rather than piece together the past through the slow accumulation of facts, they plunder legitimate historical studies to build huge edifices out of odd and unrelated elements" (33). Pipes himself assumes, however, that pseudohistorians of this ilk "build edifices," that is, construct narratives into which they, willy-nilly, stuff the facts, while responsible historians simply collect facts—painstakingly. In this he reveals his allegiance to a view of history as "the slow accumulation of facts" as if more acceptable historians do not also "build edifices."

It seems just as likely that Angebert's and Ravenscroft's accounts of the past have been ignored by historians because their narratives about the Third Reich deviate so dramatically from the narratives authorized by conventional histories. They self-consciously ignore the traditional narratives of politics, economics, and social change. Indeed, like Hitler, they contend that the truth of Nazi Germany cannot be found in the empirical reality favored by mainstream historical narratives. Angebert writes: "It seems to us that numerous interpreters of the Nazi phenomenon have erred in insisting that the occultism and astrology of this period was merely a passing fancy, a whim of some madmen. Once and for all we must stop seeing Nazism as just a political system" (191). Ravenscroft claims that historian—and Hitler biographer—Alan Bullock was simply wrong when he contended that "the shock of Germany's surrender was the decisive experience in Hitler's life. Everything with which he had identified himself had been defeated and swept away" (Ravenscroft, 96). Ravenscroft argues that Hitler's biographers have not "understood the real significance of what Hitler was reading and what lay as motive behind his choice of subjects and the books he avidly consumed" (25). In fact Ravenscroft dismisses entirely the empiricism that has dominated twentieth-century historiography. He claims that the "wealth of historical material" contained in the scholarship of his teacher, Walter Johannes Stein, had been gathered through some quite new techniques of historical research involving "the use of occult faculties and the practice of mind expansion" (xv). *The Occult and the Third Reich* and *Spear of Destiny* both dismiss conventional explanations of "the Nazi phenomenon" such as national defeat, economic depression, and endemic anti-Semitism and locate the reality of Nazism in the transcendent spiritual realm of the occult. Hitler rose to power not because he was an astute politician who could play on the fears, uncertainties, and bigotries of a defeated and impoverished Germany, but because he was controlled by supernatural powers.

In other words, the narratives these historians produce are not acceptable to historians steeped in the methods of scientific historiography and empiricism. To be understood as a history by the community of late-twentieth-century historians, narratives must be grounded in verifiable empirical reality. They are not the idiosyncratic production of historians but are produced within interpretive communities that bring together readers and writers who share particular assumptions. Ravenscroft, at least, seems to appreciate that any historical narrative can only be understood within an interpretive community, that it requires some collaboration between readers and writer. He says that his history had to wait to be told until there were readers who were equipped to recognize it as a coherent narrative; he is only willing to bring his findings forward because the publication of Aldous Huxley's *The Doors of Perception,* which "attacked the prevailing skepticism regarding the validity of occultism and the existence of higher levels of consciousness and further dimensions of time within reach of the human mind," prepared readers to experience history at the level of the "supersensible," of "transcendent consciousness" (xiv). This is where he parts company with the majority of historians who locate history at the level of the "sensible."

We do not finally care whether or not the histories written by Angebert and Ravenscroft are true; they are almost certainly, like Geoffrey of Monmouth's narrative, ludicrous. But the story they tell about how historians construct a "useable past," a past from which at least some of us would like to be descended, is compelling. What interests us is the manner in which they bring the Arthurian story—which they both insist is a matter of historical record—up-to-date, incorporating it as a template for world history. In a world in which more people believe in angels and aliens than in evolution (to paraphrase Detective Munch on the TV series "Homicide"), there are those who are convinced that Angebert and Ravenscroft have found the truth about Nazi Germany in the story of Arthur and the Holy Grail, and we would like to understand the appeal these narratives have for this group. In offering an escape from the trauma of fascism, these narratives end up reinscribing its fantasies of racial science and medieval chivalry. Both Angebert and Ravenscroft offer unsettling political agendas, which, we would like to argue, expose, in a number of ways, the fascist ideology inherent in the Arthurian legend. Despite frequent disavowals of the excesses of the Third Reich, these narratives are disturbing in the ways they nevertheless manage to dignify the Nazi quest for the Holy Grail.

Higher Paranoid Scholarship: History as Psychomachia

What distinguishes higher paranoid scholarship, according to Hofstadter, "is not that its exponents see conspiracies or plots here and there in history, but that they regard a 'vast' or 'gigantic' conspiracy as the motive force in historical events. History is a conspiracy, set in motion by demonic forces of almost transcendent power" (29). Umberto Eco, writing in *Foucault's Pendulum* about authors who turn their efforts to exposing grand conspiracies, speaks of "their extraordinary capacity for tying everything together" (219). Angebert and Ravenscroft offer to expose the conspiracies covering up the secrets surrounding the Holy Grail, conspiracies that go back nearly to the beginnings of humanity and are particularly significant to twentieth-century life because the Third Reich drew much—if not all—of its power from possession of Grail objects. It would be easy to dismiss both the authors and their admiring readers as so many conspiracy kooks and their accounts as so much fantasy, as Eco seems to do, at least initially, when he refers to conspiracy theorists as "diabolicals." To do so, however, begs the question of how paranoia and fantasy operate in the practice of conventional history. "All human knowledge," writes Jerry Aline Fleiger, "is paranoid" (26). Paranoia pushes to the extreme history's claims to truth and its desire for a coherent narrative; it is a pathological extension of a completely human need to make sense of our world. Fantasy is also a mechanism for making sense of the world. All paranoid scholarship is in some sense fantastic because it offers illusions that manage the ineptitudes and horrors of history.

It is not, in the final analysis, terribly difficult to understand the appeal of fantastic narratives like those proposed by Angebert and Ravenscroft. It has become almost a commonplace for historians of the Third Reich to apologize for the inadequacy of their narratives to comprehend their subject—especially as it relates to the Holocaust; there is always some surplus in excess of any explanation. In an interview, *Shoah* director Claude Lanzmann criticized *Schindler's List* for not being real enough, as if his eight-hour documentary could satisfactorily contain the trauma of the death camps (Rosenbaum, 253).[6] Despite all the explanations of Hitler and the Holocaust, all the recountings of the torture, terror, and murder, there remains an inert presence that resists symbolization, "a traumatic point" that "persists as a surplus and returns through all attempts to domesticate it" (Žižek, 69). Žižek calls this "real traumatic kernel" in the midst of the symbolic order variously the Real, the Thing, the blot, the symptom. This may be what Theodor Adorno meant when he said that "to write poetry after Auschwitz is barbaric," that after Auschwitz there can be no poetry (Rosenbaum, 253). It may be that after the Holocaust there can be no history either. There has been endless writing about the Holocaust, both poetry and history, all of which attempt to manage the trauma by displacing it into narrative. But whatever strategies we employ to integrate this blot into the symbolic order can never satisfy us, can never be commensurate with the trauma. Angebert and Ravenscroft offer a fantasy—in the form of history—to overcome the terrifying pain of the blot by relocating reality in a Neoplatonic and transcendent psychomachian struggle.

Neither Angebert nor Ravenscroft care about Nazism as a cultural phenomenon. They have no interest whatsoever in the political, social, or economic forces that led to the creation of the Third Reich. Both *The Occult and the Third Reich* and *Spear of Destiny* see the rise of Nazism as a psychomachia, an episode in the ongoing battle between forces of darkness and those of light. While their discussions of ancient conspiracies are impossibly complex, these texts ultimately conceptualize the world in the simplest of divisions, wherein evil wars with good for dominance. This totalizing of human history tends to push the Holocaust—as well as World War II—to the side. The mass murders of "undesirables" as well as the multitude of battles that constitute the Second World War are, for Angebert and Ravenscroft, a diversion, a sideshow to the "real" conflict associated with Hitler's rise. Angebert writes that "[r]ecalling the worldshaking crimes in which the Third Reich indulged kept us from pursuing our study further" (120). According to Ravenscroft, Hitler's decision to go ahead with the "final solution" occurred on the very same night that the Führer marched into Vienna and took possession of the Spear of Destiny (319); it is the acquisition of the spear, "a happening so potent with evil that it would cause an eruption more violent and destructive than the world had ever known" (320), that interests Ravenscroft; the Holocaust is merely a by-product of that event. Both Angebert and Ravenscroft find the "real" history of the Third Reich in the opposition of Nazi "black magic" to "white magic." Angebert claims this psychomachian confrontation took place while "Europe was altogether unaware," and the information about it offered by *The Occult and the Third Reich* functions as a corrective to "those simple minds and those practitioners of historical science who refuse, even now, to acknowledge the existence of occult forces waging war from the shadows" (162). The objective of Nazism, Ravenscroft suggests, was to mold the souls of followers "into a selfless chalice for the incorporation of demonic spirits of a high order. For Hitler's God-Men would have been none other than the legions of Lucifer, the hosts of the anti-spirit associated with the Spear of Destiny" (252). In their efforts to explain everything, Angebert and Ravenscroft, at least by the standards of traditional historiography, explain nothing. But the simplicity and the sheer excessiveness of their narratives provide the illusion of explanation, provide a fantasy that the trauma can be somehow comprehended.

Žižek writes that "The usual definition of fantasy ('an imagined scenario representing the realization of desire') is . . . somewhat misleading, or at least ambiguous: in the fantasy-scene the desire is not fulfilled, 'satisfied,' but constituted (given its objects, and so on)—through fantasy we learn 'how to desire'" (118). For Žižek, fantasy is a frame, a "window," a screen through which the desired object is simultaneously regarded and constructed. The Holy Grail is the perfect fantasy object for Angebert and Ravenscroft; its illusiveness (we do not even know what it really is) allows it to become a window through which fascism is constituted as a chivalric quest. In fact, Angebert and Ravenscroft seem to balance two separate fantasies; they appear to be looking simultaneously through two mirroring screens. On the one hand, they reconfigure the antique past, make Arthurian history relevant to the twentieth century, through the fantasy-frame of Nazi ideology, the suppositions of racial science. On the other hand, they attempt to make the incomprehensible, the horrific excesses of National Socialism, coherent through the fantasy-frame of Arthurian history.

To constitute Arthurian material as an object of desire, Angebert and Ravenscroft must reconfigure it. They must excise the "Matter of Britain." Their fantasy is not a national fantasy, not the myth of the nation Anthony Smith calls a *mythomoteur* (see chapter 4); rather it is cosmic in scope. The histories produced by Angebert and Ravenscroft are not interested in the origins of England, the origins of Europe, or even the origins of the Indo-Europeans. They explain the origins of everybody. In their hands Arthurian history loses its specific connection to the island of Britain and comes to signify the cosmos. For Angebert, Nazi history finds its origin in the legacies of the lost continent of Atlantis and the vanished master race of Hyperborea: "The mysterious continent was believed to have once existed at the site of Greenland and Iceland.... Inhabited by 'giants several meters tall,' Hyperborea was thought to be a land even more developed than Atlantis and which perhaps had been civilized by extraterrestrial beings" (64). These legacies, though somewhat corrupted, survived—and are traced in an almost incomprehensibly complex manner by *The Occult and the Third Reich*—in Druidism, Gnosticism, Zoroastrianism, Manichaeanism, Rosicrucianism, Freemasonry, Hindu mysticism, and, most importantly, Catharism (especially as it was influenced by the discoveries of the Knights Templar). They exist, complete, in the Holy Grail, "the sacred Book of the Aryans, lost and then found again, to be finally hidden at Montségur by the Cathars who were unable to decipher it" (17). Ravenscroft follows the Grail spear from Gaius Cassius—the Roman centurion Ravenscroft identifies as having kindly killed Jesus while he suffered on the cross—through, among others, Mauritius, "the Commander of the Theban Legion," Constantine the Great, Theodosius, Alaric the Bold, Aetius, "the Last of the Romans," "the mighty Visigoth Theodoric," Justinian, Karl "the Hammer" Martel, Charlemagne, Heinrich I, "The Fowler," Otto the Great, Frederick Barbarossa, and Frederick II. In all, Ravenscroft claims that "forty-five Emperors had claimed the Spear of Destiny as their possession between the coronation in Rome of Charlemagne and the fall of the old German Empire exactly a thousand years later" (16–

17). Ravenscroft suggests, however, that Hitler acquired special powers to activate the Spear of Destiny through his knowledge of The Secret Doctrine, "a new religion which sought to bring every facet of life into relationship with the divine universal order of the world" (244), originally formulated on the lost continent of Atlantis and then used as an inspiration by the Aryan people.

The method by which Angebert and Ravenscroft transform Arthurian history into world history, the fantasy-frame through which they construct their desire for a chivalrous past, recalls myths of Aryan identity; thus, even as they disapprove of Nazism, Angebert and Ravenscroft rehearse histories of the world offered by nineteenth-century racial science. Announcing its disdain for Nazis, condemning them as "Luciferian"—a word that, interestingly enough, Angebert glosses as "luminous"—*The Occult and the Third Reich* nevertheless admires their resourcefulness in decoding those texts (the Grail) that baffled the greatest minds of Western civilization: "it remained only for some modern specialists versed in the decipherment of pagan inscriptions to rediscover the Grail stone and to translate it into a clear language in order that the Aryan Tradition not be lost" (17). This writing on the Grail stone connects Arthurian history with those of Atlantis and Hyperborea:

> the end of Atlantis [was] explained by a racial mix, by a corrupting of the blood which saw the pure race of the white Atlanteans assimilated with the "demoniacal" and "inferior" races of the Asian-Semitic type.
>
> We can well understand the interest that certain occultists (whose groups have propagated its implications throughout the world) have shown concerning the myth of Atlantis, since it established an historical continuity of the white race by demonstrating its material and spiritual ascendency over all other races since time immemorial. (62–63)

According to Angebert's account of history, racial destiny brought the Nazis to the Grail and sanctioned their inheritance of it. *The Occult and the Third Reich* does not necessarily approve of National Socialism, but it needs racial science to frame its Arthurian history; it needs to believe that certain races are superior to others and that this superiority must inevitably be known.

Ravenscroft also writes Arthurian history through the screen of racial science. He describes the utopian continent of Atlantis where inhabitants "reached heights of social and technological perfection" (236), and "lived in direct self-conscious vision of the celestial hierarchies in the Macrocosm with whom [they] had a magical means of communication" (237). Unfortunately some Atlanteans practiced black magic rituals, "involving the perversion of the powers of human reproduction" (240), and the continent fell victim to eventual destruction. Before this destruction, however, Atlantean racial scientists created a new "Master Race," "the Aryan Race . . . not formed by mere refinements of the previous sub-races of Atlantis. A sort of leap in the whole process of human evolution was achieved in order to fashion the Root Race which would live on in the new conditions of environment" (241). The Aryans who, according to Ravenscroft, warred against the jealous, "degenerating races in the south of the continent" (242) developed, "[u]nder the symbol of the 'Sun Wheel' or 'Four-Armed Swastika,'" the ability to open their vision to "the spiritual hierarchies" (243). This ability, The Secret Doctrine, was learned by Adolf Hitler and put to use in activating the powers of the Spear of Destiny. Like Angebert, Ravenscroft provides a myth of origin to explain not only the survival of Arthurian Grail symbols but also why Hitler and the Third Reich were destined to appropriate them.

But fascism holds no more reality for Angebert and Ravenscroft than does Arthurian history. It too is an inexplicable "other" that requires a fantasy-frame to be understood. Indeed, it is the incomprehensibility of National Socialism that haunts these two narratives. As Angebert and Ravenscroft struggle to make sense of the trauma of National Socialism through the fantasy-frame they construct—Arthurian history—they learn to desire its cause. In both *The Occult and the Third Reich* and *Spear of Destiny*, Nazism becomes validated by a history of Arthurian origin that explains that the Grail belongs, has always belonged, and will continue to belong to Aryans, and that the Grail can only be used to the advantage of Aryan peoples. Having dissociated Arthurian history from its original connection with Britain—and, to a lesser extent, France—Angebert and Ravenscroft provide a new cast of twentieth-century Arthurian knights. These figures dovetail interestingly with Hitler's desire to reconceive the Knights Templar in the image of National Socialism. As Malcom Barber has recently suggested, the Order of the Temple was created to bring about a "new knighthood," one that emphasized not only hypermasculine aggression but spirituality as well (38–63). *The Occult and the Third Reich* and *Spear of Destiny* locate, however, a kind of hypermasculine aggression in spirituality. They suggest that the real conflicts demanding the services of twentieth-century knights took place not on battlefields but rather on the spiritual plane and were of world-shattering consequence. For Angebert and Ravenscroft, knights need not be the muscle-bound, physical presence that attracts the alienated, fascist male teenager looking for posters to decorate his room. Their knights are professors and politicians, who, taking on spiritual armor, clash on a higher plane.

Angebert and Ravenscroft offer Rudolf Steiner, the Austrian-born scientist, editor, educator, and founder of anthroposophy—a movement based on the notion that there is a spiritual world comprehensible to pure thought—as the principal adversary to the darkness of National Socialism; he is the embodiment of "white magic." Neither book, however, identifies Steiner as having a major effect on world events—perhaps because Steiner died in 1925. While *The Occult and the Third Reich* argues that "white magic" organizations offered resistance throughout the reign of National Socialism, it also notes that the "war between Steinerian white magic and Hitlerian black magic took place well before the Nazis came to power" (Angebert, 161–62). That Nazi "black magic" outlasted—and appears to have fairly well crushed—Steinerian "white magic" is a matter Angebert never addresses, and seems to care little about. Steiner is described by Ravenscroft as "the prophet of the Cosmic Christ in our time and the solitary herald of the eternal significance of the Spiritual Self, which seeks to come to birth in the soul of men in our age" (262), whose primary success was the design and construction of the Goetheanum at Dornach, Switzerland—burnt to the ground by "a German-Swiss watchmaker who was both a fanatical Nazi and a zealous member of an established Church. His payment for the deed in gold coins was found on his charred corpse beside the ashes of the building" (289). These descriptions reinforce Ravenscroft's notion of history as allegory and as psychomachia. Behind Steiner and Hitler, spirits of good and evil, Jesus—like Steiner, betrayed for coins—and Satan contest for world power. Ravenscroft includes a photograph of Steiner, "working on the figure of Jesus Christ as the Representative of Humanity. On the Left is a picture of a clay model of the projected woodcarving which stands 32 feet high. The carving shows Christ at the moment of conquest of the hierarchies of evil—Lucifer, Ahriman, and the Azuras" (figure 17 fol. p. 170). Nevertheless, Ravenscroft is at a loss to demonstrate a parallel victory for Steiner. Either the allegory does not quite hold, or the forces of darkness are very powerful indeed.

Walter Johannes Stein, Ravenscroft's teacher, an intellectual/historian who, according to Ravenscroft, both knew Hitler and opposed him, functions in *Spear of Destiny* as the twentieth-century's positive version of the Grail knight. Seeing the "Spear of Destiny" in Vienna, Stein:

> Found himself transported into the very midst of an astounding scene which forcibly clothed itself in his spiritual imagination. And with this newly-born cognition he found himself a witness to a Manichaean War of the Worlds between Spirits of Light and Darkness.
>
> Above him he could discern a mighty figure leading an array of angelic hosts, a transcendent spirit girded around the breast in white raiment which fell in folds of living beauty, an outward expression of absolute purity of heart. In joy and wonder he beheld the majesty and spirit power of this heroic Being whose countenance was the "Countenance of the Lord." (195)

But Stein, though he is cast by Ravenscroft as the hero of his story, like Steiner, is a fairly inconsequential figure in cosmic history. He is more a reporter than a player. Stein's relationship with allied forces is noted—he supposedly serves as an advisor to Churchill on the occult—but his influence seems to have made small difference in the war effort. He is even something of a failure as a historian. Although he devises a new historical method based on "mind expansion," Stein never records his findings. He dies before he can begin composing his book on Hitler's quest for the Grail spear—leaving the composition to his "reluctant" student, Ravenscroft.

It is the forces of darkness, however, that really seem to capture the imaginations of Angebert and Ravenscroft, and both *The Occult and the Third Reich* and *Spear of Destiny* use Arthurian history to fantasize Nazis as Arthurian knights. The hero of Angebert's study is the "brilliant" Otto Rahn, who, according to *The Occult and the Third Reich*, directed the Nazi search for the Grail and likely found it. Rahn, archeologist, author, intellectual, SS officer, is transformed by Angebert's study into a Grail knight, a seeker of truth. The book includes a number of pictures of Rahn, but the most striking, a back-lit silhouette, shows him standing in a cave, straddling large rocks, facing the heavens, the angles of his body imitative of the cave opening (Figure 7.4). In this picture Rahn is inserted into the fantasy-frame that constitutes him as the romanticized quester. The idealized medieval knight is replicated in the idealization of the young Nazi scholar/soldier. Rahn, Angebert notes, may have killed himself because he was not sufficiently in step with Hitler's ambitions. But Rahn's political positions, as they are praised by Angebert, are only slightly less fanatical than those

Fig. 7.4. Otto Rahn at Montségur. From Jean-Michel Angebert, *The Occult and the Third Reich*.

of the government he represented: "All too aware of the significance of his findings, he would have preferred to the total war being prepared by the Third Reich the revelation to the white race of its true nature, which would have as its corollary the transformation of Germany into a community of 'pure ones,' or (Cathar) perfecti" (15). *The Occult and the Third Reich*'s glorification of Rahn and the purposes of his Grail quest completely exposes the book's fascist fantasy, a fantasy that is extended to Hitler himself who would be transformed into "the Messiah of the eternal religion, the theocratic head of a new Europe with Germany at its center and principal beneficiary of Absolute Knowledge (since the white race would renew its eternal becoming)" (21). Angebert's narrative offers Nazi Germany as the last Grail kingdom, the last effort of the world's white peoples to reclaim their heritage. Now that the Nazis are done with the sacred object—and the world done with the Nazis—it is forbidden to anyone else.

For Ravenscroft, Hitler is not an ordinary man; he is a Grail knight, a perverted one to be sure, but still one worthy of capturing the imagination. Ravenscroft's discussion of Hitler's psychic evolution as a Grail master encompasses the Nazi leader's use of psychedelic drugs, his membership in organizations devoted to black magic, his attempts to uncover the powers of the pineal gland and the Cyclops's eye, and his experiments with reincarnation. Reading *Parzival* as a medieval roman à clef and a history of sorts, he claims that Hitler embodied the reincarnated spirit of Landulf of Capua, a historical figure whose life and deeds provided Wolfram von Eschenbach with the material for his character Klingsor. He suggests that Hitler "had quickly discovered that Wolfram von Eschenbach's *Parsival* [*sic*] was not in the ordinary sense a book. He recognized it as an initiation document of the highest order. He had been shrewd enough to perceive that within its verses was a prophetic picture of the contemporary time; a sort of magic mirror which predicts the cataclysmic events of the passing decades of the twentieth century and makes visible the inward and hidden countenance of this critical historic period in which humanity is thrown against the very threshold of the spirit" (87). Ravenscroft thus, on the one hand, seems to indicate that Hitler was never really Hitler; he was a weak spirit dominated by the universe's varied malevolent forces. On the other hand, he paints a picture of Hitler as a romantic psychic quester who risked plunging all of humanity into unbearable chaos to appease his own desire for knowledge. Hannah Arendt's notion of Nazism as "the banality of evil" is nowhere to be found in Ravenscroft's analysis. Hitler and his accomplices are presented as mystical journeyers, not twisted bureaucrats. Hitler's second encounter with the Spear of Destiny is recorded by Ravenscroft as a moment of revelation:

> All cynicism about himself, all skepticism about the genuineness of his first eerie experience before the ancient Spearhead in the Hofburg now melted away as he read again with bated breath these words of Hegel which seemed to confirm the role played by the long chain of claimants to the Spear of Destiny. His sense of mission was now enkindled to the point of pain. The Spear in the Treasure House held the key to Power! The key to his own world historic destiny!
>
> Somehow he too must unravel its secrets and harness its powers to his own personal ambitions for the German people. Might he himself not be the immortal Siegfried destined to reawaken men of German blood from the great sleep which followed Götterdämmerung? The Sun Hero fated to raise the eyes of all Germans to the greatness of their spiritual heritage? (19–20)

Hitler draws the primary focus of Ravenscroft's attention. *Spear of Destiny*'s attempt to explain Hitler, and those who followed him, shades into absolution. Ravenscroft contends that Hitler was a sinister character, possessed by demons who drove him in pursuit of the Holy Grail. According to Ravenscroft, Hitler was more than a student of Wagner, he was a very careful scholar of medieval literature. Ravenscroft writes, for instance, of Stein's reaction after reading Hitler's personally annotated copy of Wolfram von Eschenbach's *Parzival*: "It suddenly dawned on him that he was reading the footnotes of Satan!" (48). In his portrayal of Hitler, Ravenscroft has it both ways. Hitler is both the dupe of a cosmic conspiracy and a dark romantic figure, like Milton's Satan, titanic, erotic, inspired, brought down by lesser men of trifling ambition.

In *Ordinary Men*, Christopher R. Browning describes Nazi Germany's Reserve Police Battalion 101 as its members carried out "actions" ordered by the SS after the invasions of Eastern Europe. Having arrived at Józefów, Poland, the men of Reserve Police Battalion 101 rounded up the Jewish population and forced them to dig large ditches. Jews were then executed: "At first we shot freehand. When one aimed too high, the entire skull exploded. As a consequence, brains and bones flew everywhere. Thus we were instructed to place the bayonet point on the neck.... Through the point-blank shot that was thus required, the bullet struck the head of the victim at such a trajectory that often the entire skull or at least the entire rear skullcap was torn off, and blood, bone splinters, and brains sprayed everywhere and besmirched the shooters" (Browning, 64). The officer corps offered their men increased rations of alcohol both to encourage their brutality and to dull its repugnance. Most did what was asked of them, however appalling—and would do so again, repeatedly. Nevertheless some wept, some vomited, some hid, and some openly refused to participate. It is perhaps the violence of those who gave the orders—and those who took pleasure in carrying out those orders—that provides the incentive for rehabilitative histories like Angebert's and Ravenscroft's. Describing the Nazi assault on Biatystok, Russia, Browning writes that "The action began as a pogrom: beating, humiliation, beard burning, and shooting at will as the policemen drove Jews to the marketplace or synagogue. When several Jewish leaders appeared at the headquarters of the 221st Security Division of General Pflugbeil and knelt at his feet, begging for army protection, one member of Police Battalion 309 unzipped his fly and urinated on them while the general turned his back" (11–12). Angebert and Ravenscroft envision incomprehensible horrors like this through the frame of Arthurian history, fantasizing thugs as noble knights dueling on some spiritual plane. Like medieval Arthurian histories that masked the ambitions of the noble classes—and the unspeakable horrors performed in support of those ambitions—Angebert and Ravenscroft offer the fantasy of chivalry to those whose realities were considerably less glorious. Perhaps the reason the excesses of National Socialism seem so inexplicable to us is that we occlude similar atrocities of the European past when we accept at face value the noble tales—like those of King Arthur—invented to justify them.

Afterword

In the previous pages we have argued that pseudohistories can, and should, be read as historical documents that enable the historiographer to explore the social and political agendas of the cultures that produced them. As we have presented portions of this book (especially chapter 7) to audiences both in the United States and Europe, this argument has exposed us to the charge not so much of practicing Holocaust denial, but of opening the door to accepting Holocaust denial as a legitimate subject for historical inquiry. In fact, the Holocaust has become a kind of limit case for poststructuralist approaches to history.[1] For this reason, although the specifics of Holocaust denial are far outside the scope of this book, we feel it would be appropriate to conclude our study of Arthurian history with some remarks on the ways in which our poststructuralist and postcolonial historiography might understand and critique Holocaust denial.

Practitioners of Holocaust denial claim that the systematic extermination of more than six million Jews and other "undesirables" by the Third Reich never happened, that these were simply a portion of the many lives lost in the collateral damage of World War II, and they offer alternative histories (in fact, they refer to themselves not as Holocaust deniers but rather as "historical revisionists") to support their beliefs. The histories produced by Holocaust deniers in many ways resemble those of Ravenscroft and Angebert; they are "higher paranoid scholarship" with a decidedly anti-Semitic twist. The reason our study has provoked anxiety in our audiences is because it considers such "higher paranoid scholarship" as a kind of historiography. They are nervous that arguments like ours might give the revisionists credibility, the opportunity to be viewed as they would view themselves, as historians.

Poststructuralist theory, in general, has been particularly susceptible to charges that it enables Holocaust denial—especially in the aftermath of revelations concerning the Nazi past of deconstructionist critic Paul de Man (Hartman, "Blindness and Insight"). Citing Jean Baudrillard's *The Transparence of Evil,* however, Geoffrey Hartman argues that Holocaust revisionism is not so much the result of poststructuralist historiography as of the radical skepticism of the postmodern condition itself:

> There is a new amnesia . . . produced by an endless process of image-substitution, or representation after representation, of one theory after another. . . . The negationist paradox concerning the supposed impossibility of proving that the Holocaust occurred is only another expression of this sense of the unreality of the present; we have reached "the impasse of a hallucinatory *fin de siècle,* fascinated by the horror of its origins, for which oblivion is impossible. The only way out is by denial or negation." (*The Longest Shadow,* 45)

Hartman draws a very sharp distinction between the postmodern "perfectly reasonable suspicion of the world of appearances" and the discourse of Holocaust denial, in which "a *civilized* fear of reality-loss is contaminated by a savage anti-Semitism that preceded the Holocaust and still continues" (46). Holocaust deniers have replaced history's "critical and evidential impact," he argues, with a mythology of origin through which "[t]hose who seek an identity, personal, national, or racial, with an intensity that is equivalent to religious passion, seem to have returned to that delusive moment" (51). The questions posed of historiography by the rigorousness of poststructuralist theory should expose Holocaust denial as little more than perverse nostalgic desire.

We would insist that the criticism that poststructuralist historiography enables Holocaust denial rests on certain misunderstandings or caricatures of poststructuralist arguments, particularly the belief, expressed by Deborah E. Lipstadt in *Denying the Holocaust,* that "[a]t its most radical [the poststructuralist critique] contended that there was no bedrock thing such as experience. Experience was mediated through one's language." While Lipstadt admits that "the scholars who supported this deconstructionist approach were neither deniers themselves nor sympathetic to the deniers' attitudes" and that "most had no trouble identifying Holocaust denial as disingenuous," she asserts that

> because deconstructionism argues that experience was relative and nothing was fixed, it created an atmosphere of permissiveness toward questioning the meaning of historical events and made it hard for its proponents to assert that there was anything "off limits" for this

skeptical approach. The legacy of this kind of thinking was evident when students had to confront the issue. Far too many of them found it impossible to recognize Holocaust denial as a movement with no scholarly, intellectual, or rational validity. (18)[2]

More so than more positivistic approaches to the Holocaust, Lipstadt insists that the politics of poststructuralist theory open a Pandora's box, allowing the corrosive discourses of Holocaust denial into the mainstream.

Lipstadt's critique of poststructuralist approaches to history, however, rests on at least two assumptions about poststructuralism that we believe to be faulty. The first is that poststructuralism denies experience. No poststructuralist thinker that we know of denies that experiences happen to individuals, and no poststructuralist historian would argue that events did not happen in the past. What poststructuralism questions is any epistemological certainty that we can know experience or historical events in any unmediated way. Lipstadt writes as if "experience" were something we could simply take for granted as a given and that "experience" provides the axiom from which debate can begin but which itself must never be unpacked. Lipstadt's study requires that some "experiences" be undeniable and their interpretations indisputable—the facts of the Holocaust, for example. But the facts of the Holocaust, and how we interpret them, are not disputed only by deniers like the authors published in *The Journal of Historical Review*. They are in dispute all the time, by scholars whose reputation is beyond question—the highly publicized disagreements between Christopher Browning and Daniel Jonah Goldhagen come immediately to mind.[3] What, then, differentiates interpretations of facts that merit serious consideration from those regarded as fraudulent? In many ways this has been the central question of *King Arthur and the Myth of History*.

Poststructuralism requires that we explore what we mean by terms like "experience" and "event." As Lipstadt quite rightly points out, poststructuralists argue that experience and historical events are always mediated by cultural semiosis, by the symbolic structures, language included, that are our only source of access to either experience (our own and others) or past events. Teresa de Lauretis, in *Technologies of Gender*, defines "experience" as "a complex of meaning, effects, habits, dispositions, associations, and perceptions resulting from the semiotic interaction of self and outer world (in C. S. Peirce's words)" (18). Furthermore, to designate something that happened in the past as an "event" is to give the flux of experience a narrative, not an ontological, structure. Michel Foucault, in trying to argue for a philosophy of the event, describes it as a "materialism of the incorporeal." He insists on *both* the narrativity and the materiality of the "event," which offers a way out of the textuality of much poststructuralism ("there is no *hors* text"). He describes the "event" as "neither substance nor accident, neither quality nor process; the event is not of the order of bodies. And yet it is not something immaterial either; it is always at the level of materiality that it takes effect, that it is effect; it has its locus and consists in the relation, the coexistence, the dispersion, the overlapping, the accumulation, and the selection of material elements. It is not the act or the property of the body; it is produced as an effect of, and within, a dispersion of matter" ("The Order of Discourse," 231). The historian does not find events already in place; she makes them by making sense of the "relation, the coexistence, the dispersion, the overlapping, the accumulation, and the selection of material elements."

A second, related, assumption Lipstadt makes is that all "permissiveness toward questioning the meaning of historical events" makes it "hard for its proponents to assert that there was anything 'off limits'" for questioning. Leaving aside the difficulties of determining who gets to decide what historical events are "off limits" to questioning, it is worth pointing out that the radical skepticism of poststructuralist history, which involves a relentless questioning of the bases of ontology and epistemology, is not the same kind of skepticism practiced by Holocaust deniers. Holocaust denial is, as we note above, a form of higher paranoid scholarship and, like all paranoid scholarship, its effectiveness, such as it is, rests on its claim that we can know the past, that it exists independent of our interpretations of it, and that we can make verifiable truth claims about it. Holocaust denial's allegiances are with positivist, not deconstructive, approaches to history. Pipes, for instance, emphasizes that *"The Journal of Historical Review* sounds akin to the *American Historical Journal;* more than that, both quarterlies share a recognizably academic tone and list professorial boards of editors. But while the latter is a leading scholarly periodical, the former exists exclusively to disprove the reality of the Jewish Holocaust" (35). Lipstadt too notes that *The Journal of Historical Review* "imitates the serious and highbrow language of academia" (142), in particular, we would add, in its belief that it has the final word on "what really happened." The practitioners of Holocaust denial would agree with Lipstadt that there are facts that are absolute; they simply disagree on which facts those are. Holocaust deniers have no truck with poststructuralism's rigorous philosophical wrangling over the meanings of "experience" or "event" cited above.

Lipstadt contends that all discussions of Holocaust denial as history, even those that emphasize the bigotries of the genre, give it credibility, thus exposing a naive audience—our students, for instance—to its ideological dangers. If our study demonstrates anything, it is that Lipstadt's concerns about the impact of Holocaust denial "histories" on uncritical readers are well founded. At the heart of our readings of Arthurian pseudohistories, medieval and modern, is the suggestion that narratives "with no scholarly, intellectual, or rational validity" have had important consequences. The history of pseudohistories clearly demonstrates that they have commanded public attention and have influenced the course of cultural events. For this reason, we would like to go beyond simply rejecting the belief that poststructuralism enables Holocaust denial. We would like to make the bolder claim that, far from providing a context that confuses bigotry with truth, poststructuralism offers tools that might be helpful in exposing the ideological agendas of Holocaust deniers who hope to perpetrate such confusion. At the very least, it might illuminate the processes by which such beliefs take root.

In our opening chapter we turned to the scientific writings of Latour and Woolgar to characterize the process by which cultures construct "facts" of all sorts, including historical facts. For Latour and Woolgar, the fact is an utterance whose history has been erased. Every fact is held together by a specific network of alliances of people (eyewitnesses, historical actors, scholars, readers, teachers, students) and of things (books, manuscripts, articles, archives, photographs, letters, diaries, buildings, artifacts). When that network becomes so strong that it would be too costly for any one individual or even a group of individuals to stand against it, the network itself can be erased and the fact stands alone; it "speaks for itself," though in fact it is this tightly woven network of alliances that speaks for it. Thus, the Holocaust as a "fact" is held together by an alliance of people (survivors, scholars, readers, teachers, eyewitnesses, and those who claim what Walter Map called "the certainty of the things which they did not see") and things (photographs, letters, texts, diaries, records, buildings, museums, concentration camps). This is what Hartman means when he critiques Holocaust deniers who write "as if the Book of Destruction were not open, as if the massive facts and testimonies were not totally available" (*The Longest Shadow*, 43). Debate about historical "fact" occurs only when a new network of alliances (consisting of both people and things) stands against the network that holds the fact together. As one network assembles more and better allies, isolating dissenters, it may become too costly to stand against it; at such a point the new network is packaged as a fact and the old one discarded. When both networks are equally strong, a controversy ensues. Formulations like Latour's can help historians to understand the ways in which Holocaust denial might at some point become a credible form of history and to take appropriate steps to ensure that that day never comes. For this reason, the injunction "never forget" has been the byword of Holocaust survivors and historians alike. The appeal to memory reminds us that the Holocaust will be kept alive in our histories not by passive appeals to a preexistent reality but only by the active participation of all in forging the network of alliances that holds this fact in place, isolating those dissenters who offer alternative networks shaped by bigotry or opportunism.

The Arthurian pseudohistories of the Middle Ages were authorized as history because they could contain and advance culturally useful agendas. The Arthurian pseudohistories of the twentieth century are believed as history by those who, whatever their politics, long for a past structured by institutionalized hypermasculine militarism. Just as poststructuralism enables us to engage the social apparatuses that have produced Arthurian pseudohistories, it allows us to read through the historical pretense of Holocaust denial to reveal the ideology that shapes it, an ideology informed by hatred and fear.

Notes

Chapter 1. "To Mend the Interrupted Sequence of Time": The Narrative Logic of Medieval History

1. This term is used by the ninth-century historian Nennius and is variously translated duke or leader of battle, which appears to have been an old Roman military title.

2. For contemporary historiographic theory, see White, *Metahistory* and *Tropics of Discourse*; Foucault, *The Order of Things*; Certeau, *Writing of History*; La Capra; Zagorin; Ankersmit; Markley; and Chakrabarty (especially chapter 4). Among medieval historians, see Partner, *Serious Entertainments*; Otter; Ward; and Spiegel.

3. Spiegel makes much the same point in *Romancing the Past*, 1.

4. In 1956 when the book was finally published, no doubt the same words could have been applied to England's cold war enemies.

5. We do not disagree with Ingham's argument in *Sovereign Fantasies* that Arthurian histories also provided narratives of resistance for the colonized Celts. Our interest, however, is primarily in the uses made of indigenous material by the colonizing Normans and afterward by other dominant groups anxious to legitimate their hold on political power.

6. See, for instance, on Geoffrey of Monmouth, Leckie; on Laȝamon, Le Saux and Bryan.

7. Rosamund Allen's 1992 translation of the *Brut* replaced the translation in Frederick Madden's 1847 edition, and Judith Weiss's 1999 translation was the first full English translation of Wace.

8. The only edition of Hardyng's *Chronicle* is Henry Ellis's 1812 edition. Kingsford's article contains a transcription of the prologue of the unpublished early version, London, British Library, MS Lansdowne 204.

9. Only in its most recent edition has the *Norton Anthology of English Literature* (2000) begun to include Norman material (Geoffrey, Wace, and Marie de France among others) in its medieval section. On the place of Chaucer in the formation of a specifically *English* national literature, see Patterson, *Chaucer and the Subject of History*, and Lerer, 1–21; on the fifteenth century, see Lawton.

10. The term was coined by Stephen Greenblatt; see "Towards a Poetics of Culture"; see also Montrose. On the relationships between history and literature, see White, "The Historical Text as Literary Artifact," in *Tropics of Discourse.*

11. Monika Otter has also argued that these histories' mixing of history and fiction ought not to be considered a defect in the histories. Her analysis, however, differs from ours in its focus on these texts' exploration of newly emerging notions of fiction; her interests produce a more formalist account that brackets off the context of these works' production; see Otter, 1–19. We are more interested in how these texts participated in and shaped the social reality of their day.

12. Ingham makes much the same point in *Sovereign Fantasies,* see p. 3, though we will focus in what follows more on Norman than on Celtic uses of King Arthur during this period.

13. For an introduction to this body of work see Cohen, *Postcolonial Middle Ages.* "Medieval Temporalities and Colonial Histories," a conference held at Princeton in May 2003, brought medievalists together with scholars from later periods to discuss theoretical and historical issues of postcolonialism; papers can be downloaded from http://web.princeton.edu/sites/english/colloquium/. Michelle Warren in *History on the Edge,* Patricia Ingham in *Sovereign Fantasies,* and Geraldine Heng in *Empire of Magic* have all recently brought postcolonial theory to bear on Arthurian materials, Warren by examining so-called border writing about Arthur, Ingham by exploring fantasies of insular wholeness, and Heng by investigating the relationships between the genre of romance and the medieval crusades. While we have benefited from these excellent books, our study differs from theirs in its focus on the problem of historiography within postcolonial discourse; see also Robertson.

14. Postcolonialism, according to Bhabha, "bears witness to the unequal and uneven forces of cultural representation involved in the contest for political and social authority" ("Postcolonial Criticism," 437).

15. Warren describes the "shifting status of *barbarian* in the twelfth century, from foreigner at the beginning to degraded culture by the end" (*History on the Edge,* 50); Ingham adopts Felipe Fernandez-Armesto's term "internal primitives" to describe groups like the Welsh (*Sovereign Fantasies,* 11).

16. Among medieval scholars who have argued for the existence of the nation in the Middle Ages are Heng, *Empire of Magic,* Turville-Petre, Kathleen Davis (who locates the emergence of national writing in the ninth-century works of Alfred the Great), Biddick, Bowers, and Ingham, *Sovereign Fantasies.*

17. Lee Patterson has examined this phenomenon in the context of the Alliterative *Morte Arthure;* see *Negotiating the Past,* 197–230.

18. It is perhaps ironic, given the frequency with which this passage is recited as an argument about the objectivity of history (see Zagorin, 274), that Huizinga's own work was dismissed by his contemporaries as "lacking scientific rigor" (Ankersmit, 288).

19. Lévi-Strauss, *Savage Mind,* 257. John O. Ward makes the same point about medieval historians; see 108.

20. Nancy Partner makes much the same point in her analysis of narrative and history; see *Serious Entertainments*, 194–211. Ingham provides a fascinating discussion of the pleasurable role of fantasy in the historical process; see *Sovereign Fantasies*, 28–29. For a different view, see Appleby et al. Here the authors argue for a pragmatic idea of "workable truths," based on a shared, rational understanding of historical facts and evidence. Historical truth must be maintained so that institutions and groups can adjudicate among conflicting stories and interpretations. For a challenge to this argument, see Chakrabarty, especially chapter 4.

21. See also Markley, 877–94.

22. Indeed, if readers refuse to engage with the events related as "what really happened," then the text also ceases to be a history. We will examine this phenomenon in more detail in chapter 7.

23. We use the term *genre* here not to describe a formal classification of literary texts; rather we are drawing on the Russian theorist M. M. Bakhtin's notion of "speech genres," which he describes as complexes, clusters, or "congealed events" that competent speakers draw upon "to suggest the social relations between speakers and their relation to outsiders; to indicate a set of values; to offer a set of perceptions and ways of perceiving; to outline a field of possible, likely or desirable actions; to convey a vague or specific sense of time and space; to suggest an appropriate tone; to rule in or rule out various styles and languages of heteroglossia; and to negotiate a set of purposes" (Morson and Emerson, 290).

24. As Donna Haraway and others have pointed out, the terms "fact" and "fiction" derive from the same Latin verb, *facere*, to make. *Fiction* comes from the active present of the root and emphasizes the process of making, while *fact* derives from the past participle, suggesting something already made (Haraway, 3; Finke, *Feminist Theory*, 18).

25. Cyberneticians use a black box as a symbol to designate a piece of machinery or a set of commands too complex to be repeated when the only information needed for a particular operation is its input and output; see Latour, 2–3. Facts are history's black boxes.

26. We will examine this network more closely in chapter 2.

27. We use the pronoun *it* because, for Latour, the spokesperson need not be human; it could also be a thing, a book for instance.

28. See Otter's discussion of this passage, 8.

29. In chapter 7, we will look at modern histories that express an almost medieval belief that reality is to be located in the spiritual, not the physical realm.

30. See Patterson, *Negotiating the Past*, 199–202; Geoffrey Koziol's article on ritual in twelfth-century England and France is particularly useful in understanding the Norman kings' need for ideological legitimation. See Lerer, 14–17, for a discussion of the need the Lancastrian monarchs felt to authenticate their claims; the short version of Hardyng's *Chronicle* quite loudly proclaims its intention of providing the duke of York with a pedigree that traces his claim to the throne back to Edward I.

31. Patricia Ingham makes this point in *Sovereign Fantasies*; see especially her discussion of the *Historia* (40–50).

32. Though Bakhtin's concept of dialogism is frequently criticized for lacking an analysis of power, we would argue that Bakhtin, who experienced censorship firsthand throughout his life and who was reduced to using his own writings to roll cigarettes during the war, understood the dynamics of power all too well. Even in the face of such violence, however, he refused to abandon his belief that language was fundamentally dialogic and that even the most powerless are able to patch together more or less subversive forms of resistance.

33. Our analysis draws on Bakhtinian dialogics, as well as the work of the anthropologist James Scott and analyses of ideology by Slavoj Žižek and Raymond Williams.

34. Cohen suggests adapting Gloria Anzaldúa's term to describe the shifting and multiple identities created in postconquest England: "Hybrids, Monsters, Borderlands," 96.

35. See chapter 4 for a discussion of the translations of William's Latin terms for ethnic groups.

36. Otter (12) discusses William's textile metaphor in terms of the Bakhtinian chronotope, the relation in narrative between space and time.

37. For a discussion of the ways in which William dismisses Welsh claims about Arthur, see Ingham, *Sovereign Fantasies*, 21–24.

38. This passage would seem to call into question the evenhandedness of William's praise and criticism; his encomium is no less fawning than Geoffrey's oft-criticized dedication to Robert.

39. For a description of the discovery of Arthur's body at Glastonbury Abbey see Giraldus Cambrensis, who claims in *Speculum Ecclesiae* (1216) to have been an eyewitness to Arthur's exhumation. In *Journey Through Wales*, he writes, "In our own lifetime, when Henry II was reigning in England, strenuous efforts were made in Glastonbury Abbey to locate what must have once been the splendid tomb of Arthur. It was the King himself who put them on to this" (Gerald of Wales, 284). Echoing William's disdain for the "credulous Britons," he contrasts the "stupidity of the British people" who "maintain that he is alive": "The fairy-tales have been snuffed out, and the true and indubitable facts are made known, so that what really happened must be made crystal clear to all and separated from the myths which have accumulated on the subject" (284–85).

Chapter 2. Profiting from the Past: History as Symbolic Capital

1. See Green; Cronne; *Gesta Stephani*.

2. For discussions of the Christian tradition of medieval historiography, see Tatlock; Hanning, *Vision of History*; Southern; Gransden; Partner, *Serious Entertainments*, 212–30; and Schwartz.

3. On the dating of the *Historia Regum Britanniæ*, see Geoffrey, ed. Wright, x–xvi.

4. Geraldine Heng writes about the *Historia* as romance (see "Cannibalism"); however, it strikes us that the division between romance and history was much more blurred in the twelfth century than it is for us. Geoffrey's narrative is governed not by the synchronic and episodic structure of the romance, but by the sequential and diachronic narrative of the history (see chapter 5).

5. Michelle Warren takes exception with our language here, arguing that Arthur was "an effective antecedent but not a unifying ancestor" (*History on the Edge*, 11). Yet our choice of the words "smooth over" was deliberate, suggesting that at the same time that Arthurian histories turn "strategies of difference" into "resemblance" (Warren, *History on the Edge*, 13), they also continue to remain sites of ideological contestation and struggle. See our remarks in chapter 1 (pp. 6–10) on the unevenness of ideological development.

6. On modern receptions of the *Historia Regum Britanniæ*, see Brooke, 77–91.

7. For a discussion of Geoffrey's choice of Latin, see Robertson, 46.

8. As Leckie notes, Geoffrey of Monmouth violated even the very loose standards of twelfth-century historical writing: "A medieval historian's ability to render critical judgments on the reliability of his sources is a function of the availability of data. Only in cases where a basis for comparison exists, can a writer exercise some modicum of control. Geoffrey of Monmouth undoubtedly traded on this fact. That his stunning achievement represented a gross violation and willful manipulation of accepted historiographic practice was often suspected, but difficult to prove"; see Leckie, 40. On William of Newburgh's criticisms of the *Historia Regum Britanniæ*, see Partner, *Serious Entertainments*, 62–68.

9. See Foucault, *The Order of Things*, 17–44; Partner, *Serious Entertainments*, 186–93. Chapter 1 explores this attitude toward history more fully; see pp. 10–21.

10. On the influence of the *Historia*, see Keeler; Fletcher, *Arthurian Materials*; Matheson; Crick, 4:218–26. Kendrick examines the use of Geoffrey's history during the Tudor period in *British Antiquity*. On Renaissance appropriations of Geoffrey, see Finke, "Spenser for Hire."

11. On the decline in the number of manuscripts in the *Historia Regum Britanniæ* following the fifteenth century, see Crick, 4:216–17. On the seventeenth-century uses of Arthurian materials, see Carlson.

12. For discussions of the persistence of the Western myth of *translatio imperii et studii* in European histories that trace this myth through Geoffrey of Monmouth back to Virgil, see Waswo and Hieatt.

13. Kendrick, 19–53, and, more recently, Levine, 73–106, document the skepticism among humanist historians about Geoffrey's account of early Britain.

14. Much has been written, however, on the possibility of the source book's existence; see especially Ashe.

15. Here we are drawing upon Austin's notion of the performative speech act, particularly as it is understood by Derrida in "Signature, Event, Context" to include the nonserious speech act as a constitutive performative. For any speech to occur, Derrida argues, "it must be recognizable as the repetition of a conventional proce-

dure" (Culler, 119). The so-called nonserious speech act becomes an excellent model for such iteration. For a summary of the Austin-Searle-Derrida debate, see Culler, 110–34. Geoffrey's text, to paraphrase Derrida, is recognizable as the repetition of the conventional procedures for writing history in the Middle Ages.

16. On the *Historia Regum Britanniæ* as a self-deconstructing text, see Patterson, *Negotiating the Past*, 201–2; on Geoffrey's education, see Echard, 31, 34–35.

17. On the distinction between historical truth and narrative truth, see Spence, 24–25, and above, chapter 1.

18. On the history of prophetic writing, see Jarman; on Merlin's prophecies, see Ingham, *Sovereign Fantasies*, 34–40.

19. On Geoffrey's name and his biography, see Padel; Geoffrey, ed. Wright, ix–xx; Roberts; and Gillingham.

20. The *Gesta Stephani* describes Stephen's difficulties with Welsh rebels at the beginning of his reign; see 9–14.

21. The sheer number and variety of manuscripts make the choice of an edition itself difficult. There is currently no critical edition of the text. In this chapter, we use Neil Wright's edition, though it is based on a single witness that David Dumville argues circulated only in Normandy ("Early Text," 22–25). Further investigations of individual manuscripts should reveal more about the complex reception of this text.

22. *Gesta Stephani*, 4–8. This anonymous chronicler of Stephen's reign dismisses the oaths Henry's barons swore to Matilda by claiming that Henry never intended such a preposterous oath to bind them.

23. In Bern, Burgerbibliothek, MS 568, upon which Wright bases his edition, King Stephen is the subject of this dedication; see Geoffrey, ed. Wright, 1. Crawford calls this a "fawning address" (157). The language of the dedications is, in fact, little different from countless other dedications of the period. See above, for instance, the discussion of William of Malmesbury's dedication of his *Chronicle* to Robert of Gloucester.

24. Gransden discusses the importance of patronage in twelfth-century history; see 187–88.

25. The following story from the *Gesta Stephani* is illustrative of the period's attitude toward the accumulation of wealth: "Among others came William, Archbishop of Canterbury, a man with the countenance of a dove and a truly religious bearing; but he was more eager in keeping the money he had got than lavish in spending it. For when at length he died and departed from life among men the king's agents found a countless quantity of coin laid up secretly in his strongboxes; and if during his life he had distributed it in alms, imitating the man in the gospel, who making himself friends by the mammon of unrighteousness, shared it out and gave it to the poor that his justice might endure forever, he would have shown in greater perfection the character of the perfect pastor" (6). The citations from the *Gesta Stephani* should make it clear that our discussion of patronage extends beyond the literary patronage being invoked in Geoffrey's dedications, which is a special in-

stance of a pervasive means of arranging all kinds of political, economic, military, and social relations.

26. Spenser, for instance, appends seventeen dedicatory sonnets to his *Fairie Queene*, alongside a dedication to Elizabeth; see Finke, "Spenser for Hire," 214–19.

27. See also Scott, *Weapons of the Weak*, 307. Georges Duby attests to the power of "symbolic capital" in feudal Europe when he notes that the word "honour" referred not merely to a code of chivalry followed by the feudal aristocracy, but also to the hereditary seignorial lands, the estate and the material wealth that attached to it. One might refer to the honor of Beaumont or the honor of Dunster; see *Knight*, 291 n. 14.

28. It is worth reiterating that it is not necessary to believe in the truth of Geoffrey's *Historia* to understand how the practice of genealogical history helped to create a certain kind of imagined political community.

29. It might be possible to argue that Leir's daughters Regan and Goneril represent female villainy. However, we must be careful not to read Geoffrey's version of King Leir through the lens of Shakespeare's *King Lear*. In Shakespeare's tragedy, Regan and Goneril are the villains. But Geoffrey's account is not a tragedy. Leir regains his kingdom not from his daughters (who never rule), but from their husbands. He finally dies of old age, not from his daughters' treachery, and Cordelia succeeds him. While Regan and Goneril may provide examples of not very pious daughters (*pia filia*), Geoffrey focuses this narrative of a family feud on other issues. Perhaps more interesting in this episode than Regan and Goneril's behavior is the rebellion of their sons against Cordelia because "they became indignant at the fact that Britain was subjected to the rule of a woman" (trans. Thorpe, 86).

30. See Akbari, Biddick, Burger, Kathleen Davis, Ganim, Heng, and Tomasch in *The Postcolonial Middle Ages*, ed. Cohen; for important exceptions, see Cohen and Ingham in the same volume.

31. As late as the fourteenth century, Chaucer's *Man of Law's Tale* creates a formal narrative parallel between the orientalized exoticism of the pagan "sultan" and his court and that of pre-Christian Northumbria; see Bowers, 58.

32. For a useful discussion of women as gifts, see Hyde, 93–108, and Rubin.

33. For a discussion of erotic magic in the Middle Ages, see Kieckhefer.

34. Endogamy—marriage within the family—was an important strategy for second marriages within the twelfth-century biopolitics of lineage. A dead man's spouse might be married to a relation as a means of preventing her family from gaining access to the husband's wealth.

35. We will examine anxieties about miscegenation more fully in our discussion of the Mont Saint Michel giant episode in chapter 4.

36. See our discussion below of this scene in Laȝamon's *Brut*.

37. A number of medieval chronicles from Scotland question Arthur's birth and the legitimacy of his rule. They suggest that the children of King Lot have a more genuine right to the throne. See Alexander, and Shichtman, "Sir Gawain in Scotland."

38. We have stressed throughout this chapter the usefulness of the *Historia* to the Norman ruling class. In *Sovereign Fantasies,* Ingham examines the ways in which Geoffrey's text encodes oppositional discourses; see especially 38–40.

39. Technically Geoffrey never calls Merlin a magician outright. But he does indicate that Merlin must vanquish Vortigern's magicians (*magis*), calls him a "prophet" (*uates*), and credits him with supernatural powers (*numen*, "divine will"; see Geoffrey, ed. Wright, 73; trans. Thorpe, 169). Perhaps Geoffrey's very refusal to call Merlin a "magician" suggests the imbrication of magic and technology in the figure.

40. Green, 139–57. On the place of the *magister* in Anglo-Norman court culture, see Echard, 1–30. Thomas Keefe has argued that the presence of lower-born royal servants in the Anglo-Norman and Angevin courts has been overstated; however Ralph Turner's recent study of six royal servants in *Men Raised from the Dust* illustrates the ways in which bureaucratic service was a means of advancement and social mobility at the courts of the Angevin kings.

41. We examine the issue of intellectual property in Marie's *lais* in our essay "Magical Mistress Tour."

42. Michelle Warren offers a persuasive reading of the colonial implications of Aurelius's appropriation of Stonehenge; see 40–41.

43. It is worth pointing out that this intersection of magic and technology as a means of protecting intellectual property is the basis of much of the humor in Mark Twain's *Connecticut Yankee in King Arthur's Court* (and the many film versions that have been made of that novel).

Chapter 3. The Romance of Empire: Vernacular History and the Structuration of Power

1. On dominant and emerging hegemonies, see Williams, "Base and Superstucture" in *Marxism and Literature.*

2. The *Peterborough Chronicle* may be the exception that proves the rule; chapter 4 will examine some further exceptions.

3. On the debate over whether the so-called "feudal revolution" of the tenth to twelfth centuries ought to be considered in terms of continuity or discontinuity, see Bisson. Historians have long debated whether the prime mover of history is evolution or revolution, whether epochal changes represent continuity or a radical break from the past. Žižek's analysis suggests that this debate is at bottom about whose histories we will reconstruct—those of the winners or of the losers.

4. In *From Memory to Written Record,* Clanchy argues that the Norman aristocracy had at least a nodding acquaintance with Latin. Henry II, for instance, was considered *literati* by some contemporaries (186). However, it seems likely that those members of the royal family who were literate in Latin would fall into the category Malcolm Parkes describes as "pragmatic" readers, readers who read primarily for business rather than for scholarship or recreation (555).

5. We borrow the term "chronotope" from M. M. Bakhtin to designate "the in-

trinsic connectedness of temporal and spatial relationships"; see "Forms of Time and Chronotope in the Novel," in *Dialogic Imagination*, 84–85, for Bakhtin's definition of chronotope.

6. For a discussion of the Norman patronage system, see chapter 2. On Wace's patronage, see Blacker, 31–40.

7. All quotations from the *Roman de Brut*, cited by line number, are from the edition by Ivor Winters. All translations will be from the translation of Judith Weiss unless otherwise noted.

8. See Ingham's discussion of Welsh "lies" in William of Malmesbury: *Sovereign Fantasies*, 21–24.

9. Françoise Le Saux argues that Laȝamon's *Brut* was written sometime between 1185 and 1216. Others have set the date as late as the mid-thirteenth century; on the dating of the poem, see Le Saux, 2–10.

10. For a discussion of the status of the Otho manuscript, see Bryan.

11. It is also possible, as Allen suggests, that Laȝamon's patron might also have been an English merchant (Lawman, trans. Allen, xxii).

12. Spiegel uses the term "social logic" to describe the historical circumstances that are displayed openly in a given text, as well as those that appear in its silences, gaps, and contradictions (84). We have borrowed her concept and extended it to an examination of the ways in which the formal features of a genre (in this case history) carry social meanings.

13. Chrétien de Troyes, for instance, author of the first Arthurian romances, was the client of Marie, the countess of Champagne, who was the daughter of Wace's patron, Eleanor of Aquitaine. The poet Marie de France dedicated her *lais* to Henry II, whom Wace also claims as a patron.

14. See *Gesta Stephani*, 102: "Ad tantorum autem accedebat cumulum malorum, quod effera barbarorum multitudo, quae gratia militandi, facto grege, Angliam confluxerat, nec uisceribus pietatis, nec humanæ compassionis affectu super tot tantisque miseries frangebatur: sed ubique per castella in scelus et flagitum committendum unanimiter conspirare, in rebus pauperum diripiendis insatiabilitir uacare, in discordiis alterutrim promouendis, in cædibus passim peragendis toto malitiosi animi studio intendere."

15. Presumably one of the evil customs abolished was the practice of hiring mercenaries to fight wars, although Giraldus Cambrensis in his *Itinerarium Cambri* suggests that use of mercenaries was not entirely abandoned during Henry's reign: "Vidimus quippe nostris diebus, et indubita veritate comperimus, principes ecclesiasticarum possessionum usurpatores, præcipue vero Anglorum regem Henricum secundum, nostris diebus regnantem, et hoc vitio præ aliis laborantem, modico fermento massa corrupta, novis semper ea occasione emersis in commodis, thesauros universos profudisse, stipendiario dantes militi quæ dari debuerant sacerdoti" (21–22) [We have undoubtedly seen in our lifetime and proved it to be true that the great leaders who seize the possessions of the Church squander all the treasure that they have acquired and hand over to mercenaries what they should have left in the hands

of the priests. This is particularly true of Henry II, the king of the English, the reigning monarch, who has indulged in the malpractice more than most people (Gerald of Wales, 82)].

16. King John, as late as 1215 in the Magna Carta, was still promising to rid the kingdom of mercenaries: "Et statim post pacis reformacionem amovebimus de regno omnes alienigenas milites, balistarios, servientes, stipendiarios, qui venerint cum equis et armis ad nocumentum regni" [Immediately after concluding peace, we will remove from the kingdom all alien knights, crossbowmen, sergeants and mercenary soldiers who have come with horses and arms to the hurt of the realm] (Holt, *Magna Carta* 330–31).

17. Though see Keefe, 93–96, for the argument that the distinction between the "new men" and the hereditary aristocracy was not nearly as great as historians have claimed.

18. For this and the next quotations we have used our own translations to emphasize the distinction between abduction and rape (forced sexual intercourse) we believe the text creates. Weiss's translation blurs the semantic nuances of Wace's Anglo-Norman vocabulary.

19. Medieval historians portray Mordred's abduction of Guenevere variously as consensual or forced, depending on their political loyalties, but the distinction is beside the point; if rape is defined by abduction, it cannot be obviated by the woman's consent; the crime lies in stealing a woman from the man under whose authority she lives.

20. On "internal colonization," see Hechter; as noted before (see p. 7), we have some discomfort with this term applied to the Middle Ages, as it implies a coherence and unity to Europe that does not appear to exist in the twelfth century, but are unable to come up with a better term.

21. On the history of Christian–Muslim interaction in eleventh- and twelfth-century Spain, see Fletcher, *Moorish Spain*, 79–130.

Chapter 4. Discontinuous Time: History in the Eyes of Its Losers

1. This statement begs the question of why either the Welsh or the English should be considered legitimate inhabitants when they too held the island by right of conquest.

2. All references to Laȝamon's *Brut* are to the edition of Brook and Leslie. Translations are from Rosamund Allen, *Lawman's Brut*. Line numbers are noted parenthetically in the text.

3. We have already noted, for instance, the mixed parentage (Norman and Saxon) of both William of Malmesbury and Wace.

4. On the modernity of nationalism, see Anderson, *Imagined Communities*, 4; Hobsbawm, 5, 14–15; Gellner, 1–7; Smith, *Theories of Nationalism*, x; Armstrong, 4. In *Ethnic Origins of Nations*, Smith devotes an entire chapter to this question; see 6–18.

5. Heng places the emergence of the nation in England in the thirteenth century.

Among medieval scholars who join Heng ("The Romance of England") and Turville-Petre in the consensus on the existence of the nation in the Middle Ages are Davis, who locates the emergence of national writing in the ninth-century works of Alfred the Great ("National Writing"), Bowers, Stein, Ingham (*Sovereign Fantasies*), and Michelle Warren.

6. Nazism is a good case in point. See chapter 7 below.

7. For an argument that the "community of the realm" was current in thirteenth-century English political life, see Reynolds, *Kingdoms and Communities*, 250–76.

8. The most recent translation by R.A.B. Mynors, R. M. Thomson, and M. Winterbottom tends to retain Giles's use of a nationalist vocabulary.

9. Christine Fell suggests that the Anglo-Saxon verb *agan*, from which *aʒen* derives, could be understood to designate the responsibilities of the person legally in charge of a community; such responsibilities were determined interpersonally rather than contractually; see 16–17.

10. While Turville-Petre attributes to the propaganda of patriotism Henry III's address to his subjects as "alle hise holde, ilærde and ileawede" in the 1258 Provisions of Oxford, the MED suggests that *holde* refers to a kingdom, domain, or possession. Henry addresses not his fellow citizens, but his subjects (9); that is, he does not imagine the horizontal ties Anderson attributes to the nation-state.

11. Indeed the Round Table, Laʒamon writes, is conceived not out of any abstract concept of egalitarianism but as a practical means of avoiding food fights and worse forms of violence among the various members of Arthur's court (11421–41).

12. We will discuss this point more extensively in the next chapter.

13. These terms are sometimes used to designate distinct populations (the pre-Saxon Celts and the island after the Saxon occupation).

14. Transactions involving symbolic capital are difficult to understand if we think of them only in terms of the kinds of impersonal economic exchanges we are used to. Lewis Hyde's description of symbolic capital in academia is helpful for understanding both how the system works and how it has survived even market forces in certain sectors of society. It is a general (if unstated) rule in academia that original research is rarely, if ever, rewarded financially. The royalties authors receive for academic books and articles are paltry compared to the labor involved. Instead, authors receive symbolic capital—reputation, prestige—that can subsequently be converted to financial rewards like jobs, tenure, grants, promotions, endowed chairs. Conversely, authors of popularizations or textbooks often receive large financial rewards but little symbolic capital, little prestige. In modern academia, there is then an inverse relationship between symbolic and financial capital (Hyde, 77–78).

15. Bear in mind that our comments about patronage are not confined only to literary patronage, which we see as a special case of a social structure that organized social, political, and economic relations at every level of medieval society. Laʒamon's relation to the "cniþht" who was his patron is not qualitatively different from that of the Picts to Vortigern. The power Eleanor of Aquitaine exercised as a patron of the arts cannot easily be separated from her political influence.

16. This calls to mind Fredric Jameson's pronouncement that history "is what hurts, it is what refuses desire and sets inexorable limits to individual as well as collective praxis." See Ingham's discussion of this statement in *Sovereign Fantasies*, 25–29.

Chapter 5. Mapping Ambition: Imperialism, Nationalism, and the Logic of Seriality in the *Chronicle* of John Hardyng

1. London, British Library, MS Harley 993; cited in Bartlett, *Medieval Authors*, 166.

2. An earlier appeal to Henry had secured for Hardyng only the manor of Willoughton in Lincolnshire with an income of about ten pounds per year, "a quarter of what he believed Henry V had promised him" (Riddy, "John Hardyng's *Chronicle*," 95).

3. BL, MS Lansdowne 204, fol. 2v; see also Kingsford, 740. All references to the 1457 version of the *Chronicle* will refer to the manuscript. Kingsford prints only the prologue to the text.

4. It was quite common for poets in the fifteenth century to imitate Chaucer and even to invent an "aureate" style they dubbed Chaucerian to increase the legitimacy of English as a poetic language.

5. See: seat, place of sitting; royal seat on throne (OED).

6. Pretend: to put oneself forward, to profess or claim (OED).

7. On medieval maps, see Harvey and Akbari.

8. Akbari, 21; on Jerusalem as the center of the world, see also Harvey, 32, and Higgins.

9. BL, MS Harley 661, fol. 188; Ellis prints the accompanying text (Hardyng, ed. Ellis, 420).

10. It is instructive to compare Hardyng's representations of the Scots as an enemy with the representations of the French in a text like London, British Library, MS Royal 18.B.xxii, *The Book of Noblesse*, a treatise, produced in the household of Sir John Fastolf, urging Edward IV to renew the war against France and reclaim its lost territories. While the French are generally treated as rebellious subjects, the Scots, in Hardyng, are imagined as an alien and barbaric "other."

11. On the importance of foundational myths to the coherence of the community of the realm, see Reynolds, *Kingdoms and Communities*, 256–61. Warren discusses the complex roles origins play in colonial histories (*History on the Edge*, ix).

12. Dioclesian appears to be a textual corruption of the name Diodicias, which appears in the earliest Anglo-Norman texts of this story (Johnson, 21).

13. For a discussion of the history of *Des Grantz Geanz* and its earliest exemplar, London, British Library, MS Cotton Cleopatra D.ix, see Johnson, 20–24; Carley and Crick discuss the Latin manuscripts, including those incorporated into *Brut* manuscripts, in their edition of the Latin *De origine gigantum*.

14. See, for instance, John of Fordun's *Chronicle of the Scottish Nation*, written in about the 1380s (Göller, 174; Kennedy, 191).

15. Hardyng includes two stories of Scotland's foundation. In chapter 15 he describes how Brutus "departed Britaine in thre partes to his thre sonnes, the two yonger to holde of the elder" (ed. Ellis, 42), showing why Wales and Scotland must do homage to England. Later, in chapter 50, he describes how "Gadelus and Scota in the yere / Of Christe seuenty and fiue, by assise, / At Stone inhabitte as might suffise / And of hir name that countre there aboute / Scotlande she called that tyme with outen doubt" (ed. Ellis, 86). In his account, Scota, "kyng Pharois doughter," gives only her name to a territory already partitioned hundreds of years earlier by Brutus.

16. For our purposes, it hardly matters whether Hugh de Genesis (possibly a reference to Hugh of St. Victor) actually existed or not as we are not interested in the accuracy of Hardyng's sources. Undoubtedly he used some source. We are more interested, however, in his performance (see chapter 1) of historiography and especially his strategy of playing the truth of one source off against another. On Hardyng's sources, see Riddy, "Glastonbury."

17. It may seem odd that in the next chapter we argue that Caxton's edition of the *Morte Darthur*, produced only twenty years later, does evince a kind of emergent nationalism. But ideologies are not lockstep programs into which entire communities fall; they are always applied and understood unevenly, and this is a good example of such unevenness. Hardyng, a provincial writer from a contested border area (the Scottish marches), may have had less investment in the idea of "nation" than contemporaries located in London and enjoying real royal patronage (Caxton). After all, Caxton used the technology of printing to disseminate his edition of Malory, while Hardyng was still using the older technology of the manuscript.

18. On the historical accounts of Joseph's foundation of a British church, see Lagorio, 209–12; Kennedy, 186–87; and Riddy, "Chivalric Nationalism," 400–401.

19. The second stanza, which describes Joseph forming the red cross with his own blood, is found only in the Harley manuscript, fol. 28r; cited in Riddy, "Chivalric Nationalism," 401–2.

20. Hardyng does not associate the Grail with Joseph as his sources did. The long version in London, British Library, MS Lansdowne 204, presumably drawing on John of Glastonbury, has Joseph bring with him to England "two fyols, full of the swete to sayne / Of Ihu Cryste, as red as blode of bayne" (fol. 39v; cited in Riddy, "Chivalric Nationalism," 401), but even this has disappeared from the shorter versions.

21. Sarras, the reading of the Harley manuscript, is most likely the correct reading here.

22. On the secular rule of the kingdom of Jerusalem, see Prawer.

23. The term is Anderson's, from *Spectre of Comparison*, 47.

24. See Anderson's discussion of the Lincoln Memorial, *Spectre of Comparison*, 47–48.

Chapter 6. Patronage, Printing, and the Symbolic Economies of Nationalism in Caxton's *Morte Darthur*

1. Kindrick demonstrates the extent to which the Winchester/Caxton debate has dominated conversation among Malory scholars. *Arthuriana* 7 (1997), the issue in which his essay appears, also contains several previously unpublished essays by William Matthews suggesting that Caxton's edition of the *Morte Darthur* most closely approximates Malory's authorial intention. The most recent overview of the arguments pertaining to the Winchester/Caxton controversy can be found in *The Malory Debate*, ed. Wheeler et al.

2. The copy owned by the Pierpont Morgan Library is the only complete copy of Caxton's text surviving; the John Rylands Library at Manchester owns a copy that is missing some leaves.

3. Compare this, for example, to the uniqueness of BL MS Lansdowne 204, the 1457 version of Hardyng's *Chronicle*, discussed in chapter 5.

4. For examples, see Caxton.

5. We are not alone in reading late medieval works about Arthur through the lens of the chronicle history; see Patterson's reading of the Alliterative *Morte Arthure* in *Negotiating the Past*, 197–230.

6. See Ingham, *Sovereign Fantasies*, 197–99, for a discussion of the Welsh "nationalism" that preceded Henry's accession to the throne.

7. The controversy surrounding the actual authorship of Caxton's version of Arthur's wars with Lucius have pitted the likes of William Matthews, R. M. Lumiansky, and Charles Moorman (who argue that Malory made the changes to the text Caxton printed) against Terence McCarthy, Sally Shaw, and, most recently, John Withrington (who believe Caxton responsible). Matthews's "Who Revised the Roman War Episode in Malory's *Morte Darthur*," presented posthumously by Roy Leslie at the 1975 meeting of the International Arthurian Society in Exeter, was not published until 1997, when it appeared in *Arthuriana* 7.

8. The changes Caxton makes to the Pentecostal Oath from the Winchester manuscript consist almost exclusively of omissions in the so-called "lady clause." Caxton omits widows from the list of ladies and cuts the phrases "strengthe hem in hir ryghtes" and "never to enforce them"; see Malory, *Works*, 1:120.

9. For a reading of Malory based on the King's Two Bodies, see Pochoda, 39–46, and Ingham, *Sovereign Fantasies*, 194–99.

10. Citations of the Middle English *Body of Polycy* are from the 1524 edition by John Scot, a.i–a.iv.

11. Anamorphosis is a distorted projection or drawing of anything made so that when "viewed from a particular point, or by reflection from a suitable mirror, it appears regular and properly proportioned; a deformation" (OED). The point is that

the viewer sees one image from one perspective and a quite different image from another. The most famous example of an anamorphic painting is Hans Holbein's "The Ambassadors."

12. Bourdieu's notion of symbolic capital, as we argue in chapter 2, is crucial to understanding the medieval political economy. Even in the fifteenth century, symbolic capital in the form of honor, prestige, reputation, and status was as important as material wealth in medieval politics and business. The centrality of symbolic capital to success explains why a family of Norfolk lawyers and landowners like the Pastons would invest so significantly to send one of their younger sons to court, literally to curry favor with more important men in hopes of furthering their business interests. And why, lacking any real symbolic capital to leverage, John Paston II could fail so miserably at court, "for he is not bold enough to put himself forth" as his uncle Clement writes; see Bennett, 83–84. Malory only mystifies what the Paston letters discuss so openly, the struggle to accumulate symbolic capital and to convert it to material wealth and social power.

13. Felicity Riddy, for example, writes that "early readers of both manuscript and print must ... have had a very specific understanding of the instability and division on which the *Morte Darthur* rests." She writes of Malory himself as "an unstable and divided figure" (*Sir Thomas Malory*, 2).

14. On the relationship between centripetal and centrifugal forces in social formations, see Bakhtin, *Dialogic Imagination*, 270–75. On carnival, see Bakhtin, *Speech Genres*, and Stallybrass and White, especially chapter 1.

15. For an examination of the ways in which Malory structures masculinity in the *Morte Darthur*, see Finke and Shichtman. For discussions of the significance of the impenetrable male body, see Ingham, *Sovereign Fantasies*, 221, and Kelly.

16. It is worth pointing out that the Grail story begins with Balin's act of utterly gratuitous violence when he smites King Pellam with Longinus's spear; see Finke and Shichtman.

Chapter 7. Paranoid History

1. On the relation of fantasy to social reality, see Louise Fradenburg who argues that, far from separating us from reality, fantasies have the power to remake the social realities we live and desire (206–8).

2. Historians have been uncomfortable with Rauschning's accuracy as an eyewitness, nervous about the excesses and biases he brings to his historical performance, the possibility that he exaggerated both his friendship with Hitler and his account of Hitler's conversations. We would argue that it does not matter whether these words belong, finally, to Nazi leader or Nazi stooge; Nazi medievalism was not the fantasy of a single individual, but part of an ideology that pervaded German life. Rauschning's account, even if it does not tell exactly what Hitler really said, is consistent with—and illuminates—that ideology.

3. Nazi fear of sexual pollution is reflected in the belief that Jews were the source

of syphilitic infection. Novels of the period, such as Zoberlein's *Befehl des Gewissens* (*Conscience Commands*), warn of Judenpest (Jewish pox), a sexually transmitted blood disease—syphilis—that causes sterility; see Theweleit, 2:13–15.

4. In Wolfram von Eschenbach's *Parzival* the Grail procession is preceded by the appearance of a page bearing a lance: "Blood gushed from the point and ran down the shaft to the hand that bore it and on to the sleeve" (127). This lance is usually described as Longinus's spear.

5. In the third chapter of his book *Conspiracy,* Pipes acknowledges that "telling the real conspiracy apart from the imaginary one—or, in the terminology used here, the conspiracy from the conspiracy theory—is a subjective process" (37). He offers in this chapter on "Unmasking Conspiracy Theory" a number of tools to identify "higher paranoid scholarship." He suggests that "higher paranoid scholarship" demonstrates certain "distinct patterns" such as "Obscurity," "Reluctance to divulge information," "Reliance on forgeries," "Inconsistencies," "Overabundant learned factoids and pedantic references," "Piling on conspiracy theories," "Dismissing contradictory evidence as a sign of conspiracy," "Indiscriminately accepting any argument that points to conspiracy," "Oblivious[ness] to the passage of time. Generations and centuries go by, but little changes," and a "Cavalier attitude toward facts. At times conspiracy theorists make these up out of whole cloth" (see 40–42). Similarly, conspiracy theories contain "several recurring assumptions": "POWER IS THE GOAL," "BENEFIT INDICATES CONTROL," "CONSPIRACIES DRIVE HISTORY," "NOTHING IS ACCIDENTAL OR FOOLISH," and "APPEARANCES DECEIVE" (*sic*, 43–45). Ultimately, however, Pipes admits that "I have done my best to separate conspiracism from conspiracy, reality from fantasy. Yet no one can be sure in every case which is which, and I make no claim to certainty. Conspiracism manages to insinuate itself in the most alert and intelligent minds, so excluding it amounts to a perpetual struggle" (49).

6. Rosenbaum writes that Lanzmann "insisted that if he ever found a secretly made film that shows the actual killing of three thousand Jews in a death camp, say, not only would he refuse to use it, but he would seek to destroy it . . . for Lanzmann, 'after *Shoah*,' there is no argument: Certain matters are settled, certain things are forbidden. His film is not merely superior to reality; it replaces, substitutes for, and demands the literal destruction of the merely real" (253).

Afterword

1. For a discussion of the events of September 11, 2001, as a limit event for poststructuralist histories, see Stanley Fish, "Condemnation without Absolutes," where he argues against the charge that "the ideas foisted upon us by postmodern intellectuals have weakened the country's resolve." "According to the critics," he writes, "since postmodernists deny the possibility of describing matters of fact objectively, they leave us with no firm basis for either condemning the terrorist attacks or fighting back." Does this spell the end of poststructuralist relativism? "If by relativism one means the practice of putting yourself in your adversary's shoes, not in

order to wear them as your own but in order to have some understanding (far short of approval) of why someone else might want to wear them, then relativism will not and should not end, because it is simply another name for serious thought."

2. This issue, among others, relating to writing the Holocaust was taken up by a number of international historians at a conference, "Nazism and the 'Final Solution': Probing the Limits of Representation," held at the University of California, Los Angeles, April 26–29, 1990. A number of papers from this conference are included in *Probing the Limits of Representation*, ed. Friedlander.

3. In his landmark study, *Ordinary Men*, Christopher Browning points to psychological experiments performed in American institutions of higher education by Philip Zimbardo and Stanley Milgrim to help explain the actions of Hitler's *einsatzgruppen*, those who, following closely behind as the German army moved through Eastern Europe, enacted the "Final Solution," often killing Jews by shooting them at close range in the back of the head. In *Hitler's Willing Executioners*, Daniel Jonah Goldhagen argues that the explanation for Nazi genocide can be found in "eliminationist antisemitic German political culture, the genesis of which must be and is explicable historically." It was "the prime mover of both the Nazi leadership and ordinary Germans in the persecution and extermination of the Jews, and therefore was the Holocaust's principal cause" (455). *The Journal of Historical Review* claims to publish historical revisionist thinking of all kinds, but it is, in fact, primarily an organ of Holocaust denial.

Bibliography

Abu-Lughod, Janet L. *Before European Hegemony: The World System* A.D. *1250–1350*. Oxford: Oxford University Press, 1989.
Akbari, Suzanne Conklin. "From Due East to True North: Orientalism and Orientation." In *The Postcolonial Middle Ages*, ed. Cohen, 19–34.
Alexander, F. "Late Medieval Scottish Attitudes to the Figure of Arthur: A Reassessment." *Anglia* 93 (1975): 17–34.
Anderson, Benedict. *Imagined Communities: Reflections on the Origin and Spread of Nationalism*. London: Verso, 1983.
———. *The Spectre of Comparison: Nationalism, Southeast Asia, and the World*. London: Verso, 1998.
Angebert, Jean-Michel. *The Occult and the Third Reich: The Mystical Origins of Nazism and the Search for the Holy Grail*. Trans. Lewis A. M. Sumberg. New York: Macmillan, 1974.
The Anglo-Saxon Chronicles. Trans. A. Savage. New York: St. Martin's, 1983.
Ankersmit, F. R. "Reply to Professor Zagorin." *History and Theory* 29 (1990): 275–96.
Appleby, John T. *Henry II: The Vanquished King*. London: G. Bell and Sons, 1962.
Appleby, Joyce, Lynn Hunt, and Margaret Jacob. *Telling the Truth About History*. New York: Norton, 1994.
Arendt, Hannah. *Eichmann in Jerusalem: A Report on the Banality of Evil*. Rev. and enlarged. New York: Penguin, 1965.
Armstrong, John A. *Nations Before Nationalism*. Chapel Hill: University of North Carolina Press, 1982.
Ashe, Geoffrey. "'A Certain Very Ancient Book': Traces of an Arthurian Source in Geoffrey of Monmouth's History." *Speculum* 56 (1981): 301–23.
Bakhtin, M. M. *The Dialogic Imagination*. Trans. Caryl Emerson and Michael Holquist. Austin: University of Texas Press, 1981.
———. *Speech Genres and Other Late Essays*. Ed. Michael Holquist and Caryl Emerson, trans. Vern W. McGee. Austin: University of Texas Press, 1986.
Barber, Malcom. *The New Knighthood: A History of the Order of the Temple*. Cambridge: Cambridge University Press, 1994.

Barlow, Frank. *The Feudal Kingdom of England: 1042–1216.* London: Longmans, Green and Co., 1955.

Bartlett, Anne Clark. *Medieval Authors, Female Readers: Representation and Subjectivity in Middle English Devotional Literature.* Ithaca: Cornell University Press, 1995.

Bartlett, Robert. *The Making of Europe: Conquest, Colonization, and Cultural Change.* Princeton: Princeton University Press, 1993.

Batt, Catherine. *Malory's Morte Dartur: Remaking Arthurian Tradition.* New York: Palgrave, 2002.

Baudrillard, Jean. *Transparency of Evil.* Trans. James Benedict. New York: Verso, 1993.

Benjamin, Walter. "Theses on the Philosophy of History." In *Illuminations,* trans. Harry Zohn, 253–64. New York: Schocken Books, 1968.

Bennett, H. S. *The Pastons and Their England: Studies in an Age of Transition.* Cambridge: Cambridge University Press, 1932.

Berenbaum, Michael. *The World Must Know: The History of the Holocaust as Told in the United States Holocaust Memorial Museum.* New York: Little, Brown, and Co., 1993.

Bhabha, Homi K. "DissemiNation: Time, Narrative, and the Margins of the Modern Nation." In *Nation and Narration,* ed. Bhabha, 291–322.

———. "Postcolonial Criticism." In *Redrawing the Boundaries: The Transformation of English and American Literary Studies,* ed. Stephen Greenblatt and Giles Gunn, 437–65. New York: Modern Language Association, 1992.

———, ed. *Nation and Narration.* London: Routledge, 1990.

Biddick, Kathleen. "The ABC of Ptolemy: Mapping the World with the Alphabet." In *Text and Territory,* ed. Tomasch and Gilles, 268–93.

———. "Coming Out of Exile: Dante on the Orient Express." In *The Postcolonial Middle Ages,* ed. Cohen, 35–52.

Bisson, Thomas N. "The Feudal Revolution." *Past and Present* 142 (1994): 6–42.

Blacker, Jean. *The Faces of Time: Portrayal of the Past in Old French and Latin Historical Narrative of the Anglo-Norman Regnum.* Austin: University of Texas Press, 1994.

Bloch, Howard. *Etymologies and Genealogies: A Literary Anthropology of the French Middle Ages.* Chicago: University of Chicago Press, 1983.

Boswell, John. *Christianity, Social Tolerance, and Homosexuality: Gay People in Western Europe from the Beginning of the Christian Era to the Fourteenth Century.* Chicago: University of Chicago Press, 1980.

Bourdieu, Pierre. *Outline of a Theory of Practice.* Trans. Richard Nice. Cambridge: Cambridge University Press, 1977.

Bowers, John M. "Chaucer After Smithfield: From Postcolonial Writer to Imperialist Author." In *The Postcolonial Middle Ages,* ed. Cohen, 53–66.

Breisach, Ernst, ed. *Classical Rhetoric and Medieval Historiography.* Kalamazoo, Mich.: Medieval Institute Publications, 1985.

Bromwich, Rachel, A.O.H. Jarman, and B. Roberts, eds. *The Arthur of the Welsh: The Arthurian Legend in Medieval Welsh Literature*. Cardiff: University of Wales Press, 1991.

Brooke, C.N.L. "Geoffrey of Monmouth as a Historian." In *Church and Government in the Middle Ages*, ed. C.N.L. Brooke, D. E. Luscombe, G. H. Martin, and D. Owen, 77–91. Cambridge: Cambridge University Press, 1976.

Browning, Christopher. *Ordinary Men: Reserve Police Battalion 101 and the Final Solution in Poland*. New York: Harper Perennial, 1992.

Brundage, James A. *Law, Sex, and Christian Society in Medieval Europe*. Chicago: University of Chicago Press, 1987.

———. "Rape and Seduction in Medieval Canon Law." In *Sexual Practices and the Medieval Church*, ed. Vern L. Bullough and James A. Brundage, 141–48. Buffalo: Prometheus, 1982.

Bryan, Elizabeth J. *Collaborative Meaning in Medieval Scribal Culture: The Otho La3amon*. Ann Arbor: University of Michigan Press, 1999.

Burger, Glenn. "Cilecian Armenian Métissage and Hertoum's *La Fleur des histoires de la terre d'Orient*." In *The Postcolonial Middle Ages*, ed. Cohen, 67–83.

Carley, James P., and Julia Crick. "Constructing Albion's Past: An Annotated Edition of *De Origine Gigantum*." In *Arthurian Literature*, ed. Riddy and Carley, 41–114.

Carlson, David R. "Arthur Before and After the Revolution: The Blome-Stansby Edition of Malory (1634) and Brittains Glory (1684)." In *Culture and the King*, ed. Shichtman and Carley, 234–53.

Caxton, William. *The Prologues and Epilogues of William Caxton*. Ed. W.J.B. Crotch. EETS OS 176. Oxford: Oxford University Press, 1928.

Certeau, Michel de. *Heterologies: Discourse on the Other*. Trans. Brian Massumi. Minneapolis: University of Minnesota Press, 1986.

———. *The Practice of Everyday Life*. Trans. Steven F. Rendall. Berkeley: University of California Press, 1984.

———. *The Writing of History*. Trans. Tom Conley. New York: Columbia University Press, 1988.

Chakrabarty, Dipesh. *Provincializing Europe: Postcolonial Thought and Historical Difference*. Princeton: Princeton University Press, 2000.

Chambers, E. K. *Arthur of Britain*. Cambridge: Cambridge University Press, 1927.

Chatterjee, Partha. *The Nation and Its Fragments: Colonial and Postcolonial Histories*. Princeton: Princeton University Press, 1993.

Chenu, M. D. *Nature, Man, and Society in the Twelfth Century*. Ed. and trans. Jerome Taylor and Lester K. Little. Chicago: University of Chicago Press, 1968.

Christine de Pizan. *Body of Polycye*. London: John Scot, 1524.

Churchill, Winston S. *The Birth of Britain: A History of the English Speaking Peoples*. Vol. 1. New York: Dodd, Mead and Co., 1956.

Clanchy, M. T. *From Memory to Written Record: England, 1066–1307*. Cambridge: Harvard University Press, 1979.

Cohen, Jeffrey Jerome. "Hybrids, Monsters, Borderlands: The Bodies of Gerald of Wales." In *The Postcolonial Middle Ages*, ed. Cohen, 85–104.

———. "Introduction." In *The Postcolonial Middle Ages*, ed. Cohen, 1–17.

———, ed. *The Postcolonial Middle Ages*. New York: St. Martin's Press, 2000.

Cohn, Norman. *Warrant for Genocide: The Myth of the Jewish World-Conspiracy and the Protocols of the Elders of Zion*. New York: Harper and Row, 1966.

Colley, Linda. *Britons: Forging the Nation, 1707–1837*. New Haven: Yale University Press, 1992.

Crane, Susan. *Insular Romance: Politics, Faith, and Culture in Anglo-Norman and Middle English Literature*. Berkeley: University of California Press, 1986.

Crawford, T. D. "On the Linguistic Competence of Geoffrey of Monmouth." *Medium Ævum* 51 (1982): 152–62.

Crick, J. C. *The Historia Regum Britannie of Geoffrey of Monmouth*. Vol. 3, *A Summary Catalogue of the Manuscripts*. Cambridge: Cambridge University Press, 1989.

———. *The Historia Regum Britannie of Geoffrey of Monmouth*. Vol. 4, *Dissemination and Reception in the Later Middle Ages*. Cambridge: Cambridge University Press, 1991.

Cronne, H. A. *The Reign of Stephen, 1135–54: Anarchy in England*. London: Weidenfeld and Nicolson, 1970.

Culler, Jonathan. *On Deconstruction: Theory and Criticism after Structuralism*. Ithaca: Cornell University Press, 1982.

Davies, R. R. "Law and National Identity in Thirteenth-Century Wales." In *Welsh Society and Nationhood: Historical Essays Presented to Glanmor Williams*, ed. R. R. Davies, Ralph A. Griffiths, Ieuan Gwynedd Jones, and Kenneth O. Morgan, 51–69. Cardiff: University of Wales Press, 1984.

Davis, Kathleen. "National Writing in the Ninth Century: A Reminder for Postcolonial Thinking about the Nation." *Journal of Medieval and Early Modern Studies* 28 (1998): 611–37.

———. "Time Behind the Veil: The Media, the Middle Ages, and Orientalism Now." In *The Postcolonial Middle Ages*, ed. Cohen: 105–22.

Davis, Natalie Zemon. *Society and Culture in Early Modern France*. Stanford: Stanford University Press, 1975.

De Lauretis, Teresa. *Technologies of Gender: Essays on Theory, Film, and Fiction*. Bloomington: Indiana University Press, 1987.

Derrida, Jacques. "Limited Inc. abc . . ." *Glyph* 2 (1977): 162–254.

———. "Signature, Event, Context." *Glyph* 1 (1977): 172–97.

Douglas, Mary. *Purity and Danger: An Analysis of Concepts of Pollution and Taboo*. New York: Praeger, 1966.

Duby, Georges. *The Early Growth of the European Economy: Warriors and Peasants from the Seventh to the Twelfth Century*. Trans. Howard B. Clarke. Ithaca: Cornell University Press, 1974.

---. *A History of Private Life: Revelations of the Medieval World.* Trans. Arthur Goldhammer. Cambridge, Mass.: The Belknap Press, 1988.

---. *The Knight, the Lady, and the Priest: The Making of Modern Marriage.* Trans. Barbara Bray. New York: Pantheon, 1983.

Dumville, David N. "An Early Text of Geoffrey of Monmouth's *Historia regum Britanniae* and the Circulation of Some Latin Histories in Twelfth-Century Normandy." *Arthurian Literature* 4 (1984): 1–33.

---. *Histories and Pseudo-histories of the Insular Middle Ages.* Aldershot: Variorum, 1990.

Echard, Siân. *Arthurian Narrative in the Latin Tradition.* Cambridge: Cambridge University Press, 1998.

Eco, Umberto. *Foucault's Pendulum.* Trans. William Weaver. San Diego: Harcourt, Brace, Jovanovich, 1989.

Edwards, A.S.G. "The Manuscripts and Texts of the Second Version of John Hardyng's *Chronicle.*" In *England in the Fifteenth Century,* ed. Daniel Williams, 75–84. Woodbridge, Suffolk: Boydell and Brewer, 1987.

Eisenstadt, S. N., and Luis Roniger. *Patrons, Clients, and Friends: Interpersonal Relations and the Structure of Trust in Society.* Cambridge: Cambridge University Press, 1984.

Eliade, Mircea. *The Sacred and the Profane: The Nature of Religion.* Trans. Willard R. Trask. New York: Harcourt Brace Jovanovich, 1959.

Evans, Ruth. "Translating Past Cultures?" In *The Medieval Translator IV,* ed. Roger Ellis and Ruth Evans, 20–45. Exeter: University of Exeter Press, 1994.

Fell, Christine, with Cecile Clark and Elizabeth Williams. *Women in Anglo-Saxon England and the Impact of 1066.* Bloomington: Indiana University Press, 1984.

Filmer, Sir Robert. *Patriarcha and Other Political Works.* Ed. Peter Laslett. Oxford: Blackwell, 1949.

Finke, Laurie A. *Feminist Theory, Women's Writing.* Ithaca: Cornell University Press, 1992.

---. "Spenser for Hire: Arthurian History as Cultural Capital in *The Faerie Queene.*" In *Culture and the King,* ed. Shichtman and Carley, 211–33.

Finke, Laurie, and Martin B. Shichtman. "Magical Mistress Tour: Patronage, Intellectual Property, and the Dissemination of Wealth in the *Lais* of Marie de France." *Signs* 25 (2000): 479–503.

---. "No Pain, No Gain: Violence as Symbolic Capital in Malory's *Morte d'Arthur.*" *Arthuriana* 8 (1998): 115–34.

Fish, Stanley. "Condemnation without Absolutes." *New York Times,* October 15, 2001.

Fletcher, Richard. *Moorish Spain.* Berkeley: University of California Press, 1992.

Fletcher, Robert Huntington. *Arthurian Material in the Chronicles: Especially those of Great Britain and France.* 2nd ed. New York: Burt Franklin, 1966.

Flieger, Jerry Aline. "Listening Eye: Postmodernism, Paranoia, and the Hypervisible." *Diacritics* 26 (1996): 90–107.

Forde, Simon, Lesley Johnson, and Alan V. Murray, eds. *Concepts of National Identity in the Middle Ages.* Leeds Texts and Monographs, n.s., 14. Leeds: University of Leeds, 1995.
Foucault, Michel. *History of Sexuality.* Vol. 1. Trans. R. Hurley. New York: Pantheon, 1978.
———. "The Order of Discourse." In *The Archeology of Knowledge,* trans. A. M. Sheridan Smith, 215–37. New York: Pantheon, 1972.
———. *The Order of Things: An Archeology of the Human Sciences.* New York: Pantheon, 1970.
———. "What Is an Author?" In *Textual Strategies: Perspectives in Postmodernist Criticism,* ed. Josué V. Harari, 141–60. Ithaca: Cornell University Press, 1979.
Foulon, Charles. "Wace." In *Arthurian Literature in the Middle Ages,* ed. R. S. Loomis, 94–103.
Fradenburg, Louise O. "'Fulfild of fairye': The Social Meaning of Fantasy in the Wife of Bath's Prologue and Tale." In *The Wife of Bath,* ed. Peter Beidler, 205–20. Boston: Bedford Books, 1996.
Friedlander, Saul, ed. *Probing the Limits of Representation: Nazism and the "Final Solution."* Cambridge: Harvard University Press, 1992.
Ganim, John. "Native Studies: Orientalism and Medievalism." In *The Postcolonial Middle Ages,* ed. Cohen: 123–34.
Geary, Patrick J. *The Myth of Nations: The Medieval Origins of Europe.* Princeton: Princeton University Press, 2002.
Gellner, Ernest. *Nations and Nationalism.* Ithaca: Cornell University Press, 1983.
Geoffrey of Monmouth. *Historia Regum Britannie of Geoffrey of Monmouth.* Ed. N. Wright. Vol. 1, *Bern, Burgerbibliothek MS. 568.* Cambridge: Cambridge University Press, 1985.
———. *The History of the Kings of Britain.* Trans. Lewis Thorpe. New York: Penguin, 1966.
Gerald of Wales. *The Journey Through Wales and the Description of Wales.* Trans. Lewis Thorpe. New York: Penguin, 1978.
Gesta Stephani. Ed. and trans. K. R. Potter. London: T. Nelson, 1955.
Gillingham, J. "The Context and Purposes of Geoffrey of Monmouth's History of the Kings of Britain." *Anglo-Norman Studies* 13 (1991): 99–118.
Given, James. *State and Society in Medieval Europe.* Ithaca: Cornell University Press, 1990.
Goldhagen, Daniel Jonah. *Hitler's Willing Executioners: Ordinary Germans and the Holocaust.* New York: Knopf, 1996.
Goldstein, R. James. *The Matter of Scotland: Historical Narrative in Medieval Scotland.* Lincoln: University of Nebraska Press, 1993.
Göller, Karl Heinz. "King Arthur in the Scottish Chronicles." In *King Arthur: A Casebook.* Ed. Edward Donald Kennedy, 173–84. New York: Garland, 1996.
Goodman, J. R. "Malory and Caxton's Chivalric Series, 1481–1485." In *Studies in Malory,* ed. Spisak, 257–74.

Goux, Jean-Joseph. "The Phallus: Masculine Identity and the 'Exchange of Women.'" Trans. Maria Amuchastegui, Caroline Benforado, Amy Henrix, and Eleanore Kaufman. *Diacritics* 4.1 (1992): 40–75.
———. *Symbolic Economies After Marx and Freud.* Trans. Jennifer Curtiss Gage. Ithaca: Cornell University Press, 1990.
Gransden, Antonia. *Historical Writing in England, c. 550–1307.* Vol. 1. Ithaca: Cornell University Press, 1974.
Green, J. A. *The Government of England Under Henry I.* Cambridge: Cambridge University Press, 1986.
Greenblatt, Stephen. "Towards a Poetics of Culture." In *The New Historicism,* ed. Veeser, 1–14.
Haahr, Joan Gluckauf. "William of Malmesbury's Roman Models: Suetonius and Lucan." In *The Classics in the Middle Ages,* ed. Aldo S. Bernardo and Saul Levin, 165–73. Binghamton, N.Y.: Medieval and Renaissance Texts and Studies, 1990.
Hanning, Robert W. *The Individual in Twelfth-Century Romance.* New Haven: Yale University Press, 1977.
———. *The Vision of History in Early Britain: From Gildas to Geoffrey of Monmouth.* New York: Columbia University Press, 1966.
Haraway, Donna. *Primate Visions: Gender, Race, and Nature in the World of Modern Science.* New York: Routledge, 1989.
Hardyng, John. *Chronicle.* London, British Library, MS Lansdowne 204.
———. *Chronicle.* Ed. Henry Ellis. London: J. C. and J. Rivington, 1812.
Hartman, Geoffrey. "Blindness and Insight." *New Republic,* March 7, 1988, 225–54.
———. *The Longest Shadow: In the Aftermath of the Holocaust.* Bloomington: Indiana University Press, 1996.
Harvey, P.D.A. *Medieval Maps.* Toronto: University of Toronto Press, 1991.
Hechter, Michael. *Internal Colonialism: The Celtic Fringe in British National Development.* New Brunswick, N.J.: Transaction Publishers, 1999.
Helgerson, Richard. *Forms of Nationhood: The Elizabethan Writing of England.* Chicago: University of Chicago Press, 1992.
Hellinga, Lotte. "The Malory Manuscript and Caxton." In *Aspects of Malory,* ed. Toshiyuki Takamiya and Derek Brewer, 127–41. Woodbridge: Brewer, 1981.
Heng, Geraldine. "Cannibalism, The First Crusade, and the Genesis of Medieval Romance." *differences* 10 (1998): 98–174.
———. *Empire of Magic: Medieval Romance and the Politics of Cultural Fantasy.* New York: Columbia University Press, 2003.
———. "The Romance of England: *Richard Coer de Lyon,* Saracens, Jews, and the Politics of Race and Nation." In *The Postcolonial Middle Ages,* ed. Cohen, 135–72.
Henry, Archdeacon of Huntingdon. *Historia Anglorum.* Ed. and trans. Diana Greenway. Oxford: Oxford University Press, 1996.
Herlihy, David. *Medieval Households.* Cambridge: Harvard University Press, 1985.
Hieatt, Kent. "The Passing of Arthur in Malory, Spenser, and Shakespeare." In *The*

Passing of Arthur: New Essays in the Arthurian Tradition, ed. Christopher Baswell and W. Sharpe, 173–92. New York: Garland, 1988.
Higden, Ranulf. *Polychronicon.* Trans. John Trevisa, ed. Joseph Rawson Lumby. London: Longman, 1874.
Higgins, Iain Macleod. "Defining the Earth's Center in a Medieval 'Multi-Text.'" In *Text and Territory*, ed. Tomasch and Gilles, 29–53.
Hobsbawm, E. J. *Nations and Nationalism Since 1780.* Cambridge: Cambridge University Press, 1990.
Hofstadter, Richard. *The Paranoid Style in American Politics and Other Essays.* New York: Vintage, 1967.
Holt, J. C. *Magna Carta.* Cambridge: Cambridge University Press, 1965.
———. *Magna Carta and Medieval Government.* London: Hambledon Press, 1985.
Höhne, Heinz. *The Order of the Death's Head: The Story of Hitler's SS.* Trans. Richard Barry. London: Pan Books, 1972.
Huizinga, Johann. "A Definition of the Concept of History." In *Philosophy and History*, ed. Raymond Klibansky and H. J. Paton, 1–10. Cambridge: Cambridge University Press, 1936.
Hyde, Lewis. *The Gift: Imagination and the Erotic Life of Property.* New York: Vintage, 1979.
Ignatieff, Michael. *Blood and Belonging: Journeys into the New Nationalism.* New York: Farrar, Straus and Giroux, 1993.
Ingham, Patricia Clare. "Making Time: *Branwen, Daughter of Llyr* and the Colonial Refrain." In *The Postcolonial Middle Ages*, ed. Cohen, 173–92.
———. *Sovereign Fantasies: Arthurian Romance and the Making of Britain.* Philadelphia: University of Pennsylvania Press, 2001.
Ingledew, Francis. "The Book of Troy and the Genealogical Construction of History: The Case of Geoffrey of Monmouth's *Historia regum Britanniae.*" *Speculum* 69 (1994): 665–704.
Jaeger, C. Stephen. *The Origins of Courtliness: Civilizing Trends and the Formation of Courtly Ideals: 939–1210.* Philadelphia: University of Pennsylvania Press, 1985.
Jarman, A.O.H. "The Merlin Legend and the Welsh Tradition of Prophecy." In *The Arthur of the Welsh*, ed. Bromwich, Jarman, and Roberts, 117–45.
Jauss, Hans Robert. *Toward an Aesthetic of Reception.* Trans. T. Bahti. Minneapolis: University of Minnesota Press, 1982.
Johnson, Lesley. "Return to Albion." In *Arthurian Literature*, ed. Riddy and Carley, 19–40.
Kantorowicz, Ernst H. *The King's Two Bodies: A Study in Medieval Political Theology.* Princeton: Princeton University Press, 1957.
Keefe, Thomas. *Feudal Assessments and the Political Community Under Henry II and His Sons.* Berkeley: University of California Press, 1983.
Keeler, L. *Geoffrey of Monmouth and the Late Latin Chroniclers, 1300–1500.* Uni-

versity of California Publications in English 17. Berkeley: University of California Press, 1946.
Keen, Maurice. "Chivalry, Heralds, and History." In *The Writing of History in the Middle Ages: Essays Presented to Richard William Southern*, ed. R.J.A.I. Catto and M. H. Keen, 393–414. Oxford: Clarendon Press, 1981.
Kelly, Kathleen C. "Malory's Body Chivalric." *Arthuriana* 6 (1996): 52–71.
Kendrick, T. D. *British Antiquity*. London: Methuen, 1950.
Kennedy, Edward Donald. "John Hardyng and the Holy Grail." In *Arthurian Literature*, vol. 8, ed. Richard Barber, 185–206. Woodbridge, Suffolk: D. S. Brewer, 1989.
Kibbee, Douglas. *For to Speke Frenche Trewely: The French Language in England, 1000–1600: Its Status, Description, and Instruction*. Amsterdam: Benjamins, 1991.
Kidd, Colin. *British Identity Before Nationalism: Ethnicity and Nationhood in the Atlantic World 1600–1800*. Cambridge: Cambridge University Press, 1999.
Kieckhefer, Richard. "Erotic Magic in Medieval Europe." In *Sex in the Middle Ages: A Book of Essays*, ed. Joyce Salisbury, 30–55. New York: Garland, 1991.
Kindrick, Robert L. "A Select Pertinent Scholarship Since 1975." *Arthuriana* 7 (1997): 22–26.
Kingsford, C. L. "The First Version of Hardyng's *Chronicle*." *English Historical Review* 27 (1912): 462–82, 740–53.
Kipling, Gordon. "Henry VII and the Origins of Tudor Patronage." In *Patronage in the Renaissance*, ed. Guy Fitch Lytle and Stephen Orgel, 117–64. Princeton: Princeton University Press, 1981.
Kirk, Elizabeth. "'Clerkes, Poetes and Historiographs': The *Morte Darthur* and Caxton's 'Poetics' of Fiction." In *Studies in Malory*, ed. Spisak, 275–95.
Knight, Stephen. *Arthurian Literature and Society*. New York: St. Martin's Press, 1983.
Koziol, Geoffrey. "England, France, and the Problem of Sacrality in Twelfth-Century Ritual." In *Cultures of Power: Lordship, Status, and Process in Twelfth-Century Europe*, ed. Thomas N. Bisson, 124–48. Philadelphia: University of Pennsylvania Press, 1995.
Kristeva, Julia. *Revolution in Poetic Language*. Trans. Leon Ruidez. New York: Columbia University Press, 1984.
Kuhn, Thomas. *The Structure of Scientific Revolutions*. 2nd ed. Chicago: University of Chicago Press, 1970.
La Capra, Dominick. *History and Criticism*. Ithaca: Cornell University Press, 1985.
Lagorio, Valerie M. "The Evolving Legend of St. Joseph of Glastonbury." *Speculum* 46 (1971): 209–31.
Lagorio, Valerie M., and Mildred L. Day, eds. *King Arthur Through the Ages*. New York: Garland, 1990.
Latour, Bruno. *Science in Action*. Cambridge: Harvard University Press, 1987.
Latour, Bruno, and Steve Woolgar. *Laboratory Life: The Construction of Scientific Facts*. 2nd ed. Princeton: Princeton University Press, 1986.

Lawman. *Brut.* Trans. Rosamund Allen. New York: St. Martin's Press, 1992.
Lawton, David. "Dullness in the Fifteenth Century." *ELH* 54 (1987): 761–99.
Laȝamon. *Brut.* Ed. G. L. Brook and R. F. Leslie. EETS OS 250. London: Oxford University Press, 1963.
Le Goff, Jacques. *Time, Work, and Culture in the Middle Ages.* Trans. Arthur Goldhammer. Chicago: University of Chicago Press, 1980.
Le Saux, Françoise H. M. *Layamon's Brut: The Poem and Its Sources.* Woodbridge, Suffolk: D. S. Brewer, 1989.
Leckie, R. W., Jr. *The Passage of Dominion: Geoffrey of Monmouth and the Periodization of Insular History in the Twelfth Century.* Toronto: University of Toronto Press, 1981.
Lerer, Seth. *Chaucer and His Readers: Imagining the Author in Late Medieval England.* Princeton: Princeton University Press, 1993.
Levine, J. M. *British Antiquities and Humanism and History: Origins of Modern English Historiography.* Ithaca: Cornell University Press, 1987.
Lévi-Strauss, Claude. *Elementary Structures of Kinship.* Trans. James Harle Bell, John Richard von Sturmer, and Rodney Needham. Rev. ed. Boston: Beacon Press, 1969.
——. *The Savage Mind.* Trans. G. Weidenfield. Chicago: University of Chicago Press, 1966.
Lewis, C. T. *Elementary Latin Dictionary.* Oxford: Clarendon, 1979.
Lipstadt, Deborah E. *Denying the Holocaust: The Growing Assault on Truth and Memory.* New York: Free Press, 1993.
Long, Pamela O. "Invention, Authorship, 'Intellectual Property,' and the Origins of Patents: Notes Toward a Conceptual History." *Technology and Culture* 4 (1991): 846–84.
Loomis, Roger Sherman, ed. *Arthurian Literature in the Middle Ages: A Collaborative History.* Oxford: Clarendon Press, 1959.
Lumiansky, R. M. "Sir Thomas Malory's *Le Morte Darthur*, 1947–1987: Author, Title, Text." *Speculum* 62 (1987): 878–97.
Malory, Sir Thomas. *Caxton's Malory.* Ed. James W. Spisak. 2 vols. Berkeley: University of California Press, 1983.
——. *Works.* Ed. Eugène Vinaver, revised by P.J.C. Field. 3 vols. Oxford: Clarendon Press, 1990.
Map, Walter. *De Nugis Curialium.* Ed. and trans. M. R. James, revised C. L. Brooke and R.A.B. Mynors. Oxford: Clarendon Press, 1983.
Marie de France. *Fables.* Ed. and trans. Harriett Spiegel. Toronto: University of Toronto Press, 1987.
Markley, Robert. "History, Literature, and Criticism." In *Literary Criticism and Theory: The Greeks to the Present*, ed. Robert Con Davis and Laurie A. Finke, 877–94. New York: Longman, 1988.
Matheson, Lister M. "King Arthur and the Medieval English Chronicle Tradition." In *King Arthur Through the Ages*, ed. Lagorio and Day, 1:248–74.

Matthews, William. "The Besieged Printer." Ed. Robert L. Kindrick. *Arthuriana* 7 (1997): 63–92.
———. "Caxton and Malory: A Re-view." Ed. Robert L. Kindrick. *Arthuriana* 7 (1997): 31–62.
———. "A Question of Texts." Ed. Robert L. Kindrick. *Arthuriana* 7 (1997): 93–133.
Mauss, Marcel. *The Gift: Forms and Functions of Exchange in Archaic Societies.* Trans. I. Cunnison. New York: Norton, 1967.
McCarthy, Terence. "Caxton and the Text of Malory's Book 2." *Modern Philology* 71 (1973): 144–52.
McCash, June Hall. *The Cultural Patronage of Medieval Women.* Athens: University of Georgia Press, 1996.
McClintock, Anne. *Imperial Leather: Race, Gender, and Sexuality in Colonial Conquest.* New York: Routledge, 1995.
Millican, Charles B. *Spenser and the Table Round.* Cambridge: Harvard University Press, 1932.
Montrose, Louis. "Professing the Renaissance: The Poetics and Politics of Culture." In *The New Historicism*, ed. Veeser, 15–36.
Moore, R. I. *The Formation of a Persecuting Society.* Oxford: Blackwell, 1987.
Moorman, Charles. "*Morte Darthur:* Malory's Second Edition?" *Fifteenth-Century Studies* 12 (1987): 99–113.
Morson, Gary Saul, and Caryl Emerson. *Mikhail Bakhtin: Creation of a Prosaics.* Stanford: Stanford University Press, 1990.
Mortimer, Richard. *Angevin England: 1154–1258.* Oxford: Blackwell, 1994.
Myres, J.N.L. *The English Settlements.* Oxford: Clarendon Press, 1986.
Niranjana, Tejaswini. *Siting Translation: History, Post-structuralism, and the Colonial Context.* Berkeley: University of California Press, 1992.
Noble, James. "Patronage, Politics, and the Figure of Arthur in Geoffrey of Monmouth, Wace, and Layamon." *Arthurian Yearbook* 2 (1992): 158–78.
Norris, Christopher. *Derrida.* Cambridge: Harvard University Press, 1987.
Otter, Monika. *Inventiones: Fiction and Referentiality in Twelfth-Century English Historical Writing.* Chapel Hill: University of North Carolina Press, 1996.
Padel, O. J. "Geoffrey of Monmouth and Cornwall." *Cambridge Medieval Celtic Studies* 8 (1984): 1–28.
Painter, George D. *William Caxton: A Biography.* New York: G. P. Putnam's Sons, 1977.
Parkes, Malcolm B. "The Literacy of the Laity." In *The Mediaeval World*, ed. David Daiches and Anthony Thorlby, 555–77. London: Aldus Books, 1973.
Parry, J. J., and R. A. Caldwell. "Geoffrey of Monmouth." In *Arthurian Literature in the Middle Ages*, 72–93.
Parsons, John Carmi. "Of Queens, Courts and Books: Reflections on the Literary Patronage of Thirteenth Century Plantagenet Queens." In McCash, *The Cultural Patronage of Medieval Women*, 175–201.

Partner, Nancy F. "The New Cornificius: Medieval History and the Artifice of Words." In *Classical Rhetoric and Medieval Historiography*, ed. Breisach, 5–59.
———. *Serious Entertainments: The Writing of History in Twelfth-Century England*. Chicago: University of Chicago Press, 1977.
Patterson, Lee. *Chaucer and the Subject of History*. Madison: University of Wisconsin Press, 1991.
———. *Negotiating the Past: The Historical Understanding of Medieval Literature*. Madison: University of Wisconsin Press, 1987.
Patterson, Robert B. "Stephen's Shaftesbury Charter: Another Case Against William of Malmesbury." *Speculum* 43 (1968): 487–92.
Penninger, Frieda Elaine. *William Caxton*. Boston: Twayne, 1979.
The Peterborough Chronicle 1070–1154. Ed. C. Clark. Oxford: Clarendon, 1958.
Pipes, Daniel. *Conspiracy: How the Paranoid Style Flourishes and Where It Comes from*. New York: The Free Press, 1997.
Pochoda, Elizabeth T. *Arthurian Propaganda: Le Morte Darthur as an Historical Ideal of Life*. Chapel Hill: University of North Carolina Press, 1971.
Pollock, Dale. *Skywalking: The Life and Times of George Lucas*. New York: Harmony, 1983.
Poole, Austin Lane. *From Domesday Book to Magna Carta: 1087–1216*. Oxford: Clarendon Press, 1955.
Prawer, Joshua. *The Latin Kingdom of Jerusalem*. London: Weidenfeld and Nicolson, 1972.
Rauschning, Hermann. *The Voice of Destruction*. New York: G. P. Putnam's Sons, 1940.
Ravenscroft, Trevor. *Spear of Destiny: The Occult Power Behind the Spear which Pierced the Side of Christ*. New York: Putnam, 1973.
Reeve, M. D. "The Transmission of the Historia Regum Britanniae." *Journal of Medieval Latin* 1 (1991): 73–117.
Renan, Ernest. "What Is a Nation?" In *Nation and Narration*, ed. Bhabha, 8–22.
Reynolds, Susan. *Kingdoms and Communities in Western Europe, 900–1300*. Oxford: Clarendon Press, 1984.
———. "Medieval 'Origines Gentium' and the Community of the Realm." *History* 68 (1983): 375–90.
Rhodes, Anthony. *Propaganda. The Art of Persuasion: World War II*. New York: Chelsea House Publishers, 1976.
Riddy, Felicity. "Chivalric Nationalism and the Holy Grail in John Hardyng's *Chronicle*." In *The Grail: A Casebook*, ed. Dhira B. Mahoney, 397–414. New York: Garland, 2000.
———. "Glastonbury, Joseph of Arimathea, and the Grail in John Hardyng's *Chronicle*." In *The Archaeology and History of Glastonbury Abbey*, ed. Lesley Abrams and James P. Carley, 317–31. Woodbridge, Suffolk: Boydell and Brewer, 1991.
———. "John Hardyng's *Chronicle* and the Wars of the Roses." In *Arthurian Lit-*

erature, vol. 12, ed. James P. Carley and Felicity Riddy, 91–108. Woodbridge, Suffolk: Boydell and Brewer, 1993.

———. *Sir Thomas Malory*. Leiden: Brill, 1987.

Riddy, Felicity, and James P. Carley, eds. *Arthurian Literature*. Vol. 13. Woodbridge, Suffolk: Boydell and Brewer, 1995.

Roberts, B. "Geoffrey of Monmouth, *Historia Regum Britanniae* and *Brut Y Brenhinedd*." In *The Arthur of the Welsh*, ed. Bromwich, Jarman, and Roberts, 97–116.

Robertson, G. Kellie. "Geoffrey of Monmouth and the Translation of Insular Historiography." *Arthuriana* 8 (1998): 42–57.

Rosenbaum, Ron. *Explaining Hitler: The Search for the Origins of His Evil*. New York: Random House, 1998.

Rothwell, William. "The Role of French in Thirteenth Century England." *Bulletin of the John Rylands Library, University of Manchester* 58 (1975–76): 445–66.

Rubin, Gayle. "The Traffic in Women: Notes on the 'Political Economy' of Sex." In *Toward an Anthropology of Women*. ed. Rayna R. Reiter, 157–210. New York: Monthly Review Press, 1975.

Rutter, Russell. "William Caxton and Literary Patronage." *Studies in Philology* 84 (1987): 440–70.

Said, Edward W. *Orientalism*. New York: Pantheon, 1978.

Salter, Elizabeth. *English and International Studies in the Literature, Art and Patronage of Medieval England*. Ed. Derek Pearsall and Nicolette Zeeman. Cambridge: Cambridge University Press, 1988.

Sayles, G. O. *The Medieval Foundations of England*. London: Methuen, 1948.

Schleifer, Ronald. *A. J. Greimas and the Nature of Meaning: Linguistics, Semiotics, and Discourse Theory*. Lincoln: University of Nebraska Press, 1987.

Schwartz, S. "The Founding and Self-Betrayal of Britain: An Augustinian Approach to Geoffrey of Monmouth's Historia Regum Britanniæ." *Medievalia et Humanistica* 10 (1981): 33–53.

Scott, James. *Domination and the Arts of Resistance: Hidden Transcripts*. New Haven: Yale University Press, 1990.

———. *Weapons of the Weak: Everyday Forms of Peasant Resistance*. New Haven: Yale University Press, 1985.

Shaw, Sally. "Caxton and Malory." In *Essays on Malory*, ed. J.A.W. Bennett, 114–45. Oxford: Clarendon Press, 1963.

Shichtman, Martin B. "Gawain in Wace and Laȝamon: A Case of Metahistorical Evolution." In *Medieval Texts and Contemporary Readers*, ed. Laurie A. Finke and Martin B. Shichtman, 103–19. Ithaca: Cornell University Press, 1987.

———. "Percival's Sister: Genealogy, Virginity, and Blood." *Arthuriana* 9 (1999): 11–20.

———. "Sir Gawain in Scotland: A Hometown Boy Made Good." In *King Arthur Through the Ages*, ed. Lagorio and Day, 1:234–47.

———. "Wagner and the Arthurian Tradition." In *Approaches to Teaching the*

Arthurian Tradition, ed. Maureen Fries and Jeanie Watson, 139–42. New York: MLA, 1992.

Shichtman, Martin B., and James P. Carley, eds. *Culture and the King: The Social Implications of the Arthurian Legend.* Albany: State University of New York Press, 1994.

Smalley, Beryl. *Historians in the Middle Ages.* New York: Charles Scribner's Sons, 1974.

Smith, Anthony D. *Ethnic Origins of Nations.* New York: Blackwell, 1986.

———. *Theories of Nationalism.* New York: Holmes & Meier, 1983.

Sontag, Susan. *Under the Sign of Saturn.* New York: Farrar, Straus, Giroux, 1980.

Southern, R. W. "Aspects of the European Tradition in Historical Writing." *Transactions of the Royal Historical Society,* 5th series, 20 (1970): 173–96.

Spence, Donald P. *Narrative Truth and Historical Truth: Meaning and Interpretation in Psychoanalysis.* New York: W. W. Norton, 1982.

Spiegel, Gabrielle. *Romancing the Past: The Rise of Vernacular Prose Historiography in Thirteenth-Century France.* Berkeley: University of California Press, 1993.

Spisak, James W., ed. *Studies in Malory.* Kalamazoo, Mich.: Medieval Institute Publications, 1985.

Stallybrass, Peter, and Allon White. *The Politics and Poetics of Transgression.* Ithaca: Cornell University Press, 1986.

Stein, Robert M. "Making History English: Cultural Identity and Historical Explanation in William of Malmesbury and Laȝamon's *Brut.*" In *Text and Territory,* ed. Tomasch and Gilles, 97–115.

Stock, Brian. *Listening for the Text: On the Uses of the Past.* Baltimore: The Johns Hopkins University Press, 1990.

Stubbs, William, ed. *Select Charters and Other Illustrations of English Constitutional History, From the Earliest Times to the Reign of Edward the First.* Oxford: Oxford University Press, 1913.

Suchman, Mark C. "Invention and Ritual: Notes on the Interrelation of Magic and Intellectual Property in Preliterate Societies." *Columbia Law Review* 89 (1989): 1264–94.

Tatlock, J.S.P. *The Legendary History of Britain: Geoffrey of Monmouth's Historia Regum Britanniae and Its Early Vernacular Version.* Berkeley: University of California Press, 1950.

Theweleit, Klaus. *Male Fantasies.* Trans. Stephen Conway. 2 vols. Minneapolis: University of Minnesota Press, 1987.

Thierry, Augustin. *History of the Conquest of England by the Normans.* Vol. 1. London: J. M. Dent and Co., 1907.

Thomson, R. M. "The 'Scriptorium' of William of Malmesbury." In *Medieval Scribes, Manuscripts, and Libraries: Essays Presented to N. R. Ker,* ed. M. B. Parkes and Andrew G. Watson, 117–42. London: Scolar Press, 1978.

———. *William of Malmesbury.* Woodbridge, Suffolk: Boydell and Brewer, 1987.
Tolhurst, Fiona. "The Britons as Hebrews, Romans, and Normans: Geoffrey of Monmouth's British Epic and Reflections of Emperess Matilda." *Arthuriana* 8 (1998): 69–87.
Tomasch, Sylvia. "Postcolonial Chaucer and the Virtual Jew." In *The Postcolonial Middle Ages*, ed. Cohen: 243–60.
Tomasch, Sylvia, and Sealy Gilles, eds. *Text and Territory: Geographical Imagination in the European Middle Ages.* Philadelphia: University of Pennsylvania Press, 1998.
Turner, Ralph V. *Men Raised from the Dust: Administrative Service and Upward Mobility in Angevin England.* Philadelphia: University of Pennsylvania Press, 1988.
Turville-Petre, Thorlac. *England the Nation: Language, Literature, and National Identity, 1290–1340.* Oxford: Clarendon Press, 1996.
Veeser, H. Aram, ed. *The New Historicism.* New York: Routledge, 1989.
Von Eschenbach, Wolfram. *Parzival: A Romance of the Middle Ages.* Trans. Helen M. Mustard and Charles E. Passage. New York: Vintage, 1961.
Wace. *Roman de Brut.* Ed. Ivor Winters. 2 vols. Paris: SATF, 1938–40.
———. *Roman de Brut: A History of the British.* Trans. Judith Weiss. Exeter: University of Exeter Press, 1999.
———. *Roman de Rou.* Ed. A. J. Holden. 3 vols. Paris: A. & J. Picard, 1970.
Wagner, Richard. *Richard Wagner's Prose Works.* Trans. William Ashton Ellis. 6 vols. 1892. Reprint, New York: Bronde, 1966.
Ward, John O. "Some Principles of Rhetorical Historiography." In *Classical Rhetoric and Medieval Historiography*, ed. Breisach, 103–65.
Warren, Michelle R. *History on the Edge: Excalibur and the Borders of Britain.* Minneapolis: University of Minnesota Press, 2000.
———. "Making Contact: Postcolonial Perspectives through Geoffrey of Monmouth's *Historia regum Britanniæ.*" *Arthuriana* 8 (1998): 115–34.
Warren, W. L. *Henry II.* Berkeley: University of California Press, 1973.
Waswo, R. "The History that Literature Makes." *New Literary History* 19 (1988): 541–64.
Wheeler, Bonnie, Robert L. Kindrick, and Michael N. Salda, eds. *The Malory Debate: Essays on the Texts of Le Morte Darthur.* Woodbridge, Suffolk, and Rochester, New York: Boydell and Brewer, 2000.
Whitaker, Muriel. "Illustrating Caxton's Malory." In *Studies in Malory*, ed. Spisak, 297–319.
White, Hayden. "Historical Pluralism." *Critical Inquiry* 12 (1986): 480–93.
———. *Metahistory: The Historical Imagination in Nineteenth-Century Europe.* Baltimore: The Johns Hopkins University Press, 1973.
———. *Tropics of Discourse: Essays in Cultural Criticism.* Baltimore: The Johns Hopkins University Press, 1978.

White, Richard, ed. *King Arthur in Legend and History*. New York: Routledge, 1998.
William of Malmesbury. *Chronicle of the Kings of England*. Trans. J. A. Giles. London: Bell and Daldy, 1866.
———. *De Gestis Regum Anglorum*. Ed. William Stubbs. 2 vols. London: Eyre and Spottiswoode, 1887–89.
———. *De Gestis Regum Anglorum*. Ed. and trans. R.A.B. Mynors, completed by R. M. Thomson and M. Winterbottom. New York: Clarendon Press, 1998.
William of Newburgh. *History of English Affairs: Book I*. Ed. and trans. P. G. Walsh and M. J. Kennedy. Warminster: Aris, 1988.
Williams, Raymond. *Marxism and Literature*. Oxford: Oxford University Press, 1977.
Wincor, Richard. *From Ritual to Royalties: An Anatomy of Literary Property*. New York: Walker and Co., 1962.
Withrington, John. "Caxton, Malory, and the Roman War in the *Morte Darthur*." *Studies in Philology* 89 (1992): 350–66.
Wolf, Eric R. *Europe and the People Without History*. Berkeley: University of California Press, 1982.
Wood, Denis. *The Power of Maps*. New York: Guilford Press, 1992.
Wyld, Henry Cecil. "Laȝamon as an English Poet." *Review of English Studies* 6 (1930): 1–30.
Zagorin, Perez. "Historiography and Postmodernism: Reconsiderations." *History and Theory* 29 (1990): 263–74.
Žižek, Slavoj. *The Sublime Object of Ideology*. London: Verso, 1989.
———. *Looking Awry: An Introduction to Jacques Lacan Through Popular Culture*. Cambridge, Mass.: MIT Press, 1991.

www.ingramcontent.com/pod-product-compliance
Lightning Source LLC
Chambersburg PA
CBHW020944230426
43666CB00005B/165